Sir Fob W. Pot's Journey to Katahdin

Volume 1

STEVE JOHNSON

D1511060

Printed in the United States of America

First Printing, 2017

Scriptures taken from the Holy Bible, New International Version®, NIV®. Copyright © 1973, 1978, 1984, 2011 by Biblica, Inc.™ Used by permission of Zondervan. All rights reserved worldwide. www.zondervan.com The "NIV" and "New International Version" are trademarks registered in the United States Patent and Trademark Office by Biblica, Inc.™

ISBN: 0692838333
ISBN-13: 978-0692838334

Steve Johnson Publishing
504 Richard Street
Union, SC 29379

Cover design by Janet Johnson

To my wife, Janet…

for encouraging me to pursue my insatiable dream
by embarking on a crazy long hike.

for giving me abundant reasons to finish the trail
and be reunited with you, the love of my life.

for birthing two incredible sons…
one of whom once pooped on a trail.

CONTENTS

Appendices

FOREWORD

The first time I met Steve Johnson was in a podunk Tennessee restaurant that proudly advertised the best "aigs & biskits" in the state. I was there to rendezvous with his church youth group before guiding them on a five-day backpacking trek in Big South Fork wilderness. It was there, in the lobby, that this big man lifted me off the ground and gave me a true bear hug. As I hung helpless as a rag doll, over his shoulder I saw his wife smiling. "Ever since reading your book, he has the biggest man-crush on you!"

I've guided well over a hundred treks, but that trek would prove to be one of the most difficult. On day two, as usual, the plan was to climb down into the gorge and cross the river twice. Everything was fine, until we came to the river and saw that it had swelled into a raging current. It was the first time I had ever seen it impassable. In the end, we had to climb back out of the gorge and take a route that turned our eight-mile day into an eighteen-mile day.

To make matters worse, one of my hikers was sick and shooting the glories of nature out of both ends. We sat up with him all night, but the next morning, we had to carry him two miles to an evacuation point. Oh, and did I mention it rained those first two days?

Through it all, while some adults were having full-blown melt-downs, Steve appeared happy to take on whatever challenge was thrown at us. Whether it was helping people climb cliffs or encouraging others as they hiked with blistered feet in wet shoes, he did so with a jubilant attitude.

When Steve shared with me that he was planning to thru-hike the Appalachian Trail, I knew he had the grit to accomplish the journey. Of course, the Trail tests more than determination. It challenges you in almost every way possible and often reveals what a person is at their very core.

Enjoy the journey,

Lawrence "Baro" Alexander

Co-Founder and Program Director, ChallengePoint

ACKNOWLEDGMENTS

Many people played crucial roles in helping me tackle the Appalachian Trail and then write about it. My wife, Janet, green-lighted the entire adventure, despite the challenges and inconveniences my absence would cause her. Through phone calls, texts, the occasional romantic rendezvous, and meeting me at Mount Katahdin, she supported my journey in every conceivable way. She also reviewed and edited this manuscript over and over, each time offering insightful suggestions.

The rest of my family also assisted in significant ways. Many were at Springer Mountain to see me off. You'll read about them in chapter 6. My dad, not surprisingly, was there at the beginning and end, and proudly converted his bedroom dresser into a shrine with memorabilia related to my hike. Ellen, my oldest sister, stood by me at the beginning, mailed me a care package, and sent several encouraging texts that always arrived at a time of great need. Stacy, my other sister, used her English teaching background and a few red pens to shape this narrative.

In addition to offering writing tips, author and friend Lynne Gentry implored me to dig deeper and never be satisfied with just a "good enough" book. She convinced me I had a unique voice, to keep asking probing questions about my life and hike, and to keep putting words on paper.

I owe a debt of gratitude to the scores of Trail Angels who generously helped and encouraged me along the way. None were more important than Maurine Welch, Darrell and Alicia Brimberry, Dave and Deann Werner, and Jeff Battreall. You'll learn about them in the pages that follow. These Trail Angels may not have realized it at the time, but God was using each of them in a powerful way. If you're unfamiliar with hiking terms such as *Trail Angel*, check out the glossary at Appendix D.

Larry "Baro" Alexander's impact was felt as my trail mentor, advice provider, trail name giver, and writer of this book's Foreword. His own AT books inspired me to see a thru-hike as not just a pipe dream, but something I could achieve.

Thank you to those who read my AT blog. I'm especially grateful for your encouraging and often inspirational comments. Typing thousands of words on an iPhone, using only my right thumb, while lying in a dark tent, grew tiresome. Your comments made me feel like it was worth the effort.

I offer my heartfelt gratitude to my fellow AT hikers, whether we were huddled together for several days in the Smokies or just a few minutes at a trailside watering hole. Each of you plays a part in my AT story, and I am honored to be a part of yours. I did my best to accurately capture the myriad details using just my memory and the illegible notes scribbled in my AT guide. Forgive me wherever I missed the mark (and contact me so I can correct any mistakes). I'm especially grateful to Lou "Booknboot" Jillett, whose conversation with me at the base of Tennessee's Thunderhead Mountain, which you'll read about later, helped inspire my writing career.

To my sons, Jason and Kyle, thank you for encouraging me to pursue my dream and for your texts and phone calls during my hike. Knowing you and your wives were praying for me during my journey boosted my morale and surely had other impacts I can't even imagine. I hope this tale inspires you, and future generations, to continue tackling your own crazy bucket list dreams. Always remember…We Da Johnsons!

Finally, and most importantly, I thank God, the giver of all good things… including the magnificent Appalachian Trail.

Part One ~ Preliminaries

"Nothing splendid has ever been achieved except by those who dared believe that something inside them was superior to circumstance."

- Bruce Barton

CHAPTER 1

WHY IN THE WORLD?

"Things won are done; joy's soul lies in the doing."
- William Shakespeare

"Why in the world would you want to go and do something like that?" My mother-in-law's question was a reasonable one, considering I was about to abandon her youngest daughter for a six-month hike on the 2,189.1-mile Appalachian Trail. Still, I was taken aback by her disbelief. I had just spent a solid 10 minutes confidently explaining my plans and motivations for hiking the AT. Between sips of hot coffee at the kitchen table on this cold December 2015 morning, I had made my case. My rationale was thorough and compelling. In fact, when I finished, I was certain my mother-in-law would not only heartily endorse my trek, but might even join me.

Yet there she sat, staring me down from across the table, pulverizing a bite of strawberry strudel. It was the kind of puzzled stare a parent might give a son after being informed he planned to use his recent college degree to start a rock band. Clearly unconvinced, she looked me in the eyes, shook her head, and said, "I just don't get it. How did this crazy idea make your bucket list?"

My planned trek into a bear-infested, rocky and dangerous wilderness made no logical sense to her. A normal person would not attempt such a risky undertaking. She had doubted my normalcy in the past, but this bucket list item confirmed her suspicions. Her daughter had married an illogical, abnormal fool.

Why in the world would I willingly risk my health, the opportunity to travel in my old age, or worse yet, my life? My mother-in-law's question prompted deeper reflection, the first and most important of the many demanding exercises all aspiring thru-hikers should tackle before stepping foot on the trail. After giving this dear woman's challenge some serious thought, I determined my Top 10 reasons for tackling the dream, some of which had been swirling in my head for nearly two decades.

Perhaps someone will find them more convincing than my mother-in-law. Perhaps a few brave souls will even "get it."

1. I love adventure.

In my mind, I traveled across the continent with Lewis and Clark, thanks to the novel *Undaunted Courage* by Stephen Ambrose. I mentally journeyed into space with the crew of Apollo 13, battled snakes and Nazis with Indiana Jones, and scored the winning goal in Quidditch with Harry Potter. I imagined floating with Rose on the raft as Jack sank to the bottom of the ocean in *Titanic*, and picking up giant-slaying stones with David in his heroic battle, won against all odds.

I vicariously hiked the AT a thousand times through movies, journals, YouTube clips, and books. In fact, the original adventurous seed was planted while reading Bill Bryson's *A Walk in the Woods*. The bud grew into a full-blown desire after devouring the pages of *Through Hiker's Eyes, Parts I and II*, by Larry Alexander, my friend and mentor.

While adventure reading is thrilling and adventure watching is exciting, nothing compares to living my own adventure and telling my own story. Whether my story would be a tragedy or comedy, featuring a devastating injury or a thrilling final summit, remained to be seen. Either way, I wanted it to be an adventure—my very own adventure.

2. I love the outdoors.

Nothing lifts my spirits, gets my blood pumping, and connects me more with my Creator than a good hike. My wife, Janet, and I have explored many trails around the world. Each twist in the path or view from a rocky summit has given me a different glimpse of God's handiwork. His presence whispers to me throughout a regular day, but God shouts his awesomeness when I am hiking and thinking in nature.

I knew over the course of my AT adventure I would walk over 2,000 miles in all sorts of conditions. I would get wet and dirty and carry a stench like none other. Still, I would be outdoors, staring at countless stars from a mountaintop on a clear night. Wild ponies, squirrels, and moose would be my companions. Living outdoors would give me an opportunity to connect with God and His creation like never before.

3. I love fun experiences in new places.

The year was 1974, I was eight years old, and my family had just made the third of six moves during my K-12 years. This time, the Air Force directed we pull up our roots in Germany, say goodbye to friends, and move back to Dover, Delaware. While I didn't particularly enjoy packing my toys or observing my older sisters' teenage angst, my parents made every move an adventure.

On that snowy Christmas eve, tensions were high because Dad, distracted by details of the move, had not yet purchased a Christmas present for Mom. While my sisters fretted with him about his oversight, I knew Santa had his back. Forever my hero, Dad calmly motioned for me to put my winter coat on and join him outside in his beloved Volkswagen Beetle.

I knew what was to follow—a high stakes Christmas Eve shopping trip to find my mom a present. We'd been down that road before. I also knew he would succeed, because he was my dad. I didn't know he would take us on a detour to an empty, snow-covered parking lot and do thrilling, high-speed spin outs for 20 minutes. Coolest dad ever? You bet! Dad valued spontaneity over predictability and orneriness over toeing the line. He taught me to anticipate the excitement of a strange new place, rather than fear the unknown. I had a lifetime of training to prepare me to tackle this new trail.

What would I find around the AT's next bend? Could I run faster than the approaching bear (no), or at least faster than the person hiking next to me (maybe)? Who would I meet at the next campfire or shelter? What was their story? What could I learn from them? Could I encourage them in some way, or would I be the one needing encouragement? Would the shower be hot at the next trail town, and would there be an all-you-can-eat buffet to devour? I looked forward to the unexpected twists and turns as much as the expected ones.

4. I love a challenge.

My 45-year association with the United States Air Force presented myriad challenges. I moved 17 times and lived in 22 different homes or apartments. I said goodbye to hundreds of friends and a few girlfriends, and then made new ones. I learned new routes to school, different languages, and new blocking schemes in football playbooks.

I arrived at some schools mid-year and had to endure yet another teacher announcing, "Class, this is Steven. He's new. Everyone say 'hi' to Steven." I learned to sit at a lunch table full of strangers and introduce myself. Sometimes I sat alone at these tables, but usually not for long. Rather than sulk during my first day at a new military base and school, I learned to join the backyard football game already in progress. I walked the streets looking for moving vans and the even newer kids that sometimes came with them.

As a mobile military professional, there was the every two to three-year adjustment to a new job, boss, church family, and next-door neighbor. I've served on casualty notification teams, delivering the worst possible news a military spouse can receive. I've nervously sat behind my general officer boss as he testified before Congress, discreetly slipping him notes to help answer high stakes questions. I've counseled Airmen who had been raped, passed over for promotion, and charged with child abuse. Whether it was long duty days, frequent TDYs (military trips to perform temporary duty), or a deployment to Afghanistan, my profession presented many challenges to me and my family.

The military lifestyle was difficult at times, but I wouldn't change a thing. From seeing the world to meeting fascinating people, the rewards were immense. Each challenge I overcame prepared me for the next one. I learned to be flexible and adaptable. Through sheer necessity, I learned to view these potentially life-disrupting difficulties as challenges to overcome. Most times, I overcame them. Sometimes, I even sought them out.

Thru-hiking the AT is a really, really difficult, life-disrupting challenge. It ranks somewhere between running 84 marathons (the approximate distance of the AT) and clothes shopping with my wife while my Dallas Cowboys are playing. The total elevation change on the trail is the equivalent of hiking Mount Everest 16 times! Of the 4,000 or so crazies who attempt an AT thru-hike each year, 75-80 percent fail.

Those are bad odds. The journey has to be difficult in order for the eventual summit at Maine's Mount Katahdin to have significance. There is little joy in accomplishing the "Easy" Sudoku puzzle or beating a five-year-old in chess. Nothing ventured, nothing gained.

As my friend, Terry Reeves, once said about missionaries laboring in the mission fields of poverty-stricken third world countries, "If it were easy, everybody would be over here doing it. There's a reason why most people haven't done it." But for those who have the guts to take on difficult challenges, there are rewards. As a hiker in the movie *Everest* said, "You suffer for a few days. But for the rest of your life you're a guy who got to the top of Everest." I wanted to be that guy.

5. I love planning.

I may have been the only senior in my high school graduating class with written one, three, and five-year goals. In case you're wondering, they each had an action plan. As other members of the Class of 1984 were celebrating their academic and athletic achievements, I rejoiced that the Franklin International Institute had begun selling the first Franklin Planner, a paper-based time management system. Like a world-class nerd, I have been planning and managing my life with it ever since.

My incessant need to plan only grew during my 23-year Air Force career. There was always another plan to create, variable to assess, and general officer to please. My love for detailed plans carried over into my personal life. Our three-day trip to Italy warranted a six-page plan, with instructions to "rise and shine" at 0700 hours and "eat breakfast and brush teeth" at 0715 hours. It's a wonder I ever found someone to marry. Sure, I was willing to spontaneously divert from a plan on occasion. But the idea of leaving home without a plan? Preposterous!

Not surprisingly, my AT planning was an obsession—a truly magnificent obsession. I spent over three months studying sleeping bag specifications and over three hours researching sporks. That's right—three hours deciding what kind of eating utensil I would take! The very thought that I would have to get from Point A to Point B, in the forecasted weather, with the projected elevation changes and terrain, using nothing but prayer and what I could carry on my own back…and that my survival depended on my preparation…well, I found the challenge intriguing and exciting.

6. I wanted to get in shape.

The AT will either make or break a person physically. I intended to be one it made. I hoped to lose at least 20 pounds while hiking, and get a resting heart rate in the fifties. Hiking 10 or so hours per day is one of the few activities where I literally couldn't eat enough to replenish the 5,000-6,000 calories burned each day. Six months of pigging out and losing weight? Sign me up!

7. I wanted to help Amber and Julio Colón adopt a child.

My mom was a care-giver. Throughout my childhood, we had regular weekend visitors in our home. As a respite worker, Mom brought in mentally and/or physically disabled people for a few days to give their parents or caregivers a break.

Little Raymond wore a helmet and gloves because he liked to hit himself and bang his head against the wall. Lurleen, a gregarious teenager, had a crush on my sister's boyfriend. On one occasion, Lurleen ran outside and took her shirt off, exposing her bra. As I arrived home from school, my breathless mom was chasing the shirtless Lurleen around the yard in order to get her back inside. I told my school buddies to move along.

Marge was an older woman who couldn't speak and had the mind of a five-year-old. She and Mom would spend hours in the living room, smiling and brushing each other's hair. Mom had a big heart for people, and seemed especially sensitive to Jesus' commandment to care for *"the least of these."* (Matthew 25:31-46) Through her words, but more so her actions, she taught us to look for opportunities to help others.

I learned that while I can't always do everything to fix a problem, I should try to do what I can. Mom's example motivated me to look for opportunities to help those in need and try to make a difference in their lives. One such situation involves my friends, Amber and Julio. For eight years, these dedicated Christians have been trying, unsuccessfully, to have a child.

In recent years, Amber and Julio shifted their focus to adoption and raising the required money. Although they'd worked hard to raise the funds, they still needed $6,645 to cover adoption agency fees. I decided to use my hike to raise awareness, and some money, to help them fulfil their dream of having a child. I believe they will make great parents someday and will bless a child.

8. I hoped to inspire some 5th and 6th grade students at Foundation Christian Academy in Valrico, Florida.

Students from the school where I previously taught planned to track my journey and complete related assignments. With each 100 miles trekked and each state traversed, they would move a thumbtack on an AT map on their classroom walls. More than just giving them miles to track, I hoped in some small way, I could encourage them to dream big dreams and then pursue them.

In the *Everest* movie, Jon Krakauer asks Doug Hansen, "It hurts. It's dangerous. I gotta ask the question, you know I do. Why?" Hansen responds, "I have kids. They see a regular guy can follow impossible dreams, maybe they'll do the same." I hoped being willing to overcome fears and pursue a dream would launch at least a few of the FCA students in pursuit of their dreams.

9. The timing was right.

A few years ago, I watched a powerful video illustration entitled "Balance Beam" by preacher and author, Francis Chan. He compares living a safe, risk-free life to a gymnast whose balance beam routine consists of lying down and tightly gripping the beam. While the gymnast will likely avoid a fall or injury, she shouldn't expect high scores from the judges.[1]

For our lives to have an impact on the world, we need to take chances and assume risks. To stick a landing and reap the rewards, we must be willing to jump high off the beam. While Chan's analogy focuses on taking risks for God, the principle can be applied to many life endeavors.

Similarly, in 1989's *Dead Poets Society*, John Keeting, played by the late Robin Williams, implores his students to "Carpe diem. Seize the day, boys.

---

[1] Chan, Francis. "Balance Beam." Online video clip. YouTube. YouTube, 2 October 2008. Web. 17 January 2017.

Make your lives extraordinary." Life is simply too important, and too short, to be satisfied with mediocrity. As an English teacher, Mr. Keeting probably knew that one antonym for seize is *reject*. To not try to make the most of my life is to reject a precious opportunity given to me by God.

I realized my time to *carpe diem* had arrived. My opportunity to somersault high above the beam was now. My sons were grown and out of the house. I had recently retired so there were no job constraints. My wife lovingly and graciously gave me the green light, knowing that it was a long-time dream of mine. I embarked on this journey less than one month after turning 50. The body and mind weren't getting any younger. I needed to do this before I felt the urge to lie down on the balance beam and hold tight until the end of my life. On my deathbed, I want to look back on my life and know I took risks and didn't always play it safe.

10. I promised my mom I would do it.

In early 2015, my mom was diagnosed with stage-4 cancer. Mom was a fighter. She so wanted more time to celebrate the successes of and to love on her children, grand-children, and great-grandchildren. Eight months after the initial diagnosis, she passed from this life, but not before she made me promise I'd follow my crazy dream to hike the AT.

I don't know if people can watch things from heaven, but I intended to hike as if Mom was watching. She is among my *"great cloud of witnesses."* (Hebrews 12:1) I doubted she would care whether I finished the AT, but she would be disappointed if I didn't follow my dream and make an attempt. As added incentive, my dad agreed to let me take some of her ashes to spread at the final summit. For Mom's sake, I had to get to Katahdin.

My 10 reasons for hiking the AT may not have been compelling to my mother-in-law, or most people, but they were compelling to me. All that mattered was that I was convinced of the trek's worthiness. I wasn't a recent college graduate in my early twenties trying to figure out what to do with my life. I wasn't a guy in my fifties facing a mid-life crisis or trying to escape something. I have a great life, yet I had my reasons. Thru-hiking the Appalachian Trail was something I had to do. I had to find out if there was something inside of me superior to circumstance. I had to learn to rely on God like never before. With these motivating reasons firmly planted in my mind, it was time to formulate a strategy.

7

CHAPTER 2

KEYS TO A SUCCESSFUL THRU-HIKE

"Jesus looked at them and said, 'With man this is impossible, but not with God; all things are possible with God.'"
- Mark 10:27

I had my reasons. But were they enough? Most aspiring thru-hikers have a variety of reasons for hiking the AT, yet the vast majority don't accomplish their goal. Why would I be any different? After all, I was a pudgy 50-year-old with poor vision and a history of sprained and broken ankles. On paper, I was a long shot. But what is on paper doesn't always tell the whole story, and I had three things working in my favor. No, I'm not talking about my good looks, rock solid body and humility. I'm talking about the three keys that would make all the difference in the world.

First and foremost, I believe in God. Our God not only created the universe, but knows each of us by name. He created me, loves me, is always with me, and has sustained me for over half a century and counting. Why would my six months on the AT be any different? With God on my side, I had a majority against any problem or challenge.

Imagine being team captain for a middle school pick-up basketball game. Just before making your first selection, Lebron James walks onto the court and wants to play. You have first pick and can select Lebron or any of your middle school buddies. Naturally, you pick Lebron.

Your confidence immediately soars. In fact, your next three picks don't matter. You are no longer concerned about the weather, the playing surface, the ball's inflation, or even how good a player you are. Why? Because you are going to feed the ball to Lebron—on every play. You are going to rely on him and, in the process, elevate your own game.

Similarly, my plan was to hike the AT with God by my side, strengthening and protecting me with every step and at every turn. I would "feed the ball" to God each day and let him take over the game. In the process, he would bring out my best.

My second key to a successful AT thru-hike relates to commitment, which Webster defines as, "an agreement or pledge to do something in the future."[2] Commitment is a critical word and concept that should be taken seriously. When I commit to something, I try my best to follow through. It doesn't matter whether the commitment involves military service, marriage, or hiking the AT. If I make a commitment, a pledge to do something, I go all out to make it happen. I committed to thru-hike the AT. In effect, I promised myself I would complete the journey.

As part of that promise, I didn't give myself any easy outs. I didn't say, "I'll continue hiking so long as…" So long as it would be fun? It wouldn't always be fun. So long as I didn't get bored? It would be boring at times. So long as I didn't get homesick? I'd be homesick every day! My "so long as" list contained only catastrophic scenarios, like a death in the family, fatal bear attack, or learning my wife had gotten a tattoo of an old boyfriend.

Most people who quit the AT for non-injury reasons simply allowed a non-catastrophic "so long as" to surface. Their "so long as" reasons were mostly solid—homesickness, job opportunities, aching bodies, etc. There's no shame in exiting the trail for such reasons. But if a good, solid, non-catastrophic "so long as" was enough to have me leave the trail, I would probably leave the trail. Eighty percent of hikers do. I was determined to be among the 20 percent who finished.

For the third key, I turned to the psychoanalytical work of Sigmund Freud. Freud's model of the human psyche consists of the *id, ego,* and *super ego.* My concern was the *id,* the part of our personality and psyche that deals with our most basic, instinctual drives. When a hungry baby cries until she's fed, a parched hiker hikes until he finds water, or an obsessed shopper tramples another shopper on Black Friday, the *id* is at work.[3] The *id* also encompasses our sexual drive and impulses. (Don't worry, I'm not going there!)

The *id* acts according to the "pleasure principle." In short, this principle holds that humans have a built-in tendency to gratify impulses, seeking pleasure while avoiding pain. Before making a decision, we subconsciously ask ourselves a series of questions, to include whether the decision will bring pain or pleasure. Self-help guru Tony Robbins put it this way: "We

---

[2] "commitment." Merriam-Webster.com. 2017. https://www.merriam-webster.com (12 January 2017).

[3] "id." yourdictionary.com. 2017. https://www.examples.yourdictionary.com (12 January 2017).

make decisions that lean toward things we deem positive — our perceived pleasure. We also make decisions that move us away from things we've determined are not as pleasurable."[4]

For example, the reason I hit the snooze button on the alarm in the morning is because of the pleasure sleeping 10 more minutes brings. The reason I eventually get up is because the anticipated pain of being late to school or work is greater than the anticipated pleasure of sleeping 10 more minutes. With each decision, the relative abundance of pain or pleasure casts the decisive vote.

Applying this principle to my AT hike, I had to have enough reasons for hiking the trail so that accomplishing the task would bring overwhelming pleasure. Even more importantly, the anticipated pleasure, short-term or long-term, had to outweigh the anticipated pain.

To finish the trail, the pain associated with quitting (e.g., letting the Colón family down, disappointing classes of 5th & 6th graders, not getting Mom's ashes to Katahdin, breaking my pledge, etc.) had to be so enormous that it outweighed whatever benefits I would gain (e.g., seeing my family, foot pain relief, etc.). Incidentally, this principle applies to any goal you want to achieve. You just have to make the pleasure associated with completing the goal greater than the associated pain.

Fob Fundamental #1 – To achieve a challenging goal, the anticipated pleasure associated with achieving it must be greater than the anticipated pain.

Note to Readers: This is the first of several "Fob Fundamentals," which are adages, lessons learned, and pearls of wisdom gleaned from my AT journey. To maintain the flow and pacing of the story, you may choose to read the Fundamental and continue the story. Then, after completing the book, use the Study Guide at Appendix B for a deeper reflection on the Fundamentals. Alternatively, you may choose to read the Fundamental, immediately flip to the Study Guide, and then return to the story.

Although I really wanted to thru-hike the AT, desire alone wasn't enough. I had to have a strategy. I would rely on God, remember my commitment, and realize that the pleasure of finishing the trail would far outweigh the pain associated with quitting. Time would tell whether my strategy was sound. Time would also tell whether my hiking gear, including my prized spork, would get me to Katahdin.

---

[4] Robbins, Tony. "What Drives Your Decisions?" Robbins Research International, Inc., tonyrobbins.com/mind-meaning/what-drives-your-decisions. Accessed 12 January 2017.

CHAPTER 3

GEAR UP!

"There is no bad weather, only inappropriate clothing."
- Sir Ranulph Fiennes

As previously mentioned, my AT preparations were a magnificent obsession. Facing six months in the wilderness in all types of weather, I had to carefully choose what to wear and carry on my back. The potential consequences of poor choices included hunger, hypothermia, injury, and chronic discomfort, all of which could eventually cause me to leave the trail or die. Neither of those outcomes is appealing.

There are different philosophies and variables hikers consider when deciding on backpacking clothes and gear. Those on a tight budget mainly consider cost, sometimes sacrificing quality or functionality in search of a money saving deal. They tend to pride themselves on homemade, old school solutions, like using an old dog food can as a cooking stove, or tree branches as hiking poles.

For others, the main consideration is weight. They will invest in more expensive ultra-light gear. Some will do without a stove or sleeping pad, or cut a toothbrush in half, in order to travel as light as possible. Every fraction of an ounce counts. The lighter the load, the more likely a hiker is to finish. Just as cost cutters might boast on how little they spent, ultra-lighters might boast about how little their pack weighs.

At the other extreme, some over-pack with too many luxury or duplicate items. They falsely assume that what works on a weekend camping trip with the family (e.g., a 10-person tent, mosquito repellent lantern, mouthwash, etc.) will work on a 2,000-mile journey. Many will send gear home or quit altogether.

My approach was to purchase high quality, lightweight gear, but to bring enough for a little more comfort and functionality than what a pure minimalist would have. Yes, I could have gone lighter and cheaper. But if I failed, I didn't want it to be because I had insufficient or low quality gear. I spent a year researching and acquiring my AT clothes and gear. I painstakingly read gear reviews in hiking magazines and on successful AT hikers' blogs.

I took detailed notes in my Franklin Planner while watching gear reviews on YouTube. My custom spreadsheets recorded relevant weight and price data which allowed me to compare types, versions, and models. I knew the ExOfficio underwear specifications better than the person who invented the quick drying, moisture wicking wonders. Since detailed gear lists helped me in the past, I have provided my list at Appendix A, along with a brief review.

Once all the gear arrived, I regularly packed and unpacked my backpack. This was due more to nervous anticipation and excitement than necessity. Experts also recommend going on shake-down hikes to test everything. My shake-down consisted of a few day hikes and one overnighter in my tent, which I set up next to our RV at a campsite near Eustis, Florida.

Everything was going fine until 3:00 a.m., when heavy rain and a nearby lightning strike woke me from a deep sleep. Then my phone rang…

Steve: "Hey, hon, what's up?"

Janet: "There's a tornado warning. I think you should come in."

Steve: "But this is a good test for my tent. I've got to be able to deal with stuff like this."

Janet: "Yes, but it's a tornado warning."

Steve: "Yes, but you're in an RV. Tornados seek out RVs."

Janet: "I think you should come in."

Steve: "Okay, sweetie."

Not wanting her to worry about me, or end up alone in Oz surrounded by munchkins, I relented and came inside. For a guy wanting to spend six months in the wilderness hiking nearly 2,200 miles in all sorts of weather, I hadn't even lasted a full night in my tent on my only overnight shakedown.

I was bummed, and a little embarrassed, but not for long. In fact, I was about to have my mind blown by the generosity of others.

CHAPTER 4

THE WIDOW'S MITE

"A good character is the best tombstone. Those who loved you and were helped by
you will remember you when forget-me-nots have withered.
Carve your name on hearts, not on marble."
- Charles H. Spurgeon

My wife and I are members of the Sojourners, a group of mostly retired Christians who travel the country by RV, helping small churches, Christian camps, and children's homes. The Sojourners have several planning workshops around the country where members can sign up to work at various assignments, known as sojourns. In February of 2016, just a month before the start of my hike, we attended a Sojourner workshop in Eustis, Florida.

At the workshop, several of our fellow sojourners wondered about the crazy new guy walking around campus carrying a 35-pound backpack. I filled them in on my plans and also suggested they read my AT blog which contained my reasons for hiking.

During a break, a dear sweet lady approached me and said, "Steve, I read the blog on your friends and I want to help them with the adoption fundraiser." She then handed me a $10 bill and wished me well. I thanked her and she walked away. A short time later, I learned that her husband had passed away and she was not well-off financially. Suddenly her $10 donation took on increasing significance. In fact, Mark 12:41-44 came to mind...

"Jesus sat down opposite the place where the offerings were put and watched the crowd putting their money into the temple treasury. Many rich people threw in large amounts. But a poor widow came and put in two very small copper coins, worth only a

13

few cents.

Calling his disciples to him, Jesus said, 'Truly I tell you, this poor widow has put more into the treasury than all the others. They all gave out of their wealth; but she, out of her poverty, put in everything—all she had to live on.'"

Our sojourner friend does not live in poverty and has more than two copper coins to her name. Still, her $10 donation was not an insignificant amount to her. She was not giving out of abundance. Her generosity got me to thinking…I wonder if I should make a personal appeal to these fine people on behalf of the Colón family.

Asking for money is not something that comes naturally to me or that I enjoy. When my sons were young, I felt awkward watching them sell candles and cookies and things to raise funds for various causes. Still, I felt like these folks should hear about the Colón's adoption plan in order to decide for themselves whether they were in a position to give.

During the next round of announcements, I addressed my fellow sojourners and made a brief appeal. I told them the Colón's adoption story and that I would be hiking, in part, to help raise funds. When we went on break, several of them made their way to Janet and lined up to donate.

Within 10 minutes, these tender-hearted people pledged $1,700 toward the cause! News of their generosity spread, additional donations and pledges came in, and the total quickly surpassed $3,700! I had no idea that total would grow even larger by the end of my hike.

Fob Fundamental #2 – God can take even the smallest gifts and turn them into something grand and wonderful.

Both widows discussed above have much in common. They both gave sacrificially, not out of abundance, but out of scarcity. They both were motivated by love—one for the work of the temple and one for the adoption of a child. In both situations, God used their seemingly small contributions to do wonderful things. He included one of their stories in the Bible and turned the other widow's offering into thousands of dollars to aid an adoption.

Never underestimate how God can use small, seemingly insignificant things. With just a donkey's jawbone, Samson killed 1,000 men. Armed with just a sling and a smooth stone, young David defeated Goliath. With just five loaves of bread and two fish, Jesus fed 5,000 men, along with women and children. With a widow's gift of just $10, God re-ignited an adoption fundraiser. God can take a small gift, simple gesture, or modest act, and turn it into something grand and wonderful.

The outpouring of love and support for the Colón family's adoption effort made me more motivated than ever to begin my hike. I would be hiking for a child I had never met, and possibly one who hadn't even been born. I had my gear, a sound strategy, and all the motivation in the world. The only thing I lacked was a trail name.

CHAPTER 5

FOB W. POT

"A name can't begin to encompass the sum of all her parts. But that's the magic of names, isn't it? That the complex, contradictory individuals we are can be called up complete and whole in another mind through the simple sorcery of a name."
- Charles de Lint, *Dreams Underfoot*

Among the many cherished traditions associated with hiking the Appalachian Trail is acquiring a trail name. Hikers typically earn their names by saying or doing something stupid or at least memorable on the trail. Others are named based on a peculiar body part, interesting occupation, bad habit, or unusual talent.

A hiker can decline a suggested trail name. After all, who really wants to be known as *Butt Scratcher* or *Snot Nose* for five to seven months? On the other hand, there's pressure to go with something other than one's usual boring name, like Bob, Sue, or Steve. I assumed I would do something unusual to earn a trail name once I began hiking.

Instead, just a few days before starting my journey, Larry Alexander, my AT mentor, contacted me with an interesting idea for a trail name. Rather than base it on something I had done, he proposed a name based on something my youngest son, Kyle, had done. Here, then, is the back story, or at least a general version that I know.

Several years ago, when Kyle was in 8th grade, he went on an Adventure Trek in the hills of Tennessee with 20 other teenagers. Larry, their guide, is an experienced outdoorsman, having thru-hiked both the AT and Pacific Crest Trail. He regularly leads groups into the wilderness for several days of hiking, rappelling, and team-building.

One evening, as the group descended into their campsite, Kyle was left with the impression they would be hiking out the opposite way the following morning. About 10:00 p.m., nature called in a big way. Kyle felt the rumble in his tummy and needed to act quickly. When there is no outhouse, the proper hiking etiquette is to go into the woods, a good 30 to 50 yards from camp, dig a hole, do one's business, and bury it. The goal, to "leave no trace," is an established camping principle dating back at least to the time of Noah.

Kyle, with a still developing frontal lobe, decided to deviate from the operating manual. Motivated by some combination of fear and laziness, he headed a short distance back up the same trail from which the group descended. Then, in the light of the moon and in a moment of moral weakness, he dropped his trousers around his ankles and took a massive dump in the center of the trail. Immediately realizing his grave mistake, he picked up a handful of dried leaves, squeezed them, and sprinkled them on top of his dung pile. Somehow this would make it all better.

The next morning, Larry assembled the young hikers and told them they would be hiking out the same way they came in. Kyle's eyes widened and he immediately got a big lump in his throat—though not nearly as big as the lump he had criminally left sitting up the trail with a few leaves on it!

He wondered what to do. Would the pile still be there? Would he be implicated? Should he hire an attorney or attempt to frame Jason, his older brother? Should he even be worried? Perhaps Mount Kyle got knocked off the trail by a deer or some midnight thunderstorm. Just to be on the safe side, he decided to keep a low profile by positioning himself at the back of the line of hikers and keeping his head down.

As they approached the Kyle pile, Larry immediately spotted it and tried to shield the younger hikers' eyes. It was too late. Larry closely examined the suspicious mound and revealed what others suspected—this was a pyramid of filthy, human waste! How could this have happened? He immediately took charge of the situation and circled the troops around the disgusting, foul-smelling heap. With the ragged bunch of hikers looking on, he gave a short, passionate speech on the sanctity of trails, leave no trace principles, and accountability. He was so convincing that over half the hikers immediately tensed up and were constipated the remainder of the trip.

In no uncertain terms, Larry informed the youngsters they weren't leaving until someone owned this horrendous trail violation. After a few awkward moments of silence, Kyle shrugged his shoulders and sheepishly raised his hand. Larry sighed, shook his head, and called Kyle over to a chorus of boos. He put his hand on Kyle's shoulder and gave him his official trail name: *Trail Pooper.*

Fast forward eight years. Prior to beginning my trek, Larry contacted me to suggest a trail name…

Larry: "I think I have a trail name for you."

Steve: "But I haven't started hiking yet."

Larry: "That's okay. You've earned it…sort of. I mean, you gave birth to Kyle, right?"

Steve: "Well, not exactly. Let's just say I was partly responsible."

Larry: "Here's my thinking…since Kyle is the Trail Pooper, you should be Fob W. Pot!"

Steve: "What's a Fob W. Pot?"

Larry: "Father of Boy Who Pooped on Trail."

Steve: "Fob W. Pot! I love it! It's brilliant!"

Larry: "I know."

Steve: "It has a great story behind it. It connects me to family and to you, my AT mentor."

Larry: "And it's not Butt Scratcher."

Steve: "I'm sold!"

I was excited to have a trail name! And who knows? Perhaps someday Kyle and his wife, Laci, will have a son, an adventurer type, and all the hiking world will come to know him as the son of a boy who pooped on the trail—Sob W. Pot.

With my gear all ready and my very own trail name, it was time to head to Georgia to begin my hike. Of all the things I was counting on for a successful hike, none were as important as my friends and family.

CHAPTER 6

SUPPORT CAN BE BEAUTIFUL

"The mountains are calling and I must go."
- John Muir

Solo-hiking the AT is a misnomer. The long, dangerous trek through 14 states is not an undertaking one successfully completes alone. Rather, there are scores of people, many behind the scenes, who each play an important role.

For my hike, one such person was Maurine Welch. I met Maurine, a fellow sojourner and fairly recent widow, at our Florida Sojourner workshop. She and her family have hiked several portions of the AT in Georgia, and she quickly took an interest in my plan to thru-hike the AT. In fact, she was the only person more excited about my hike than I was.

Maurine arranged for Janet and me to spend two nights in a cabin near Springer Mountain, the AT's southern terminus. The cabin, situated along the beautiful Toccoa River, belonged to her long-time friend, Arlin. This secluded mountain abode was the perfect spot to make final arrangements, reflect on my journey ahead, and spend some quality time with my wife.

On Friday, March 11th, 2016, Janet, Maurine, Arlin, and I left his cabin and headed to Amicalola Falls State Park to meet with several of my family members. I was thrilled to see my dad, sister Ellen, her husband Vin, her daughter Elizabeth, Vin's brother Tim, Janet's sister Carol, and her husband Scott. They were intrigued about my hike and wanted to be there to encourage me and see me off. Several of us hiked the long, steep steps that run along the Falls, and then ate together at the lodge.

During lunch, Vin asked me what I feared most about my upcoming adventure. I told him my two biggest fears were disease-carrying ticks and suffering a serious injury. I worried about hard-to-detect ticks more than bears, strangers, storms, homesickness or anything else that could potentially derail a hiker. I was also susceptible to ankle injuries after spraining or breaking mine twice while in high school and later while running the Marine Corps Marathon.

After lunch, we stopped by the Amicalola Falls visitor's center. At the gift shop, I found a blue moisture-wicking shirt with a printed white blaze. I hadn't planned on buying any more clothes, but I loved its look and feel. There are approximately 165,000 white blazes (stripes) painted on trees, rocks, and posts along the AT to mark the trail. Hikers encounter a white blaze, on average, about every 70 feet. These two-inch by five-inch trail markers were about to become a big part of my life, so I figured I might as well have one emblazed across my chest.

Behind the visitor's center, I stopped by the ranger station and officially registered for my hike. I was the 564th hiker to sign-in for a northbound (NOBO) thru-hike attempt. Something about seeing my name on the log sheet and having an official number made the previously abstract hike come into focus. In less than 18 hours, my whole world would suddenly change. I was so excited; tears ran down my leg.

Back at the cabin that evening, Janet carbo-loaded me with chili and pasta. I texted Vin, my brother-in-law, and asked if he would be willing to say a prayer for Janet and me at the start of the trail the following morning. I slept surprisingly well that night, even though I was anxious and had a lot on my mind. I thought about my wife and the tremendous sacrifice she was about to make so I could fulfill this lifelong dream. I thought about my Top 10 reasons for hiking the trail and committed them to memory. Most importantly, I prayed and asked God to protect me and to look after Janet.

"Be willing to take the first step, no matter how small it is. Concentrate on the fact that you are willing to learn. Absolute miracles will happen."
- Louise L. Hay

The peaceful sound of the Toccoa River rippled through the cabin's back yard as we opened our eyes to this new, exciting day. Saturday morning, March 12th, 2016—game day had finally arrived. The ball was in my hands, and that realization made me nervous. While showering, I conditioned my hair. I never condition my hair. I have a military buzz cut and, quite frankly, don't care about my hair's shine or follicle health. Had there been a Loofah bath brush within reach, I very well might have exfoliated my hiking legs. After showering, I took everything out of my backpack and re-packed it, placing everything in the exact same spot. That was useful, I thought to myself.

As Janet and Maurine put the finishing touches on breakfast, I paced the floor, fidgeting and running through my pre-hike checklist. Everything was on track—except me. I was clearly off-track, second guessing decisions of varied importance. Should I have gone with a longer spork? Do I have enough food for the first leg of the journey? How will other hikers react to my clean, vibrant hair and healthy follicles? Am I cut out for such an undertaking? Should I even be on this journey? Am I about to make the biggest mistake of my life?

Those questions over-shadowed an otherwise wonderful breakfast. Deep in thought, I devoured more than my fair share of sausage and egg casserole. Then, before I knew it…before I had answers to all those questions in my head, we were out the door!

All 11 of us agreed to rendezvous at the Springer Mountain parking lot. Reaching our rendezvous point was no small feat as the six-mile Forest Road 42 leading to the parking lot was gravel, winding and littered with massive potholes. Our diminutive Honda Fit was somehow able to negotiate the deep potholes without any damage. The drive felt like an intense game of Mario Kart—prior to a long, intense game of walking.

After parking, I hoisted the 30-pound pack onto my back, fastened the buckles, and tightened the straps. I reached for my chin strap, then realized I wasn't wearing a helmet. After holstering two water bottles in my backpack's side pockets, I assumed the caboose position as our family train headed up the .9-mile trail to the Springer Mountain summit. At the summit, the southern terminus of the AT, we took several photos and I signed the logbook, which is stored in a vault inside a boulder. I wondered if someday Nicolas Cage might look inside this container to find the hidden clue to the secret location of the legendary Templar Treasure.

I called my sons so they could share in this moment and give me virtual high fives. I hugged Dad a bit longer and tighter than normal, with the sobering realization that he was 79 years old, the same age his father passed away. Although my dad is in good health, he was at an age where I realize every hug is important, special and possibly the last.

Next came another very special moment: With my family gathered around and my pulse racing, I took the first of what I hoped would be about five million steps on the Appalachian Trail!

Someone once said that the first step is the most difficult, and I believe that—assuming I don't later step off a cliff and die. Having the guts or tenacity to begin any journey is the biggest obstacle. More than just a beginning, my first step was the culmination of decades of dreaming and years of planning. I stared down the biggest, toughest item on my bucket list and said, "Bring it."

For the moment, at least, I left my doubts and reservations behind. I was hiking the Appalachian Trail! Whether or not I would hike the entire trail remained to be seen, but it could never be said that I didn't have the guts to try.

Fob Fundamental #3 – The first step toward a major goal is often the most difficult. Dig deep, take the first step, and your momentum will make subsequent steps a little easier.

After hiking back to the parking lot, our group circled up and I tightly gripped Janet's hand. Vin led us in prayer and specifically asked God to protect me from ticks and serious injury and to watch over Janet. I appreciated and was moved by his words. I then hugged everyone and thanked them for being there.

As I kissed Janet and told her I loved her, I almost started to cry, but held back. I knew that if I started to cry, I would open a floodgate of tears from my menopausal lover. Her wailing would cause unsightly mascara streaks, a runny nose, and possibly trail erosion. No one wanted that. So, I clenched my teeth and tried to contain my excitement, anxiousness, sadness, and profound thankfulness. Having family and friends there was a moment I will always remember.

I also appreciated the many encouraging texts and Facebook posts from supporters all over the country—even from high school friends who I hadn't seen in over 30 years! I was energized by their love and support. Some told me they were hiking vicariously through me, and I gladly carried that mantle.

Gripping my trekking poles tightly, I turned and walked away. A few steps later, I saw a white blaze, a good indication I was on the right trail. The blaze was the same size, shape, and color as the one emblazoned on my shirt—what a coincidence! I looked over my shoulder a final time, smiled, and waved goodbye to my family.

Elle King once said, "Sometimes, if you fake confidence long enough, you're going to be confident." I was counting on that. I was alone on the Appalachian Trail, confidently putting one foot in front of the other. My life would never be the same, as I would soon find out.

Part Two ~
The Southern Appalachians

"The armored cars of dreams, contrived to let us do so many a dangerous thing."

- Elizabeth Bishop

CHAPTER 7

GEORGIA ON MY MIND

March 12 – 20, 2016

"I intend to make Georgia howl."
- William Tecumseh Sherman

Day 1 – Springer Mountain to Hightower Gap
8.9 miles, 8.9 cumulative miles

"Whatever you can do or dream you can, begin it.
Boldness has genius, power, and magic in it."
- W. H. Murray

I wasn't alone for long. Two minutes into my journey, I sensed someone just a few paces behind me. I glanced over my shoulder and asked the young man if he was going to Maine. He said that he was, so I turned and gave him a fist pump and introduced myself. His name was Matt and he was a recent graduate from the University of North Carolina-Wilmington. After learning he loved and was listening to a classical jazz music mix on his headphones, I decided not to tell him my music mix was a loop of Ozzy Osbourne's "Crazy Train."

Matt decided to take a year off and hike the AT before starting law school. He is a competitive rifle and pistol shooter which might have come in handy on the trail had he been packing. Despite the 30 years in age that separated us, Matt and I quickly forged a friendship and buddied up on this first day of hiking. I was excited to have made my first friend on the trail.

The skies were clear and the day was unseasonably warm as we wound our way through narrow gaps in mountain laurel. I stopped at the Stover Creek Shelter's privy (think AT outhouse) to relieve myself because I was apparently still too shy to take advantage of the hundreds of trees in every direction. We met several other hikers there and later at Hawks Mountain Shelter. There are over 250 shelters on the AT spaced, on average, about eight miles apart. They are typically wooden, three-sided, lean-to style structures, although their designs and features vary widely.

The scene at shelters reminded me of lunchtime on the first day of a new school year. Everyone was in high spirits and glad to have our grand hiking adventure underway. The more socially awkward among us fumbled in our pockets for lunch money and tried to remember our locker combinations. We eyeballed each other's shiny new backpacks and unsoiled hiking shirts. The female hikers still smelled like rose petals, while most of the guys already reeked of early onset spoiled cabbage. As I watched the gal across from me carefully arrange kale and dab coconut oil on her whole grain tortilla, I downed an eight-pack of peanut butter crackers and flicked orange crumbs from my goatee.

Deep down, we were all nervous and didn't want to say or do anything that would mark us as inexperienced, rookie hikers. With my shiny hair and healthy follicles, I was already flirting with those labels. We especially wanted to avoid the big mistake that could cause injury or earn us an unfavorable, hard-to-shake reputation or trail name. We learned a female hiker had to be medically evacuated from a nearby shelter after spilling boiling water on her leg while cooking. Her sad tale served as a reminder of how quickly a hike can end.

Late in the afternoon, Matt and I found a suitable camping spot on top of the first hill north of Hightower Gap. We set up camp, built a roaring fire, and discussed our first day on the AT. I mostly listened, because my beef stew and peanut butter cracker meal had stuck to the roof of my mouth, making my speech indecipherable. Already, it seemed like I had known Matt for years. I told him about a few of my sons' female friends who were currently available, in case he was interested in pursuing a mate along with his law degree. He said he'd give that some thought.

After supper, we hung our food bags and settled into our tent and hammock, respectively. We had survived a near perfect 8.9-mile first day on the trail. I glanced down at my watch and saw that it was 9:00 p.m., also known as hiker midnight. Before dozing off to sleep, I pinched myself to confirm that this was a real scene and not simply one of many AT dreams I'd had through the years. I was an actual AT hiker and had made it through my first day. Now I just needed to dig deep and hike another 4.9 million or so steps.

Day 2 – Hightower Gap to Ramrock Mountain
10.1 miles, 19 cumulative miles

"The best thing one can do when it's raining is to let it rain."
- Henry Wadsworth Longfellow

The heavy rain and wind gusts started at midnight and pounded my tent for the remainder of the night. I was excited about the storm because I wanted an early test of my portable, waterproof, 34-ounce abode. Janet wasn't next door in the RV to bail me out this time. Fortunately, my tent passed its first test. I stayed dry and warm. Matt didn't fare so well in his hammock and tarp combination. In fact, he got soaked. I felt bad for him but his spirits remained high and he quickly bounced back.

After packing my tent in light rain, I ate the pop tart that had been sitting in the bottom of my food bag for the past two months of training hikes. The normally rectangular treat had been reduced to brown sugar cinnamon sawdust. But those were calories, and I would need them on my first AT challenge, Sassafras Mountain, coming in at 3,347 feet.

What makes a mountain challenging has to do with elevation, slope, terrain, and the current weather conditions. It also has to do with the hiker's weight and physical fitness. I was a 50-year-old, 236.2-pound, slightly chubby man in average condition for a normal lifestyle. However, hiking the AT is not a normal lifestyle. I was in shape but not in trail shape. I had legs but not trail legs. The way hikers get in trail shape and develop trail legs is by hiking the trail. A hiker's body will eventually adjust to the demands placed on it. I was counting on that.

In addition to not being in trail shape, there was the issue of my vision. Years ago, during an 8th grade parent-teacher conference, my teacher told my mom, "Steven squints all the time." The issue may have been my subsequently diagnosed 20-800 vision, or that I was trying to get a better look at the adorable Beth Land sitting on the front row, twirling her hair with a pencil.

On the trail, I chose glasses over contact lenses because I didn't want the hassle of trying to keep contact lenses clean. My choice was all well and good until it started to rain. In rainy conditions, I could either wear foggy glasses that impaired my vision, or wear no glasses at all…which also impaired my vision. Fortunately, the AT is usually well-marked and I didn't need 20/20 vision to stay on it, even in rainy conditions.

I left 30 minutes earlier than Matt, but the younger, faster hiker soon caught me. By noon, the rain had subsided and the sun came out just as we reached the picturesque, mountain oasis known as Justus Creek. Out of abundant caution, we filtered the cold, clear, rushing river water and ate lunch on a log along the bank. A curious salamander bobbed and weaved on the log next to me, watching my every move.

As we discussed the previous day's events, Matt shared with me that he began his hike at the parking lot, rather than at the official southern terminus at Springer Mountain's summit. I found it odd that someone wanting to hike the entire 2,189.1-mile AT would skip the first .9 miles. I didn't question him, because hikers are expected to be non-judgmental and hike their own hike. Still, the way my brain is wired, knowing I skipped the first .9 miles would have bugged me for the rest of my journey.

Later in the day, Matt and I paid a visit to Gooch Gap Shelter and talked to several hikers. One guy was a 50-year-old pastor from Belleville, Illinois (where I used to live) who had a son who spent two years studying at Harding University, the school from which both of my sons graduated. Just like being the newcomer at school lunch tables throughout my youth, I enjoyed connecting with someone with whom I had something in common.

At Gooch Gap we got our first trail magic! Trail magic is any unexpected act of kindness one encounters while hiking the trail. Whether the magic takes the form of food, a ride to town, or something else, it is encouraging and inspiring. In this case a former thru-hiker, Sticks, was spending his Spring Break grilling hot dogs for hikers. Matt and I graciously accepted his offer and I downed two Oscar Meyer wieners in four bites.

Moments later, I made my first major mistake on the Appalachian Trail. As I thanked Sticks for the hot dogs, I placed a $5 tip on the table next to his grill. He said the money wasn't necessary, but I insisted. I thought I was doing the right thing, but he looked dejected. Matt didn't say anything, but shook his head and gave me the "Dude, what'd you do that for?" look.

The lesson learned was that trail magic does just as much, and maybe more, for the giver than the receiver. While this concept hit home with me on day two, the principle has been around for 2,000 years. According to the apostle Paul, Jesus once said, *"It is more blessed to give than to receive."* (Acts 20:35)

One of the things that makes trail magic special is that it is a free gift, given from the heart, with no expectation of anything tangible in return. Giving Sticks money, however well-intentioned, had turned his kindness into a transactional event. I had reduced this kind-hearted trail angel to just a trail vendor. I had taken the magic out of the moment. It would have been different if he had a donation jar—but he didn't. I blew it and I knew it. It wouldn't be my last lesson learned on the Appalachian Trail.

Fob Fundamental #4 – Oftentimes the best response to a kind gesture is simply to smile and humbly say thank you.

We finished our day atop Ramrock Mountain in Georgia's Chattahoochee National Forest. A couple of young, section-hiking ladies from Indiana University camped near us and shared our food bag lines. Hikers typically place their food in a waterproof bag, then use a rope or cord to hoist it up on a tree branch, hopefully out of reach of hungry bears. Hanging and sharing a line was one way hikers built bonds of cooperation. By offering to share my line, I demonstrated to younger, female hikers that I was a reliable hunter-gatherer-provider for our tribal family. They usually obliged, more out of pity than necessity.

Matt used the remaining sunlight to partially dry his hammock while I treated my first two AT heel blisters. In retrospect, I should have treated the blisters the moment they started hurting, rather than waiting until the end of the day. I knew that hiking principle, but was reluctant to stop earlier while we were making good time. On a 2,000-mile journey, it is much more important to take care of my feet than to be a "tough guy" and keep pace with a younger, faster hiking partner. This second trail lesson came with considerable pain.

As I sat boiling water to cook my two packages of Ramen noodles with tabasco sauce, I reflected on our good second day. Despite two small blisters, constipation, and missing my wife, I was off to a good start. I was grateful to be there, to have met Matt, and for my friends and family cheering me on through texts and Facebook posts.

Day 3 – Ramrock Mountain to Neels Gap
12.7 miles, 31.7 cumulative miles

"There are few moments of clarity more profound than those that follow the emptying of an overcharged bladder.
The world slows down, the focus sharpens, the brain comes back on line."
- Tom Holt

Since the time I turned 40, I have dealt with two health issues: acid reflux and frequent urination. Both maladies joined forces which made for a memorable night on Ramrock Mountain. Around 2:00 a.m., the beef Ramen noodle, chicken Ramen noodle, and tabasco sauce trifecta began taking a toll on my stomach and esophagus. I popped a few Tums and things settled down. The real issue that night, though, involved urination.

As men get older, their prostates grow. At age 50, mine was the size of a can of tuna. My doctor told me the prostate pushes on the urethra which, quite frankly, sounds like a woman's name or a body part only a woman should have. This pressure irritates the bladder walls which contract, making me (and millions of other men) have to pee.

So, for most nights over the past decade, I got up at 3:00 a.m., plus or minus an hour, shuffled to the bathroom, relieved myself, and then crawled back into bed. In an RV, where my wife and I live full-time, this is really

29

easy. I take one full stride, do a left face, and fire away.

That is all well and good in a house or RV, but not so fun in the wilderness in the middle of the night in all sorts of weather. Thus, I carried a Mountain Dew pee bottle on the trail. Before judging me, hear me out. It was ultra-light, so weight was not an issue. It fit neatly in the side pocket of my backpack, so space was not an issue. Furthermore, as a newborn in 1966, I probably heard and subconsciously processed Mountain Dew's first slogan— "Yahoo Mountain Dew…It'll tickle your innards."

On the trail, I invented and mastered a technique, *The Johnson Method* (patent pending), which provided bladder relief without having to exit my tent. This innovative technique, which worked remarkably well on my first night, has regrettably not been made available for the general public's use until now.

First, I got on my knees, comfortably straddling my air mattress, with my head wedged against the top of my tent for added stability. Next, I assumed the ready position in the dark, as any illumination would have cast an embarrassing shadow against the side of my Big Agnes tent. Third, I fired away, typically filling the bottle to near capacity. The final step, an important one, involved putting the bottle cap on tightly and returning the bottle to the tent's side pocket.

Unfortunately, *The Johnson Method* didn't yield as favorable a result during my second night on the trail. I made a critical error—a classic rookie mistake. I rose on my knees and placed them on the edges of the air mattress, rather than straddling it. I grabbed the bottle, positioned myself, aimed, and fired. Six ounces later, all was well. As the Mountain Dew bottle became warm in the palm of my right hand, I knew good things were happening. In fact, my innards were tickled.

Then disaster struck! At mid-stream, my left knee slid off the side of the air mattress, and I began to fall on my side. My instincts were to reach out and catch myself, but there were no available hands! In moments like this, mid-stream, job one is to keep the Mountain Dew bottle connected to the mother ship.

I held on for dear life and toppled over sideways with my head and shoulder hitting the side of the tent. Like a teenager playing *Call of Duty* during a slumber party pillow fight, I remained focused and kept firing. As a 50-year-old, I was unable to turn off the spigot until the tank was empty. I laid there for a moment, relieved that I wasn't injured—and just relieved in general.

Exhausted and on my side, my next issue was to retrieve the bottle cap from the other side of the tent. With all the energy I could muster, I swung my legs around while maintaining the link with the mother ship. I grabbed the bottle cap with my toes, like a ballerina demonstrating toe dexterity at an audition. I leaned the bottle up, capped it, and rolled back onto the air mattress. I was fatigued, but tragedy had been averted! My handling of unexpected situations on the AT, the surprise moments, would either make or break me. I learned that if you don't keep your wits and rise to the occasion, "urine" big trouble.

Matt and I left Ramrock at 8:15 a.m. Twenty minutes into our hike, I got that rumbling feeling deep in my stomach. There was a long roaring sound like an approaching train, and then the voice of the demon from *The Exorcist* shouted, "Let me out!" through my belly button. Startled, Matt reached for his pocket knife and spun around to defend me.

The tabasco-laced Ramen noodles had worked their way through my digestive track and were now crying for freedom. I knew Woody Gap was near and had an actual rest area and toilet. I also knew I hadn't gone in four days. So, I shifted to high gear and blew past Matt in search of relief. I burst into the Woody Gap restroom just seconds before the explosion. I only know what it sounded like from inside the restroom, but there are reports the explosion could be heard as far away as Dahlonega.

After a peanut butter and beef jerky lunch at Jarrard Gap, Matt and I made our way toward Blood Mountain, the tallest AT mountain in Georgia. Some say the mountain is named after a bloody battle between the Cherokee and Creek Indians. Others say it is based on the reddish color of lichen and Catawba near the summit. Still others say the Bloods battled the Crips there in a famous gang battle. (Just one person—Fob W. Pot—said that.)

Sadly, what is for certain is that Blood Mountain is the location where 24-year-old hiker Meredith Hope Emerson was attacked and kidnapped in January, 2008. Her attacker, who killed her a few days later, was sentenced to life in prison. I stopped and paid my respects to Meredith, who hailed from Longmont, Colorado and graduated with honors in French from the University of Georgia. She loved the AT and had been on it training her dog, Ella, as a physical therapy dog. To celebrate Meredith's life, her family and friends founded Right to Hike, Inc., a non-profit organization supporting causes that were close to her heart, including hiker safety and humane societies.[5] Yes, as part of my preparations and before ever stepping foot on the trail, I had done my homework on the 11 recorded AT murders through the years.

Back on the trail, we ascended Blood Mountain in light rain and blustery wind. During the climb, we saw a few birds, the first wildlife we had seen on the trail since the Justus Creek salamander. It was a long but easy ascent, aside from my right heel bleeding from a torn blister. Matt and I hung out for a while with some hikers at the Blood Mountain Shelter and shot a

---

[5] To learn more about Meredith Hope Emerson or to make a donation to causes that were important to her, go to https://www.righttohikeinc.com

video clip that wasn't audible due to the strong wind. The descent was more challenging as we had to scramble over dozens of large, slick boulders in rain and high winds. On the way down, we passed three New Yorkers also planning to stay at the Walasi-Yi hostel at Neels Gap that evening. That would prove to be a key pass. When we arrived at the hostel, Matt and I secured the final two bunks. Sorry, New Yorkers.

My first order of business, even before showering, was to eat. As a famished hiker, I intended to eat whatever food or drink I encountered first. For an appetizer, I drank a cold Diet Coke which, after three days of water, was magical. Other hikers rightly admonished me for passing up the 140 calories from a regular Coke. Matt and I then split a large three-meat pizza. Next, I ate a burrito and an apple and then drank a Ginger Ale and a Powerade. I concluded my planned feasting with a loud belch, which was rewarded with a splattering of applause from the hikers assembled in the hiker lounge.

I was just starting to get full when 15 students from Armstrong State University in Savannah came rolling in with trail magic—specifically, large containers full of baked ziti, salad, and bread. Despite already being full, I had to partake of this amazing Italian feast. Over-eating is what aspiring thru-hikers do. These young trail angels were on Spring Break as part of a Christian ministry outreach and we were glad to be on the receiving end of their generosity. Although I had never heard of Armstrong State University, I made a note to leave them my entire estate.

After showering and doing laundry, I began conversing with a wide assortment of the assembled hiker humanity. Among the cast of characters was Booknboot, an Australian lady with a darling accent. Next to her were the two Indiana University ladies who shared our bear bag line on Ramrock Mountain. One is a competitive cyclist and the other wants to be a brain surgeon.

A very kind and interesting transgender photographer from Houston sat in the hiker lounge. I had never met or spoken to any transgender person before so I enjoyed getting to know her. We covered some basic ground, but I didn't get to the deeper, more personal questions that were on my mind. I was genuinely interested in her story, but feared a poorly worded question might offend her. Perhaps the personal details of her story were none of my business.

I also spoke with Driftwood, a lady about my age who was there with Wildwood, her strapping, 20-year-old special needs son. I admired and was encouraged by their goal to thru-hike the trail. She happily attended to his needs, which were plentiful.

Several of us stayed up until 10:30 p.m., well past hiker midnight, watching *The Matrix* and burping ziti. My final challenge of the night was climbing to the top bunk. Although I had only been on the trail for three days, my feet and body were tired and sore. For some spiritual enrichment, I finished the day listening to an excellent online sermon by my friend and former fellow teacher, Donald Ballard.

I said goodnight to Booknboot, bunked below me, just so I could hear her say "Goodnight, mate" back in her wonderful Australian accent. It made me miss my wife and her cute, Southern accent. But things were good. I was among new friends, in a warm bed, with a bathroom nearby. My Mountain Dew pee bottle had the night off.

Day 4 – Neels Gap to Sheep Rock Top
10.5 miles, 42.2 cumulative miles

The fact that *The Hunger Games* and *The Walking Dead* were both filmed in Georgia is only fitting. In my first week on the trail in Georgia, I had experienced several zombie-like stretches when all I thought about was food.

Fortunately, as the sun rose at the Walasi-Yi hostel on the morning of day four, hunger was not going to be an issue. My previously mentioned friend and fellow sojourner, Maurine, arrived with her family at 9:00 a.m. with a ton of McDonald's food and coffee! God bless her dear soul! There was enough McGrub for Matt, other hikers, and me to fill-up on sausage and egg biscuits and cinnamon swirls.

I enjoyed meeting Maurine's sweet family. After sharing a few hiking stories, we prayed together. I specifically thanked God for Maurine being a true trail angel early in my journey.

After Maurine and her family left, I filled Matt in on the entire back story which resulted in my trail name, Fob W. Pot...

Fob: "So what do you think?"

Matt: "I love the story and name. In fact, Fob W. Pot is the best trail name I've encountered so far. But it needs an edit."

Fob: "I'm listening."

Matt: "It needs to be *Sir* Fob W. Pot."

Fob: "Interesting. Why the 'Sir'?"

Matt: "Well, that sounds more dignified, especially since the story is about your son pooping on a trail. Also, you're the oldest person I've seen in three days."

Matt's points were valid and so I became knighted as *Sir Fob W. Pot*, although I usually shortened it to just *Fob*. The name would forever symbolically connect me with my family, my mentor, my first hiking partner, and my ever-advancing biological clock.

As I started to pack up, Matt informed me that his legs were bothering him and he was going to take a zero (hiker slang for a day off) and remain at Neels Gap for a second night. Since the weather was gorgeous, I felt reasonably good, and it was only day four, I decided to hike on. With Matt being a younger and faster hiker, we just figured he would catch up with me in a few days. I said goodbye to Matt and departed the hostel. Little did I know I would never see Matt again. He would exit my life as quickly as he had entered. I still don't know whether he finished the trail, but I sure hope he did. Regardless, I value our three days together and his friendship. (Matt, if you're reading this, please contact me!)

As the day progressed, the temperature and humidity steadily rose. I was glad I had trained in hot, humid Florida. By mid-afternoon, I descended into Tesnatee Gap and discovered more trail magic! Trail angels King Tut and Angela were serving snacks and drinks, answering questions, and offering free, crocheted winter hats, courtesy of the Crochet Group from Bethlehem, Georgia's United Methodist Church.

I tried on a hat and looked like a male centerfold in the March issue of *Crochet World* magazine. Although I already had a winter hat, I silently wondered if I could cut two holes in this one and wear it as winter boxers. Instead, I decided to take one to use as a clothes bag cover, since my clothes bag doubles as a pillow. I later sent a thank-you note to these sweet, unseen, crocheting trail angels. I didn't include a $5 tip.

The climb out of Tesnatee Gap was the toughest so far, especially for my blistered right heel. Still not in trail shape, I had to stop regularly to catch my breath and give my aching feet a rest. I missed Matt, but enjoyed taking a few breaks and getting to know other hikers. I met one hiker from California who sold all his possessions and is traveling around the country in a van with his dog. (I thought, what kind of a nut job would go and do something like that?)

At Blue Mountain Shelter, I met a medically retired Marine and his girlfriend. We shared stories from our experiences serving in Afghanistan. He was in the lead vehicle of a convoy in Helmand Province when an Improvised Explosive Device (IED) exploded, sending him and others flying through the air. His face was literally torn off and had to be reconstructed. He spent a year in the hospital and had to have multiple surgeries on different parts of his body.

He invited me over to take a closer look at his face. I had visited with several recently injured troops at the hospital at Bagram Air Base, Afghanistan, but only a few following major facial reconstruction. I was impressed with how well he looked and told him so. I had to get really close to see even the slightest evidence of scarring. Major kudos to his doctors for repairing and restoring his face.

This brave Marine said most of the physical work was done and now he's hiking the trail to restore his heart and soul. Based on his attitude, I have no doubt he'll succeed. He told me he hadn't yet earned a trail name. My suggestion was "Hero" because it fit him and he had certainly earned

34

that title.

After talking to him and continuing my hike, I felt less tired. My feet seemed to hurt less, at least for a while. I held my head higher and was prouder to be an American and to be hiking the same trail as this dedicated Marine. Semper Fi!

Fob Fundamental #5 – Take the time to tell your story. You never know how it might lift someone's spirits, change his day, or even his life.

After 10.5 miles, I called it a day atop Sheep Rock Top mountain. Today, I said goodbye to one friend but met new ones, including a courageous war hero. Settling in for the night, I rested my head on a warm, crochet-covered clothes bag. I glanced down at the backpack by my feet and noticed salt formations had formed on the front straps. It seemed the trail was getting me into shape one sweat drop at a time.

Day 5 – Sheep Rock Top to Rocky Mountain
12.1 miles, 54.3 cumulative miles

"Be brave enough to start a conversation that matters."
- Margaret Wheatley

I roused in my tent and peeked out in time to witness an amazing sunrise on which God seemed to have spent a little extra time. Before heading out, I spent half an hour shaping and customizing moleskin patches for the blisters on my heels. Clearly, my feet were not tough enough before starting this journey. Even worse, I sensed my hair had lost its shine. I blamed poor follicle health. I descended to Low Gap Shelter to get water and then spent the day doing a long series of small ups and downs.

At the Blue Mountain summit, I spoke with a young, fast-hiking, red-bearded guy from Tennessee. Over the past 22 years, he has been affiliated with a variety of different faith groups, yet was still searching for the right match. He said he was here to find himself and figure things out. I appreciated his openness and honesty in my first of what would be many trail conversations with other hikers about matters of faith. Unlike strangers back in the real world, AT hikers were often willing to share deeply held struggles or concerns with others they had just met. Our common wilderness endeavor seemed to break down facades and societal norms about keeping private things private.

I told him I hoped he would find what he was looking for during his hike. Given his fast pace, I doubted I would see him again. I just hoped this experience would help him to re-connect with a God who loves him and was evident, at least to me, at every step on the AT.

The final climb of the day out of Unicoi Gap was intense. My feet hurt with each step and I was sucking wind. Unfortunately, there are no customizable moleskins to treat wind sucking. The combination of the heat, mountain slope, and my foot pain, made the climb out of Unicoi Gap the toughest in Georgia for me. I told myself to just go slowly and focus on putting one foot in front of the other. I knew the Georgia mountains would eventually beat me into shape if I continued to grind it out and not give up.

Exhausted, I set up camp on Rocky Mountain, with wonderful views from 4,017 feet. I fired up some chicken and rice on my MSR Pocket Rocket stove and gobbled it down way too quickly—a losing play in *The Hunger Games*.

While eating, I called my wife and was thrilled to hear her voice. Unfortunately, as she updated me on happenings back in the real world, I had to put her on speaker phone as my acid reflux kicked in and I started throwing up:

Janet: "It's great to hear your voice! How are you doing?"

Fob (*gagging*): "I'm fine."

Janet: "You don't sound fine. What's wrong?"

Fob (*coughing up rice*): "Just a little reflux. Sorry about that. I really miss you."

Janet: "I miss you too. Are you with anyone tonight?"

Fob: "Hold on a second." (*vomits remaining chicken and rice by campfire ring*) "Sorry again. No, I'm flying solo tonight. Probably for the best."

It wasn't the sweet, romantic phone call that I hoped for or that she deserved. I regretted not only the less than romantic phone call and the bout of reflux, but the wasted carbs that lay on the ground before me. I would have been more upbeat had I known this would be my last bout with acid reflux during my time on the trail.

Day 6 – Rocky Mountain to Deep Gap Shelter
11.7 miles, 66 cumulative miles

As I was breaking camp on Rocky Mountain, two hikers came by with their dog and stopped for a rest. The older, bearded guy, Relic Hunter, was straight out of *Deliverance*—I mean that as a compliment. He looked and spoke as if he had been in the woods his entire life, and I was naturally interested in his story.

Relic Hunter completed half of the AT several years ago. During that thru-hike attempt, a Virginia bear grabbed a hold of his backpack which was leaning next to a tree by his tent. He scrambled out of his tent, changed underwear, and followed the bear at a distance. The bear eventually dropped the foodless pack and moved on. Relic Hunter told me he proudly hung the pack, with three bear claw punctures in it, on the wall in his garage.

The younger, thin guy, Loud Owl, looked tired and worn out. As his dog curiously sniffed the mysterious substance on the ground by the campfire ring, Loud Owl asked me about the origins of my trail name. I told him the entire, three-minute-long story. I then asked him about the origin of his trail name. In his slow, southern drawl, he explained, "Sometimes at night...those owls can get pretty loud." And then he stopped.

As his dog licked my chicken and rice vomit near our feet, I looked at Loud Owl, wanting more from his story. Did a screeching owl attack him by a campfire? Does his head spin around like an owl (or like Linda Blair's character in *The Exorcist*)? No, there was no more story to be told. Owls are loud...and he was Loud Owl. End of story.

We continued talking and I learned Loud Owl was almost out of food. So, I offered him my entire bag of trail mix. His face lit up like a great grandma's birthday cake and he said, "Seriously? Thanks, Fob!" It seemed like a good and decent thing to do, but I had other motives: 1) I never craved trail mix...especially the sweet, messy kind that left trail mix residual on my fingers; and 2) Reducing unneeded pack weight whenever possible was always a good thing on this type of journey.

Later, I came across Driftwood, the dear lady who was hiking with her 20-year-old special needs son, Wildwood. He didn't speak, but could communicate with basic sign language. I spent some time with them at Neels Gap and observed how good, caring and patient she was with him. My mom would have approved. I also noticed how well my fellow hikers related to him. By virtue of being on this long journey, we were all, in a sense, "special needs." Driftwood and Wildwood were quite an inspirational pair and I hoped they would be able to finish their hike.

White blazes led me down Rocky Mountain and then on a long climb up Tray Mountain. On the way, I approached a powerful stream cutting its own path down the side of the mountain. I looked up and saw a pair of red-headed, freckled young people who appeared to have just gotten off the train from Hogwarts. Simba and Firecracker, a brother and sister team, were gathering water and toting it several yards off the trail.

As I filtered water from the stream, I watched their ritual with bewilderment. Could these young ginger wizards be concocting a mysterious potion? On closer examination, I realized what they were doing—washing their hair! Although I had conditioned my hair for the first time a week earlier, I never considered washing my hair in a frigid Georgia stream in March. Perhaps if I had long, vibrant red hair rather than a buzz cut, I would have felt differently.

Later that day, I stopped for a break and met a French-speaking Canadian from Quebec with the trail name Diguidou. We didn't speak each other's language, but he knew enough English to communicate that *Diguidou* is French slang for "everything's good." I wanted to reciprocate in order to impress him and make him feel at home, but I only know two French expressions.

Rather than say nothing, I looked him in the eyes, smiled, and said, "Oui, Oui, omelette du frommage," which means, "Yes, yes, cheese omelet." He looked at me, understandably puzzled, and decided break time was over. As he hiked away, I realized I had set U.S.-Canadian relations back 20 years, and for that I am truly sorry.

At mile 60.9, I stopped and had a candy bar at Young Lick Knob which is followed by a dip at mile 62.2 called Swag of the Blue Ridge. The stranger these location names got, the more I wondered about the stories behind the names. In fact, if I hadn't already adopted a trail name, I would have made up a story to justify being called *Sir Swag of the Blue Ridge.*

After a final climb over Kelly Knob, I descended to Deep Gap Knob and set up camp near the shelter. There were about 25 tents set up in the vicinity, and some lively dinner conversation began around the picnic table. Most hikers were millennials in their early to mid-twenties, and the topic that evening was student loan debt and how to avoid paying it. Options ranged from "just vote for Bernie Sanders" and the debt will disappear to "just don't pay it...education is not like a house they can foreclose on...once you get a degree, you have it."

I had my thoughts on these subjects, like one should only borrow money for college (or anything) if one has the intent and ability to pay it off eventually. Or perhaps one could work hard at schooling, make good grades, and earn a college scholarship. Or perhaps one could work multiple jobs and save money for college. Or perhaps one could decide not to go to college at all. But one shouldn't expect to do nothing but reap the college benefits and then expect American taxpayers to foot the bill.

Despite my beliefs on this subject, I remained silent. I was tired. My blistered feet hurt. I was outnumbered. I really just wanted to focus on keeping my fettucine alfredo down. Besides, the last thing this group wanted was a lecture from the old, conservative guy sitting on a log with salt formations protruding from his Spanish moss-looking beard.

Fob Fundamental #6 – Pick and choose your cultural battles carefully. Sometimes it's best to remain silent, digest your food, and keep peace at camp.

After supper, I noticed two German hikers sitting off by themselves at the side of the shelter. As someone who has lived in Germany twice and speaks two French phrases, I was the perfect ambassador to meet them and break the ice. Fortunately, they spoke pretty good English and were very interested in my trail name and the story behind it. At the end of my story, one of them laughed heartily and, in his thick German accent affirmed, "Your son poop on trail!"

Even later, I struck up a conversation with a friendly young man, the pride of Jackson, Mississippi. He turned out to be Beaver, the wood-gathering son of a friend of a friend of mine. He was hiking the trail as a 17-year-old, recently graduated high school student, and that alone is impressive.

It had been a good Day 6 on the AT mainly because of the wide range of interesting people I'd met. We shared much in common, particularly our love of hiking. Still, I sensed a pretty wide cultural divide between myself and some of the millennials. Despite these differences, I was enjoying the sights and sounds of the trail. In fact, digidou! Everything was good!

Days 7 & 8 – Deep Gap Shelter to Hiawassee, Georgia
3.6 miles + 0 miles, 69.6 cumulative miles

I opened my eyes to total darkness and glanced at my watch. It was 6:00 a.m., still early, but I was already alert and highly motivated. Today, I needed to hike just 3.6 miles to catch the 9:00 a.m. shuttle into Hiawassee for some much-needed time off. I packed everything in the dark and departed at 6:45 a.m., while my new millennial friends were still asleep in our makeshift tent city. The early departure necessitated using my headlamp, a gift from my good friend and hiking buddy, John Walsh. Hiking in the dark required maximum concentration as one misstep along the narrow, steep ledges would have ended more than just my hike.

About a half-mile from the pickup point at Dicks Creek Gap, I went by a trail maintainer who was blowing leaves off the trail. I knew these folks removed trees and limbs, but never realized they use leaf blowers to keep the trail clear. I thanked him for his early morning dedication which afforded me and other hikers a clearer, safer trail on which to hike.

I arrived at Hiawassee's Budget Inn and signed up for two nights in order to reap the benefits of a full zero day. I needed time off the trail to rest my aching feet, re-supply, and re-fuel. Long ago, I promised myself to take my time, enjoy the journey, and try to experience as much of these trail towns as possible. That would mean a longer hike for me than some, but I was okay with that.

I hoped to attend church services on Sunday morning. As a Christian, I strive, with mixed results, to make every day a day of worship. On the AT, like back in the real world, every day presented an opportunity to pray, read my Bible, listen to and sing songs of praise, and honor and glorify God with my words and deeds. Still, there is something special about gathering together with other Saints in more formal settings. These periods of corporate worship provide opportunities for encouragement, fellowship, and communion that can't be found alone on a mountaintop. Thus, finding a house of worship, whenever feasible, was a priority.

While waiting for my room to be cleaned, I met Pat and Megan, a mother-daughter thru-hiking team originally from Vermont, but now living in New Hampshire. Megan graduated from Dartmouth, taught English for a while, and was getting married in September. She would eventually earn the trail name Orbit because she had a big, beautiful smile like the girl in the Orbit chewing gum commercial. If I had been named after a commercial product, I suspect it would be Suave Infusion, on account of my shiny, conditioned hair and charming, sophisticated disposition. I digress. Today was Megan's 25th birthday, and we were craving coffee, so I treated them to some hot java at the nearby Dairy Queen.

Pat, who would later earn the trail name Mom, was a year older than me. A self-proclaimed "indoor cat," she had never backpacked a day in her life. Might as well start with the Appalachian Trail! I loved her boldness, thick New England accent, and the way she and Megan engaged in friendly, mother-daughter banter. Knowing Megan was a former Dartmouth-trained English teacher, I focused on using good grammar and not dangling any participles.

Once my room was ready, I took a long, luxurious hot shower followed by a long, piping hot bath. I was initially concerned that the Hiawassee water was polluted, but then realized I was the source of the brown water and sediment pooling by my feet.

After doing laundry, I headed straight for Daniel's All-You-Can-Eat Steakhouse! For an aspiring thru-hiker, hearing or seeing the words "all you can eat" can cause heart palpitations, fanciful visions, and noticeable drooling. This multi-course feast was worth hiking 70 miles for! I had a large salad, bread, potatoes, fried chicken, fried fish, fried shrimp, peas, mac 'n cheese, baked beans, strawberry dessert, two waters, two Diet Cokes, a tall glass of chocolate milk, and a cup of coffee. Did I mention it was really good? Maybe I wouldn't lose weight after all!

Full as a fat hiker's sock, I walked back to the hotel, stopping along the way to resupply at the Dollar General. Several young hikers were gathered around a campfire next to the hotel, drinking, smoking cigarettes of various lengths, and sharing their hiking stories from week one. I stopped by to chat for a few minutes, then headed off to bed. It was good to be clean and full and back in civilization, if only for a short while.

After a restful night's sleep, I awoke on my first zero day! There would be some short walks today, but no hiking. My goals were to eat, rest, take a nap, prepare my backpack, and call my wife and father. I was glad to hear that Janet had safely returned from a trip to Florida with her sister and had gotten in some sisterly bonding. Mainly, I was just happy to hear her sweet voice.

For brunch, I gobbled down a foot-long Italian sub from Subway, as a traveling soccer team from South Carolina's Francis Marion University ate nearby. Later, I finished off the day with Taco Bell's Quesalupa combo, followed by a beefy 5-layer burrito for dessert. My decision to get a single room would turn out to be wise.

Day 9 – Hiawassee to Rich Cove Gap, Georgia
7.4 miles, 77 cumulative miles

Serendipity – "Luck that takes the form of finding valuable or pleasant things that are not looked for."[6]

Providence – "The means by which God directs all things, both animate and inanimate, seen and unseen, good and evil – toward a worthy purpose, which means His will must finally prevail."[7]

The lucky twists, the fortunate breaks, the way a series of seemingly random events can work in conjunction to produce an unexpected favorable outcome...do you call them serendipity? Or is it God's providence at work?

The older I get, the less I believe in luck or randomness...and the more I believe in a loving God orchestrating a few twists, and engineering a few breaks, to provide for and sustain His children. Even when bad things happen, God is there bringing out the good and maybe teaching us some things in the process. He is a God of redemption.

Being in a trail town on a Sunday, I had a rare opportunity to attend a worship service while hiking the AT. I knew it would do me good and that opportunities to do so would be limited over the next six months. With the help of Google, I found the meeting place for the Hiawassee Church of Christ, but it was 10 miles outside of town. After more research, I reached a guy named Bobby, whose brother is a member of this congregation. Bobby graciously offered me a ride, another form of trail magic.

---

[6] "serendipity." Merriam-Webster, Inc. 2017. https://www.learnersdictionary.com (13 January 2017).

[7] McGee, J. Vernon. "Providence is the Hand of God." Thru The Bible, http://www.oneplace.com/ministries/thru-the-bible-with-j-vernon-mcgee/read/articles/providence-is-the-hand-of-god-11044.html. Accessed 12 January 2017.

Meanwhile, there was the issue of getting from the church building back to the trail—a substantial, 20-mile journey. How would God come up with a "lucky twist" to solve this dilemma? Well, from out of nowhere, I received a message from Mark Crum, a high school (and Facebook) friend who I hadn't seen in 32 years. He said his family was in the area, had been following my journey, and would love to take me to lunch and then deliver me back to the trail. Coincidence? Not likely.

On the way to the church building, Bobby drove us by his lakeside home and I commented on its beauty. He said, "You should see inside," and then pulled in and gave me a tour of the place. I admired the incredible lake view enjoyed by Bobby, his wife, and the large deer head mounted in their living room. Bobby was a kind, generous man who was being used by God to give me a "good break."

I have attended and been affiliated with churches of Christ my whole life. Like most young people, I practiced religion primarily based on my parents' beliefs and faith. As I got older, my faith gradually became my own. I increasingly realized God is real and created the universe. His only son, Jesus, had selflessly given His life for me and all humanity. My job is to try to live like Jesus as best I can—to be obedient to God's word, the Bible. The concept is simple. The difficulty lies in the execution.

In the churches of Christ, I find a group of imperfect people trying to do Bible things by Bible ways. Just Christians. Our approach is to follow the pattern of the New Testament church of the 1st Century, even though they, like us, had issues, problems, and imperfections. As a Christian, a person, and a hiker, I'm still a work in progress.

Not surprisingly, I really enjoyed this time of corporate worship. The congregation averages 12 members but had 17 in attendance that morning due to several visitors, myself included. Despite small numbers and having their long-time preacher out due to an extended illness, they had remained faithful. They extended the invitation for me to teach their Sunday School class, so I taught on "spiritual applications from hiking the AT." They encouraged me and told me they would keep me in their prayers as I continued my northbound trek.

As planned, Mark and his kind, sweet wife and two adorable children picked me up at the church building and treated me to lunch at Brothers at Willow Ranch. As I feasted on chicken alfredo and salad, we got caught up on each other's lives. They were interested in hearing about my hike and couldn't have been more kind or encouraging. Then, before dropping me back on the trail, they gave me a bag of assorted Girl Scout cookies!

Fob Fundamental #7 – God is in and over all things for the purpose of our good and to His glory. From an eternal perspective, things will

**ultimately work out well for those who love and
obey Him. As a result, we can rest.**

Despite a 2:20 p.m. start, I was able to bang out 7.7 miles before settling
in at Rich Cove Gap. The forest felt cold, lonely, and eerily quiet. The
temperature was dropping quickly and, according to my weather app, things
were about to get nasty. As I pitched my tent just off the trail, snow began
to fall. After eating Girl Scout cookies with tortillas and crawling into my
tent, the snow turned into freezing rain.

Once again, I found myself alone, but safe, warm, and dry inside my
tent. Some would say I had experienced a lucky, serendipitous day with
various random good breaks that went my way. What I saw was the
providential hand of the sovereign God, acting deliberately on behalf of one
of His own. My AT thru-hiking strategy relied on an active, intentional God
and, so far, he was faithful. He would continue to act, even as I prepared to
cross my first AT border.

CHAPTER 8

NORTH CAROLINA –
TAR HEELS AND BRUISED HEELS

March 21 – 28, 2016

"The cold never bothered me anyway."
- Elsa, *Frozen*

Day 10 – Rich Cove Gap to Beech Gap Tenting Area
13.7 miles, 90.7 cumulative miles

Elsa lied.

I awoke to brutally cold temperatures – mid-20s with winds gusting at 20-25 miles per hour. The good news: my high-end sleeping bag and liner formed a cocoon that kept me warm through the night. The bad news: to make it to Maine, I couldn't stay in my tent all day on bad weather days. Eventually, an aspiring thru-hiker has to leave the cocoon and face the elements.

After getting dressed inside my tent, I stepped out to find an inch of snow on the ground, howling winds, and freezing temperatures. My yellow tent presented a sharp contrast to the wintry, black and white world around me. Job one was to relieve myself in the snow by a nearby tree. I took my gloves off instantly causing my cold hands to start throbbing. Trembling, I unzipped my fly and reached in. To my dismay, there was nothing there. I felt around…nothing.

Apparently, the body part I was looking for had recessed into my body cavity and was lodged in a defensive position somewhere behind my gall bladder. I was not a happy camper. Shaking all over, I sang a couple of Mountain Dew ditties to coax him out, and then spelled "AT 2016" in the fresh coat of snow. Only I ran out before I got to 6, which left the impression of a 3rd Century hiker.

I packed up camp as quickly as possible, knowing the best way to warm up is to get moving. The snowy scenery was gorgeous, like a holiday puzzle or an Osmond family Christmas album cover. However, my focus had to be on not falling flat on my face. I tried to get the pain out of my hands by squeezing my trekking poles and wiggling my fingers. Distracted by this concern for my hands, I totally missed the iconic sign marking my crossing of the border into North Carolina. One state down, 13 to go!

As I entered North Carolina's Nantahala Mountains, the snow deepened and would range from one to four inches deep for the next several hours. At the edge of Bly Gap, I stopped, out of breath, with considerable pain in my hands and wind gusting in my face. Alone, cold, and miserable, I realized I had reached the low point of my first 10 days on the trail. I celebrated this fact by finishing off a bag of brown sugar cinnamon sawdust. It instantly stuck to and dried out my mouth.

I reached back for my water bottle and discovered it was frozen...thus creating an all-new low point, surpassing the one set moments earlier. The lesson learned was to always put at least one liter of water in my sleeping bag on cold nights.

With cinnamon sawdust stuck to my tongue and cheeks, snot flowing unabated over my mustache, frozen hands and numb feet, I decided to...hike on! I just kept moving. Michael J. Fox once said, "Do the right thing. And then do the next right thing, and that will lead you to the next right thing after that." My "next right thing" was to take a step forward in the snow. I dug deep and reminded myself the discomfort was temporary and my situation would improve. I mentally reviewed the 10 reasons I was hiking the trail. I put one foot in front of the other...the next right thing...and then repeated that process over and over and over again.

Guess what? Things got better! By the time I reached Standing Indian Shelter, the sun had come out and feeling and warmth had returned to my hands. As the sun baked the tree branches that lined the trail, globs of melting snow plopped to the ground. My muddied boots led me down to a creek by the shelter to filter the coldest imaginable water. I met two Australian men who usually live in a desert and had never seen or been in snow prior to that morning. Glancing over at me, they also saw their first American snotstache.

Fob Fundamental #8 – To get through a tough section of trail, or life, focus on doing the next right thing. Put one foot in front of the other, and remember the pain is temporary and things will eventually get better.

I continued hiking and passed Once a Day, who I had met a few days earlier. Hailing from The Netherlands, she fell several times on each of her first few days on the trail. A fellow hiker told her that if she must fall, she should try to do so only "once a day" ...and the name stuck. I told her my son pooped on a trail only once, but that was enough to earn me a trail name. Speaking of that, I, too, stopped on day 10 to take care of some wilderness business for the first time at the recently named Quesalupa Gap.

The miserable morning turned into a slightly warmer and manageable afternoon. After a fairly exhausting 13.7-mile day, my longest thus far, I arrived at the Beech Gap tenting area. I found that if I interacted with a lot of hikers throughout the day, I liked the solitude and quiet of a remote mountaintop at night. However, if I had minimal human contact during the day, I liked the company and camaraderie of being with others at a shelter or tenting area at night.

After a difficult day in which I was mostly alone, I enjoyed a wonderful evening in the company of some fun, interesting hikers. A breakdown of the company I kept on night 10 on the AT...

- Maine Mike – an older guy, from Maine (duh). He reminded us that as tough as Georgia had been, it was nothing compared to what we were going to experience in New Hampshire and Maine.
- Night Whisperer – a Connecticut millennial who earned his name by talking in his sleep. He greeted each arriving hiker and handed them a miniature Reese's peanut butter cup. He earned bonus cool points by building a big campfire that night and the following morning.
- Bert – a millennial from Los Angeles. His near-term goal was to get drunk in Franklin, North Carolina. He bummed a highly coveted (for smokers) cigarette off Maine Mike, and then another. I predicted such behavior would eventually earn him a trail name.
- Maia – a millennial pastry maker from Colorado who now lives in Indiana. She was a 120-pound woman who carried at least a 40-pound backpack. Although her hiking experience was her own and shouldn't concern me, I found that I was concerned for her. She hadn't slept in three nights because of the cold. So, I lent her my sleeping bag liner for the night.
- Sir Fob W. Pot – an older dude who lives in a van down by the river. Despite showering a day earlier, he reeked of manure. He missed his wife and couldn't feel his feet. He handed out Girl Scout cookies around the campfire, courtesy of the Crum family.

After sharing war stories, we retired around 9:00 p.m., hiker midnight. The bonding around the campfire more than made up for the brutally cold morning we had all endured. Our morning pain had been temporary, as most pain usually is.

Day 11 – Beech Gap Tenting Area to Wallace Gap
17.5 miles, 108.2 cumulative miles

I regained consciousness refreshed, re-charged, and to a roaring campfire, courtesy of Night Whisperer. The notably difficult Albert Mountain notwithstanding, this had the potential to be a high mileage day. My heels felt better and I wanted to get within striking distance of Franklin and all it would offer.

I ate a pop tart and half a Baby Ruth candy bar, turned on my AT music playlist, and motored out of camp. I played Leap Frog with Once a Day—not the actual game as that would have been awkward and highly inefficient. Rather, we kept passing each other as we stopped for water and other breaks. Fortunately, she made it through this section without any more falls.

Although this was only my second day of hiking in North Carolina, I already could tell these mountains were a little meaner and tougher than their Georgia counterparts. Fortunately, so was I. Near Mooney Gap, I spotted a car, some chairs, and a table of food. Could it be? Yes, it was! Time for some trail magic, courtesy of The Wanderer! I consumed a Coke and a glazed donut and then reached for a hot dog. Before eating it, I squirted two streaks of mustard down the length of it and placed an Advil, known by hikers as Vitamin I, at each end.

Bert arrived shortly after me and bummed two cigarettes off The Wanderer—a bold move to address his nicotine deficit. He was one step closer to being named The Marlboro Man or Trail Bum, either of which would have been more exciting than *Bert*. As I sat there in pure hiker bliss, I told myself that somehow, somewhere, someday, I was going to set up a magnificent trail magic stop along the AT and encourage others the way these stops have encouraged me.

No one could accuse Albert Mountain of being easy. I measured difficult climbs by the number of times I had to stop, catch my breath, and feel regret for having been born. Albert, Big Al, Fat Albert...call him whatever you like, but he was the toughest climb to date. By the end of my journey, Albert wouldn't make the list of the top 20 toughest climbs.

Still, the Albert climb necessitated my first scramble, which means I had to store my trekking poles and climb hand over hand up, around, and over boulders and other obstacles. I climbed to what I thought was the summit, only to find there was another whole section. After grinding up the second phase and thinking I was done, I looked up and saw the Albert Mountain fire tower still another quarter mile ahead and straight up. Albert was one nasty booger.

Halfway through the vertical scramble, as I gasped for air, two young day-hikers with Fannie packs blew past me. Breathing easily, they talked and laughed as they climbed. Frustrated and inexplicably competitive, I reached my hand out and tried to discreetly trip the one in back. I wasn't quick enough and they were soon gone from sight. In this moment of exhaustion and moral weakness, I may have mumbled, under my breath, "loser punk kids." I hiked on and was eventually rewarded with a magnificent view, although the top of the fire tower was locked and inaccessible.

During the long descent off Albert, I paired with Maia, the pastry chef from Indiana. Over the next hour, I learned more about the pastry business and kitchen drama than I ever thought possible. Had we not met, I would have never known that whipped egg whites leaven soufflés. To show my interest and keep the conversation moving, I asked her probing questions like, "Do people in Indiana eat the same pastries as people in other parts of the country?" Of course, I already knew the answer: they do not, as a pastry is usually only eaten once. As our mobile pastry class moved along at three miles per hour, I seriously considered changing my trail name to Sir Creampuff or Strudel Steve.

Eventually, the conversation shifted from pastries to the difficulties she was having with her hike. Discouraged over her trouble sleeping and her heavy pack, she was considering quitting the trail. I suggested she try to make some adjustments before giving up on her hike. For example, she had an environmentally friendly but extremely heavy stove. I suggested she try a lighter stove, along with therapy to address the ensuing guilt for having destroyed the environment.

Or, perhaps my pastry-loving friend could buy a warmer sleeping bag. With all the *turnover* on the AT, a trail *cruller* than most, I didn't want her to *dessert* her trail family prematurely. In fact, I knew that if she kept *pudding* one foot in front of the other, she would get out of this *jam*. Sorry for the lame pastry puns. I *cannoli* promise to do better.

After an educational, 17.5-mile day, my longest yet, I stopped for the night on a secluded mountain between Wallace Gap and Winding Stair Gap. I had positioned myself for a short hike to Winding Stair Gap in the morning to catch a shuttle into Franklin. After eating supper, I zipped myself into my cocoon and put my earplugs in to drown out the sound of high winds. Then, as I laid there alone on that mountaintop, I thought about my wife...and the prospects for a warm, frosted Danish.

Day 12 – Wallace Gap to Franklin
1.6 miles, 109.8 cumulative miles

Franklin has a reputation for being good to hikers, and I wanted to see that for myself. I quickly covered 1.6 miles through mature hardwoods to reach Winding Stair Gap. As I approached the parking lot, I spotted a couple serving trail magic! Jim and Beth were dishing out hiker love to go along with their piping hot breakfast burritos.

Jim is a former Special Forces soldier who, like me, had formerly worked for United States Special Operations Command. Our conversation quickly revealed we knew some of the same people and shared some of the same secrets. We also shared a passion for eating large, fully loaded breakfast burritos in chilly North Carolina parking lots in winter.

A short time later the shuttle arrived, driven by the one and only Ron Haven, who was accompanied by his pal, Baltimore Jack. Both men are trail legends, folk heroes, and truly interesting guys. Ron has been a professional wrestler, promoter of gun shows, and candidate for County Commissioner. In the hiking community, he's well known for offering a free shuttle and owning a hiker-friendly hotel and hostel in Franklin.

His sidekick, sitting behind him and across from me on the front seat of the shuttle, was the legendary Baltimore Jack. A larger than life figure, Baltimore Jack had a reputation for loving hikers, history, and bourbon. He failed at his first thru-hike attempt in 1995. Undeterred, he subsequently thru-hiked the trail nine times. Nine times!

On the drive in, Ron and Baltimore Jack gave us an overview of Franklin and key points of interest. Ron made it clear that he offers the shuttle to one and all, regardless of whether one stays at his Budget Inn. Baltimore Jack, in a humble, unassuming way, offered his advice on hiking the AT. He answered a wide range of AT questions posed by us newbies. Although Ron had given this Franklin orientation tour hundreds of times and Baltimore Jack had answered thousands of AT questions, their sincerity and heartfelt desire to help and serve hikers made each of us feel like we were their first customers.

As I exited the shuttle in Franklin, I thanked Ron and Baltimore Jack for the ride and for answering my trail and town questions. I wish I had known at the time that I would never see Baltimore Jack again. I wish I had known that 42 days later, he would breathe his last breath and pass away at Franklin's Angel Medical Center.

I wish I had known Baltimore Jack's real name, Adam Tarlin. I wish I'd known he was from Brookline, Massachusetts, and that his parents had passed away when he was young. I wish I had known his father's passing had prevented him from fulfilling a promise to young Adam that they would hike the Appalachian Trail together after his high school graduation.

I wish I'd known he was homeless for many years and struggled with bad knees and alcohol. I wish I'd known he took the name Baltimore Jack from the Bruce Springsteen song lyrics, because he left behind a daughter he loved, went hiking, and never came back. I wish I had more fully known that on the Appalachian Trail, he found a community he loved and could identify with, a place he could call home. While I had 10 reasons to hike the AT once, Baltimore Jack had that one main reason to hike it nine times.

Had I known all these things, and that Baltimore Jack's time was short, I would like to think our conversation might have gone differently. Rather than just pepper him with questions, I might have asked how he was doing. Instead of being amused by his reputation for partying hard, I might have been concerned about the challenges he was facing. I might have even prayed for him or with him.

I don't know whether knowing those things would have made any difference, but I would like to believe they would have. I would like to have tried to help him. I saw the best of Baltimore Jack on a shuttle bus on the morning of Day 12. Unfortunately, Baltimore Jack didn't see the best of me.

Fob Fundamental #9 – You will eventually see every person you know one final time. Since you don't know when that time will come, leave nothing unsaid and leave no kindness undone.

After securing a room at Ron's Budget Inn, I began working the usual trail town checklist. Hot shower...check. Start laundry...check. Re-supply at Ingles...check. For lunch, I headed to the Normandie restaurant for a chopped sirloin steak wrapped in bacon along with fries, salad, and bread. At the local outfitter, I purchased a carabiner for my backpack to replace the one I gave Matt. I then stopped by Ron's hostel and paid $20 for my Smoky Mountains National Park permit.

While waiting for the rest of my laundry to finish, I spotted a tee shirt shop across the street. With my sparkling clean, white-blazed hiking shirt in hand, I had an idea. I crossed the street and entered the store to speak to the manager...

Manager: "What can I help you with, sir?"

Fob: "I was wondering if you can put letters on a shirt like this."

Manager: "Sure. What letters do you want on it?"

Fob: "F-O-B."

Manager: "S-O-B? What'd you do to deserve that?"

Fob: "No, F-O-B...Fob."

Manager: "Okay, I can do that. Just curious...what's a Fob? Free on board?"

Fob: "No."

Manager: "Fresh off the boat?"

Fob: "Not exactly. It's Father of Boy...F-O-B."

Manager: "Hmm."

Fob: "You see, the boy...my son...well, I'm his father. And one time he pooped on a trail. And now I'm hiking a trail."

Manager: "Got it. It'll just take a minute and we'll get you out of here."

Being a Wednesday afternoon, I researched options to attend mid-week Bible study that night. I found the Westside Church of Christ and called its contact number. John, the preacher, answered. He and his wife, Joan, were not only willing to pick me up, but insisted I let them treat me to the restaurant of my choice. Wow…how incredibly cool of them!

I chose a local Mexican restaurant and devoured five scrumptious enchiladas while chatting with my new friends, John and Joan. We shared a lot about our respective families. One of their sons has written a Christian evidences book, *Unraveling Evolution*, which I added to my reading list.

After dinner, we headed to the church building where John presented a Bible study on benevolence. He emphasized the importance of helping others and particularly strangers in need. As he spoke, I kept thinking that standing before me is a man who practices what he preaches. I had just benefitted from the compassion and kindheartedness of him and his wife. I also thought about a loving God who had, once again, put people in my path to provide for and encourage me.

Fob Fundamental #10 – If you want to establish credibility and have your message hit home, practice what you preach.

Day 13 – Franklin to Wayah Bald Shelter
11 miles, 120.8 cumulative miles

Franklin had lived up to its hype as a hiker-friendly town, and still had one final parting gift. A local Baptist church picked a group of us up at 7:20 a.m. and took us to their church building for a full-up pancake and bacon breakfast! In the van on the way to the building, I met a hiker named Cahootin. He earned that classic trail name because it reflected his repeated and horrible mispronunciation of our common goal, Katahdin. He would say things like, "Once we get to Cahootin, all our troubles will be over."

The church serves breakfast every morning during the two months or so of the primary AT hiking season. On top of that, they take a picture of each hiker to send with a note to a loved one of our choice. (I narrowed it down to Janet and the Cowboy's tight end, Jason Witten, but Janet ultimately won out.) During breakfast, one of their ministers shared a brief devotional message about God's love and the saving power of Jesus' blood. I love how these people use their position along the AT to physically and spiritually feed hikers.

They returned us to the Budget Inn and Ron Haven delivered us to the trail. As an odd AT purist, I felt the need to walk across the parking lot to the actual spot I had left the trail before resuming my journey. If the AT has five million steps, I planned to hike all five million. Several hikers stayed behind in Franklin to take a zero day because of the likelihood of strong thunderstorms and tornadic activity later that afternoon. Unsure whether I'd end up in Oz, Katahdin, or even Cahootin, I hiked on.

With abundant mountain laurel, grassy meadows and sunlit balds, the next several hours of hiking were even more amazing than usual. At Silers Bald I met Moose, a high school student from Clemson, South Carolina. Since Moose sightings in North Carolina are rare, I decided to stop and chat.

As a former Dean of Students, I asked Moose why he wasn't in school and whether he had a hall pass. He avoided a demerit by convincing me he attended a private school and had taken extra courses to finish 11th grade early. While talking to him, I used tweezers and a pin to perform surgery on a right heel blister, then covered it with a customized piece of moleskin.

By late afternoon, I reached Wayah Bald which featured an impressive, historic stone tower offering the best views of the day. Moments later, I reached my target, Wayah Bald Shelter, and called it quits an hour before the thunderstorms began.

I preferred my tent over shelters most of the time because a tent provides privacy, protection from bugs, and the absence of loud snorers (other than myself). However, a shelter was a better choice in heavy thunderstorms, especially if I would be arriving or departing in nasty conditions. Not wanting to pack a wet tent the following morning, I secured a spot in the shelter.

My first shelter experience was quite a doozy. I was initially joined by T-Rev, Squid, and Stitch, and there was plenty of space for the four of us. Later, three Swiss hikers in matching hiking outfits arrived and asked if we could make room for them. We obliged, placing two of them parallel with us and the third at the edge of the platform, running along the length of our feet.

Later, several other hikers, one with a dog, arrived and had to set up their tents in the thunderstorm which raged off and on throughout the night. We enjoyed a fun night of bonding, eating, and sharing trail stories. My hiking comrades even helped me make a short video for Janet to wish her a happy 28th wedding anniversary.

As I tried to sleep wedged in along a row of hikers, I kept thinking about the shelter mice I had read about in AT books. Would they crawl over me? Would they get in my sleeping bag? Would they chew a hole in my face? To my knowledge, none of that happened.

What did happen was my usual urgent need to pee at 3:00 a.m.—in a crowded shelter, with no accessible Mountain Dew bottle, and Mr. Swiss Family Robinson at my feet, blocking my exit. With my canned tuna-sized prostate pressing against my Urethra Franklin, I needed to act quickly.

I quietly crawled out of my sleeping bag, flipped over on my back, and noticed the young Swiss foreigner in a deep sleep down by my feet. Like Sebastian the anthropomorphic crab in Disney's *The Little Mermaid*, I instinctively crab walked toward my new Swiss friend. As I passed over him, with my butt a mere six inches from the tip of his nose, I reminded myself to keep my hips high and to not cut the (Swiss) cheese. After relieving myself behind the shelter in a drenching thunderstorm, I crab walked back over the slumbering Swiss hiker and sought refuge in my sleeping bag.

Day 14 – Wayah Bald Shelter to A. Rufus Morgan Shelter
15.5 miles, 136.3 cumulative miles

This mass of hiker humanity simultaneously roused and sat up, as if on cue. Sprawled and contorted around the shelter, we had survived the thunderstorm and the crab-walking Fob. During the night, I had thought of a clever, borderline brilliant, collective trail name for the group of foreigners. After breakfast, I excitedly called over Fisherman, their English-speaking representative…

Fob: "Dude, I think I have a trail name for you!"

Fisherman: "I'm Fisherman."

Fob: "I know. But this would be more of a team name for your group."

Fisherman: "I'm listening."

Fob: "I think you guys should be called ABBA! You know, Dancing Queen ABBA."

Fisherman: "I'm familiar with this group."

Fob: "So what do you think? Brilliant, huh?"

Fisherman: "We are from Switzerland, not Sweden."

Fob: "My bad. So sorry."

Switzerland... Sweden... whatever. Once again, I had embarrassed myself and set international relations back 20 years. Had I not crab-walked over Fisherman's face a few hours earlier, my naming snafu would have been my most egregious foul on Wayah Bald.

As I climbed out of the wet, chilly Burningtown Gap toward Cold Spring Shelter, my feet ached along with my left knee. To make matters worse, I switched my music to shuffle mode and the song "Always and Forever" came on. Although it's a beautiful song, it may be the worst possible song to listen to during a strenuous uphill climb. All it did was zap my adrenalin and make me miss my wife.

As I made my way around Cold Spring Shelter, a section hiking couple graciously offered me a cup of coffee. Later, after the long climb out of Tellico Gap, I scaled the Wesser Bald observation tower and was rewarded with arguably the most scenic, 360-degree view to date. As I made the long, wet descent, I came across my first AT snake. The harmless black snake was hanging out along the edge of a tree stump. He was the first of more than 80 snakes I would see on the trail.

After a grueling 15.5 miles, I arrived at A. Rufus Morgan Shelter and set up my tent downhill from the shelter by a stream. At the shelter, T-Rev and The Hikers Formerly Known as ABBA were settling in for the night. A short time later, Booknboot, the friendly Aussie who had slept in the bunk below me at Neels Gap, arrived and set up her tent.

Still later, Stitch arrived and pitched her tent nearby. Stitch is a friendly, outgoing former Army troop from Gainesville, Georgia. She earned her trail name by laughing like the cartoon character of the same name. She loved the story behind my name and laughed like Stitch each of the multiple times she heard it.

I built my first campfire of the journey and we sat around joking, laughing, and getting to know one another. After extinguishing the fire, I returned to my tent to enjoy a heartwarming 28th Anniversary phone call with my wife. John Denver was right in believing that nights in the forest are enchanting, mountains in springtime are majestic, and walks in the rain are exhilarating. I had experienced all that over the past two weeks. And yet, nothing filled up my senses quite like sharing a sweet moment with Janet, my best friend and the love of my life.

Day 15 – A. Rufus Morgan Shelter to Sassafras Gap Shelter
7.7 miles, 144 cumulative miles

"The hero is commonly the simplest and obscurest of men."
- Henry David Thoreau

After a one mile descent, I arrived at the Nantahala Outdoor Center (NOC), a paradise for outdoorsmen. Across a sprawling campus with a river running through it, one can take advantage of an outstanding outfitter, restaurant, general store, white water rafting, kayaking, and more. The NOC pulled me in and made me want to stay awhile and perhaps raise a family there.

My first stop was to the outfitter to pick up my first food mail drop. Before getting on the trail, some hikers will dehydrate food and assemble other food and supplies to be later shipped to them at trail town post offices. I prepared two such shipments, and this first one had three days' worth of food I didn't need. Between trail magic food and eating less than expected while on the trail, I way over-estimated my food needs. In retrospective, I wish I hadn't sent either of my two food mailings.

Next door at the restaurant, I chowed down on Fontana Hash Browns—a large pile of hash browns covered with onions, peppers, broccoli, sautéed tomatoes, two eggs, melted cheese, and several shakes of tabasco sauce. As I devoured this mound of calories, along with four cups of coffee and five glasses of water, I watched kayakers practicing their craft in the raging rapids below. I thanked God for carrying me this far on the journey and for yet another moment of being warm, full, and dry.

Full and rejuvenated, I began the long—really long—ascent to Cheoah Bald. In fact, with 3,000 feet of elevation gain over 5.8 miles, the climb is rated the 5th longest on the AT. While the ascent is not technically difficult, it just keeps going and going…like an Energizer Bunny in the NOC's bathroom after eating tabasco-laced Fontana Hash Browns. During the climb, I spoke with Simba and Firecracker, the Hogwarts brother and sister team with the sparkling red hair. She planned to hike the entire AT and he was here to support her for just a couple of weeks.

At mile 140, near Grassy Gap, I approached the Wade Sutton Memorial. According to the memorial plaque, on December 7, 1968, about 783 feet southwest of the memorial, Mr. Sutton of the North Carolina Forest Service "gave his life suppressing a forest fire, that you might more fully enjoy your hike along this trail." I stopped and paid my respects to this man and considered the horror he faced as he succumbed to a fire on that steep mountainside when I was two years old. He didn't become a hero that day; rather, his heroic character was revealed as he willingly went into harm's way to protect lives and natural resources.

As I stood there for a moment, I also thought about my nephew, David Watts, and friend, Les Rydl, two men who have made similar commitments to fight fires and respond to other emergencies. Little did I know that eight months later, dozens of devastating forest fires would strike the Southeast, burning thousands of acres, and shutting down nearly 70 miles of the AT, including this North Carolina section.

After 7.7 uphill miles, I reached Sassafras Gap and tented directly behind the shelter. Once again, an interesting cast of characters gathered around the campfire that night, including…

- Stone – from Roanoke, Virginia. He was a traveling missionary and his hike was being funded by his church. His trail name was based on 1) his hiking speed, particularly how he moved like a rolling stone on the downhill sections; and 2) he loves Matthew 21:42, which reads, *"Jesus said to them, 'Have you never read in the Scriptures: 'The stone the builders rejected has become the cornerstone; the Lord has done this, and it is marvelous in our eyes'?'"* So, the trail name reminded him of who he is and whose he is.

- Abbie – an Alabama gal who liked to continuously rotate by the campfire to stay warm. She rejected my suggestion to take the trail name Rotisserie.

- Amelie – a 2nd grade teacher from Birmingham, Alabama and Hoover High School. She was on the trail for a week to support her friend, Abbie's, thru-hike attempt.
- The Hikers Formerly Known as ABBA – they hailed from Switzerland or Sweden or maybe Swaziland. Individually, I called them Swiss Miss, Fernando, and Dancing Queen—all names they outright rejected.
- Moses – a red-bearded, fast hiker from Louisville, Kentucky. He was trail named by members of a church youth group as he sat in all his bearded glory atop Preaching Rock. Due to previous basketball injuries, his joints were held together with brightly colored, elastic Kinesiology Tape. He was also known for his regular trail video updates posted on his Phollowing Phil YouTube channel.
- Stitch – as previously mentioned, she was ex-Army, had an odd laugh, and hailed from Gainesville, Georgia.

Campfire was a place to eat, relax, warm up, bond, tell stories, and get caught up on trail news. For example, I learned that Wildwood, the 20-year-old special needs hiker, injured his feet and had to get off the trail with his mom for X-rays and a couple days of rest. Also, Maia, my pastry chef friend, went to the NOC outfitter to get new shoes. The foot guy told her that her toes were badly infected and she needed to get off the trail for a couple of days. Foot injuries were quickly becoming the biggest source of thru-hikes ending or being delayed.

I suffered through a rough night's sleep because I mistakenly thought tenting on a modest slope would be fine. As I crawled onto my sleeping pad, I slid to the bottom of my tent like a fat man on a greased Slip 'n Slide. I had to keep my tired legs extended throughout the night to avoid folding in a fetal position at the bottom of my tent. While I still prefer a tent over a hammock, finding a flat spot to set up is one issue hammock dwellers didn't have to deal with.

Day 16 – Sassafras Gap Shelter to Cable Gap Shelter
15.2 miles, 159.2 cumulative miles

"If Jesus rose from the dead, then you have to accept all that he said; if he didn't rise from the dead, then why worry about any of what he said?
The issue on which everything hangs is not whether or not you like his teaching but whether or not he rose from the dead."
- Timothy J. Keller

Strangely, I began this Easter Sunday away from family, scrunched at the bottom of my tent. Sadly, there would be no Easter egg hunts, chocolate bunnies, or yellow marshmallow Peeps. After untangling myself and regaining feeling in my legs, I crawled out to the sound of a voice over by the shelter.

The voice belonged to Stone, who was giving a thoughtful, encouraging sunrise message about God's love, Christ's sacrifice, and the meaning of the resurrection. Great stuff! He also reminded us that what Christ did is a gift, a present, and each of us has the option of whether to open, accept, and enjoy the present or leave it wrapped and in the box. What have you done with Christ's gift?

**Fob Fundamental #11 – God's gift of His son,
Jesus, is like any other gift in that it can be opened,
enjoyed, and its blessings reaped...or left unopened.**

Today I would hit the toughest, short, non-scramble section of the trail so far—the brutal Jacob's Ladder! As I climbed the incredibly steep slope, I gasped for air and my calves burned. Desperate times call for desperate measures, so I did what any child of the 80s would do—I put on *Def Leppard's Greatest Hits* and climbed the ladder! At the top, I proudly looked back, surveyed the ground I had just covered, and bolted out the chorus of "Bringin' on the Heartbreak." Before moving on, I told Jacob I was his new daddy.

By late afternoon, I chose a tenting spot near Cable Gap Shelter, along with Terrible Lizard, Stone, Moses, Stitch, and the Hikers Formerly Known as ABBA. Terrible Lizard earned her trail name when a salamander somehow managed to crawl down into her 2-liter Platypus bag.

While crawling into my tent, two thoughts came to mind: 1) I was less than six miles from the Fontana Lodge and all the good things that would bring; and 2) I had unintentionally and creepily placed myself directly below the privy, giving myself an awkward view of the knees and ankles of hikers doing their business. Not wanting to be renamed Terrible Creeper, I quickly zipped my tent and inserted my earplugs.

**Day 17 – Cable Gap Shelter to Fontana Village
5.5 miles, 164.7 cumulative miles**

Bubble - noun – "a good or fortunate situation that is isolated from reality or unlikely to last."[8]

---

[8] "bubble." Oxord University Press. 2017.
https://en.oxforddictionaries.com/definition/bubble (13 January 2017).

I roused from a deep sleep and ate a granola bar dipped in peanut butter—another breakfast of champions. After climbing out of Cable and Black Gum Gaps, I began the long descent into Fontana Dam. Halfway through this 5.5-mile stretch, Moses zoomed past me like I was standing still.

Initially troubled by the disparity in our hiking speeds, I realized that in the wilderness, it's always best to let Moses lead. On the other hand, would following him result in 40 years of wandering on the AT? That's a lot of granola bars. Regardless, our plan was for Moses to get to Fontana Lodge first and book a room for me, Stitch, Robi Dobi (named after an elephant in her favorite children's book), and himself. He delivered as promised, as one would expect from a Moses.

Fontana Dam is a great touristy place for families to vacation and for tired hikers to re-charge and re-supply. As the gateway to The Great Smoky Mountains, the resort is also an ideal spot for AT hiking bubbles to form. A hiking bubble is a group of hikers who will generally travel together over the course of several days, weeks, or in rare instances, even months. A hiker may or may not actually hike with his bubble during the day, but would camp with them near the same shelter or campsite at night.

Being a part of a good, fun, mutually supportive bubble was, without a doubt, one of the very best things about hiking the AT. Within these bubbles, friendships were forged, burdens were shared, and memories were made. With each successive shelter, campfire, or frigid morning shared, the bonds grew tighter. A hiker could ride the bubble until his hiking pace, be it slower or faster, caused him to fall behind or move ahead. If a hiker was fortunate enough, he could eventually catch on with another bubble and ride it for a while.

At the Fontana Lodge, the first order of business was to pick up the second food package I had mailed to myself. It contained a six-day supply of food, double what I needed. It would be my last food mailing on the AT. I took a long, hot shower and ate fish-n-chips with Moses and Stitch. (To clarify, I was alone in the shower and together with them at the restaurant.)

After lunch, the three of us walked downhill to do laundry and re-supply at the General Store. Later, we had dinner together along with Mom (previously known as Pat) and Orbit (previously known as Megan). I enjoyed being reunited with the mother-daughter team I had shared a cup of coffee with on Megan's birthday in Hiawassee. As we filled our stomachs with food and souls with conversation, I wondered if I was sitting in the nucleus of what would become my first incredible hiking bubble.

CHAPTER 9

TENNESSEE –
THE RETURN TO ROCKY TOP

March 29 – April 24, 2016

"If you drive to, say, Shenandoah National Park, or the Great Smoky Mountains, you'll get some appreciation for the scale and beauty of the outdoors. When you walk into it, then you see it in a completely different way. You discover it in a much slower, more majestic sort of way."
- Bill Bryson

Day 18 – Fontana Village to Mollies Ridge Shelter
12.6 miles, 177.3 cumulative miles

"Do the thing you fear most, and the death of fear is certain."
- Ralph Waldo Emerson

For the first time in my life, I awoke next to a bearded Moses. (Words last spoken by Zipporah several thousand years ago.) I got up and, in MacGyver-esque fashion, made oatmeal by heating water with the coffee pot. I started to surprise Moses with breakfast in bed, but couldn't find his stash of manna and quail. After saying farewell to my roommates, I hitched a ride back to the trailhead and hiked two miles to the grand, alluring Fontana Dam. The dam, tallest in the Eastern United States, is among the most beautiful in the world.

After crossing the dam, I immediately entered Great Smoky Mountains National Park, the most visited park in the United States. By entering the park, I had officially cut my umbilical cord with civilization.

59

For the next week, there would be no hostels, reliable phone service, or hitches to a nearby McDonald's. At the entrance sign, I met Big Bird and hiked with him along several hundred yards of asphalt. A retired military officer, he earned his trail name by dispensing advice like the big, yellow, feathered fellow on *Sesame Street*.

I re-entered the woods, placed my park permit in the hiker permit box, and began a 2,700-foot climb that would cover the next 10 miles. Despite the challenging ascent into the Smokies, the day was gorgeous, cool, and sunny—tailor made for hiking. At mile 170.8, I came face to face with the terrifying, rickety, 1930s Shuckstack Fire Tower.

My fear of heights is palpable. The older I get, the more I fear views from steep, high places. I nearly wet myself watching *The Walk*, a movie about the guy who walked on a tightrope between the World Trade Center towers. I don't like steep roller coasters. At amusement parks, I'm the guy designated to sit on a bench, watch the roller coaster riders' stuff, and eat $9 corn dogs. However, before starting my AT journey, I told myself I needed to face my fears and climb the fire towers—even Shuckstack. My moment was at hand.

Years ago, my eldest son, Jason, preached a sermon that, to this day, has had a profound impact on me. Entitled "20 Seconds of Courage," his talk was based on this line from the movie, *We Bought a Zoo*: "You know, sometimes all you need is 20 seconds of insane courage. Just literally 20 seconds of just embarrassing bravery. And I promise you, something great will come of it."

In the movie, the boy needed just 20 seconds of insane courage to express his feelings to a girl that he liked. Sometimes you only need 20 seconds of courage to jump out of an airplane, save someone from a burning house, or take the stage for your first audition. Just 20 seconds. Don't worry about having to be brave all day, or even for an hour. Instead, just focus on being brave for the critical 20 seconds.

Fob Fundamental #12 – To overcome your greatest fears, focus on being brave for just the most critical 20 seconds.

As I approached the base of the long set of fire tower stairs, I reached deep within my soul to find the critical 20 seconds of courage. I also hoped for a miracle, like finding a "closed for repair" sign at the base of the steps. Or perhaps a giant lightning strike could take down the fire tower, a reasonable request from a guy who had just slept next to Moses. There would be no easy way out. My time to dig deep and face my fears had come.

As I approached my first step, I noticed the right rail was missing on the first set of 20 steps! Seriously? How could North Carolina, a state which brought us the Biltmore Estate, Krispy Kreme doughnuts, and the Venus Fly-Trap, not have the common decency to put another rail up on the Stairway to Fob's Death? Unbelievable!

With my palms sweating, heart pounding, and legs already tired from the climb into the Smokies, I took my first step onto Shuckstack fire tower. I stopped, six inches off the ground, and looked around. That wasn't so bad. I then took my second and third and fourth steps. The fear began to slowly creep in. I hated it. And I hated myself for hating it. I gripped the left rail so tightly that a vein popped out of the back of my hand. If I was Jacob's Ladder's daddy, then Shuckstack was his grandfather.

With each step, the earth moved farther away. I wondered why I wasn't sitting, watching the other hikers' backpacks, and eating a $9 corn dog. At the top of the first set of stairs, I looked down and nearly pooped myself. My 20 seconds of courage had passed and I needed a new strategy.

Rather than live in the moment, I decided to distract myself by making up new words to a church song; specifically, the song, *My God and I*. Weird as it may seem, with each step, the song in my head went something like this...

> *My God and I, we'll climb these stairs together;*
> *We'll walk and talk; look down and maybe puke.*
> *We'll grasp the rail, and wish there was another;*
> *My God and I, will climb to Shuckstack's view...*

That song, whether it was a God thing, simply a distraction, or both, got me to the top unscathed. For the rest of my life, *My God and I* will always remind me of the climb up Shuckstack fire tower and my struggle to overcome my fear of heights. Once again, my bravery was rewarded with magnificent views and a head nod from a Japanese tourist at the top.

Unfortunately, the climb down the fire tower was just as terrifying, and the only song I could think of was "Free Fallin'," compliments of Tom Petty. I eventually managed to make it down to solid ground, even though the rail on the final set of stairs had still not been replaced. I was relieved and maybe a little proud to have stared down one of my greatest fears. But the Smokies weren't done with me yet—not by a long shot.

Later in the day, I passed the side trail to Gregory's Bald and then the idyllic Doe Knob, two very special places to my friend, John Walsh. It was on or near Doe Knob that, years ago, John took a nap and was awakened by a deer licking him. This is a true story, one all the more plausible if you've seen the amount of deer-attracting hair on John's back.

Ironically, a few miles later, as I approached the stream at Ekaneetlee Gap, I spotted two deer in a clearing off to the left about 40 feet from the trail. As I tried to discreetly reach for my camera, one of my trekking poles dropped and the deer darted off into the deep woods. Bummer! I never had a chance to ask if one of them had once licked my friend John.

I eventually arrived at Mollies Ridge Shelter for what would easily become my favorite night on the AT so far. My previously introduced hiking bubble (Stitch, Moses, Mom, and Orbit) had picked up some familiar faces, like Booknboot, my favorite Aussie. Additionally, our bubble expanded to include...

- Nesquick – a 26-year-old from Atlanta, Georgia. His trail name is derived from his last name, Quick. I envied has massive beard and appreciated his terrific sense of humor. I didn't envy the ever-worsening condition of his feet.

- Deadwood – a 32-year-old, incredibly funny married man from North Carolina. He thought I looked like Robert Downey, Jr. During a backpacking trip earlier in his life, he was dragging behind other hikers. He noticed they all had trekking poles, thought that was the difference, and grabbed two dead sticks off the ground to propel himself forward. His buddy, Smiling Otter, gave him the name Deadwood.

- Princess Elle – a 28-year-old engineer from New Hampshire. She described herself as "adorable" which was quite accurate. A trail diva with princess-like qualities, her near-term goal was to be reunited with her Aaron Rogers look-a-like boyfriend at Newfound Gap.

- Conductor – a 61-year-old hiker from Southwest Michigan, where he has lived since retiring from the U.S. Navy. He had made two previous AT thru-hike attempts—one successful and one not. He had considerable trail expertise and was willing to share it. He earned his trail name by the graceful manner in which he waved a stick like a baton to remove spider webs from the trail.

- Master Wayne – a section hiker whose real name is Bruce. He was polite, thoughtful, and dignified, like Master Wayne before the bat suit comes on. He also wore a green jacket that made him look like The Grinch.

I built a massive campfire and we sat around laughing, eating, and telling stories and jokes. I laughed so hard that I almost forget the pain in my feet and left knee. This was good bonding time—one of the main reasons one hikes the trail—and we knew it. Everyone got along and by the end of the night, it felt like we had known each other for years. Yes, it was just a bubble... "a good situation that is unlikely to last." And yet it was our bubble and it was a great one. We were living the dream.

As I was about to doze off on the top level of the Mollies Ridge Shelter, Deadwood crawled into his sleeping bag next to me. He looked over, stared into my eyes, and proclaimed, "I'm sleeping next to Ironman. The fantasy I've had since I was seven years old has finally come true!" Everyone laughed. Ironman, aka Fob, finally dozed off to sleep. I was happy to have found a spot in the shelter, but even more so a spot in this bubble.

Day 19 – Mollies Ridge Shelter to Derrick Knob Shelter
12 miles, 189.3 cumulative miles

"Write it. Just write it...Write until your fingers hurt, then keep writing more. Don't ever stop writing. Don't ever give up on your story...Don't ever let anybody take away your voice. You have something to say, your soul has a story to tell. Write it...Love your work. Be brave. Just write."
- Melodie Ramone

Today was a nostalgic day of hiking. I would be covering familiar ground, the same section covered in a 2011 section hike with my friend, John, his brother, Scott, and my eldest son, Jason. It was a chilly and windy morning; considerably colder than the last time I was in these parts. Near privy-less Russell Field Shelter, I stopped to take care of some business behind a tree in the recently named Oats & Dark Chocolate Granola Gap, just across from Nature Valley.

Forty-one days later and just 200 feet from this shelter, a 49-year-old, aspiring thru-hiker named Bradley Veeder would suffer a bear bite in his right calf while he slept in his tent. Bear attacks on the AT are rare, but they do happen. Fortunately, Mr. Veeder survived the attack and lived to tell about it.

Later, just south of Spence Field Shelter, a two-mile stretch of the AT begins and runs to Thunderhead Mountain. With its stunning views, sprawling grassy balds, birds chirping, and interesting rock formations, I consider this section the prettiest of the first 250 miles of the AT. The only thing missing was Julie Andrews streaking across the landscape singing "Climb Every Mountain."

Some clarification is in order. By *streaking*, I don't mean "to make a sudden dash in public while naked,"[9] as such a display would be highly inappropriate for Miss Andrews and would have taken *The Sound of Music* in an entirely different direction. Anyway, I stopped, took my pack, boots and

---

[9] "streaking." 2017. http://www.dictionary.com/browse/streaking (13 January 2017).

shirt off, and lay down on a sunbaked grassy bald. As I ate an entire package of sliced salami, I wished that John, Scott, and Jason had been there to enjoy it with me.

I continued the climb to... (*drum roll*) ...Rocky Top! Yes, as a long-time, long-suffering Tennessee Volunteers fan, the song and the place have special meaning. I was joined at the summit by section hikers from Cincinnati who expressed their admiration for aspiring thru-hikers. Wanting to do something to help me on my journey, they gave me a handful of Tic Tacs, which provided two calories each and a much-needed minty fresh scent to my breath.

As I sucked on a handful of mints, I had a flashback to 2011 when Jason, my son who doesn't poop on trails, stood next to me on these same rocks. In addition to taking in the incredible views, Jason "planked" between two rocks, a fad at the time. Later that day, Princess Elle would summit Rocky Top and be greeted by a band of "Tennessee hillbillies" singing "Rocky Top" and serving shots of moonshine to weary hikers.

As I descended Thunderhead mountain, Booknboot was on my tail, drafting me as we picked up speed. For no particular reason, we wanted to see how fast we could go. Like alpine skiers, representing Australia and the USA, we tore down the mountain, with rocks and roots serving as poles or gates to maneuver around. Whenever she got close to a possible passing position, I extended my rear end to block her path. My country expected this from me.

Near the bottom, we stopped to catch our breath, get water, and delve into each other's past. She told me about her doctoral dissertation, which is based on the book *Suttree* by Cormac McCarthy, whose other works include *Blood Meridian* and *No Country for Old Men*. She was hiking the AT, in part, to gain some perspective on the character Cornelius Suttree. He left a life of privilege with his prominent family to live near Knoxville in a dilapidated houseboat on the Tennessee River. He very well could have been one of the hillbillies singing "Rocky Top" and serving shots of moonshine to Princess Elle earlier in the day. Booknboot spoke passionately about her research and made me want to read *Suttree* and her dissertation.

Booknboot then mentioned my blog and said she had read several of the AT entries. She looked me in the eyes and said, "Fob, you need to write a book. Seriously, your stories are quite good and funny and people will read it. Not everyone can be out here hiking the AT. Tell your story for them."

This sweet little Aussie, with her big brain, striped leggings, and a giant, furry winter owl hat, couldn't have been more sincere. I found her words both touching and convincing. So, I told her I would write the book. Just like that, at a watering hole at the foot of Thunderhead Mountain, in the Great Smoky Mountains, I gave my word that I'd write a book about my AT story. So, I did—and you are now holding it in your hands!

**Fob Fundamental #13 – Never underestimate the
power of your words to motivate, encourage, or
inspire someone. If you recognize talent or
potential in a person, by all means let them know.**

After 12 miles, with the temperature continuing to drop, we arrived at Derrick Knob Shelter. One by one, members of our Great Smoky Mountains Bubble came rolling in, weary and cold. The Smokies are conducive to hiking bubbles because stealth camping (tenting outside of established camping areas) is prohibited in the park. Hikers must sleep in a shelter if there is room. If not, then hikers are allowed to tent near the shelter.

Also, section hikers with shelter reservations are allowed to bump aspiring thru-hikers from shelters because they have reservations. Most aspiring thru-hikers would prefer to tent. These rules, along with the cold weather, left some hikers with a bad impression of the Smokies. Personally, I understood the rules given the popularity of the park.

After eating 2.5 servings of Mountain House Beef Stroganoff, a package of gummy bears, three Advil, and a Little Debbie, I sat on the grass feeling tired, stiff, and cold. Then, from out of nowhere, with my bubble mates gathered around, I spoke six words that I had never said before: "I want to do some yoga." I don't know where this thought came from. I barely even know what yoga is.

Before I had a chance to retract my statement, Mom offered to guide me through a yoga session. Next thing you know, I was on my back, contorted like a pretzel, trying with all my might not to shoot beef stroganoff at the food bags hanging from nearby trees. Mom explained and demonstrated a yoga move, and then looked at me pitifully as I tried in vain to execute it. The bubble members looked on in amusement, as if I were the headliner in a freak show or Julie Andrews streaking naked across the mountainside. After watching me struggle through the first two exercises, Mom mercifully suggested we stop there and build on that "progress" in future sessions.

That night we packed ourselves into the shelter and hunkered down as the temperature dropped, wind gusted, and rain fell. Little did we know that for the next four days, at elevations ranging from 4,700 to 6,700 feet, our Great Smoky Mountains Bubble would endure not only rain but some of the coldest temperatures in which any of us had ever hiked or camped. If Spring had sprung, someone forgot to tell the Smoky Mountains.

Day 20 – Derrick Knob Shelter to Double Spring Gap Shelter
7.4 miles, 196.7 cumulative miles

"I had come to realize that this whole place and experience is what you make of it. Your attitude and frame of mind determined everything. It wasn't hard to see how this undertaking could be the worst or best experience of a person's life."
- Kyle S. Rohrig, *Lost on the Appalachian Trail*

The cold, windy and rainy night carried over into a cold, windy, and rainy morning. I didn't sleep well because one of my shelter mates snored loudly and non-stop from 9:00 p.m. until dawn. He was not a part of our core group and we were previously unaware of his propensity to saw logs. He sounded like a freight train that had gotten off track and was loose in his nostrils. Had he been next to me, I would have shoved a hiking sock down his esophagus. Of course, I would have used one of Deadwood's socks in order to maintain my innocence. Deadwood would gladly take the fall for his beloved Ironman.

We hiked six miles in the nasty weather and finally sought refuge at Silers Bald Shelter. The weather was so cold that Stitch built a rare, midday fire inside the shelter. As we huddled around the flames and tried to get feeling back in our extremities, Conductor checked his weather radar. A line of heavy thunderstorms was closing in on us and was due to hit in 30 minutes.

Decision time: stay at Silers Bald Shelter by the fire and call it a day; or make a run for Double Spring Gap Shelter, just 1.7 miles away? I took a final glance at the radar and said, "I'm going for it!" I pulled my black ninja balaclava over my face and took off speed hiking in the freezing rain as fast as I could go without face-planting. The others followed behind me and we made it to the shelter just as the thunderstorm hit.

Fob Fundamental #14 – Nothing binds soldiers, teammates, friends, or hikers more quickly than overcoming adversity together.

We were partially frozen, exhausted, and a little bummed over the wimpy 7.4-mile day. However, we were very thankful to have outrun a massive thunderstorm, and that said thunderstorm would preclude my second yoga session. We removed our wet outer layers and fired up our stoves to heat food and warm our hands. Most importantly, we reminded each other that we had chosen to be here and that hiking the AT is fun.

Believe it or not, it was fun! Despite the bitterly cold, miserable conditions, everyone was surprisingly upbeat. My watch read "1:00 p.m." and our hiking day was over. What do 13 hikers do for 18 hours while stuck in a small shelter in nasty, frigid weather? A better question is what did we not do? Answer: complain. We adhered to an unwritten rule not to complain. On the AT, hikers quickly realize complaining doesn't change anything. In fact, it makes the experience worse.

We also needed to stay busy doing something—anything. Mom broke out her crossword puzzle book and began reading the clues aloud. The rest of us shouted answers from across the room. Stitch emerged from under her sleeping bag to shout "Roosevelt!" and then re-submerged. Nesquick and Deadwood, with their mouths full of Ramen noodles, tried to be the first to yell "NASA!" or "Michaelangelo!" Princess Elle's and Orbit's answers were unintelligible, as frostbite had immobilized their lips. As an expert in only two things, 80s music and Dallas Cowboys history, I patiently waited for the right question that never came.

With our core temperature dropping, we sought refuge in our sleeping bags by 7:00 p.m. We were lined up like 13 sardines, with just our mouths protruding from our sleeping bags. Given the smell, we could have been mistaken for actual giant sardines. With my headlamp on, I could see puffs of breath emerge from sleeping bags from across my row of weary campers. Our sleeping bags were literally keeping us alive.

By 8:00 p.m., we were all asleep or close to it. Suddenly, three day-hikers came stumbling into the shelter. Soaked to the bone and obviously ill-prepared for their hike, they asked if there were any available spots. Technically, they had a right to bump three of us thru-hikers, but two of them were content to sleep on the shelter floor. Without prompting, Conductor got up and said to the third one, "You can have my spot." His offer was selfless, compassionate...and accepted. We need more Conductors in this world.

As I burrowed deep into my sleeping bag, I was proud of the way our bubble had handled the day's events. Most of us had done very little backpacking, and these were extreme conditions. We had worked together, laughed together, and bonded in a way that rarely happens outside of war zones.

I considered that, on average, only two or three of us assembled in the shelter that night should successfully complete our thru-hikes. However, was it possible we were not an average group? My gut told me we were well above average and would defy the odds. Only time would tell whether my gut would prove to be right.

Day 21 – Double Spring Gap Shelter to Icewater Spring Shelter
13.4 miles, 210.1 cumulative miles

"I'm a hiker, not a thru-hiker. You can't go for a jog and then call yourself a marathoner...or take a few courses and then put a 'PhD' after your name.

The Smokies decided to serve up yet another brutally cold, rainy and foggy morning. From a tiny opening in my sleeping bag, I surveyed the shelter landscape for visible puffs of breath that would indicate life. Questions flooded my mind. Had anyone frozen to death in the middle of the night? If so, is cannibalism legal in Tennessee? If so, is there a socially acceptable, minimum time a hiker should wait before suggesting a fellow frozen hiker be eaten? I kept these questions to myself.

Princess Elle, the self-described "adorable" diva, was first out of the shoot. After swapping my warm, dry, long underwear for cold, damp hiking pants, I followed a few minutes behind her. Despite the dismal weather, I was looking forward to climbing the 6,643-foot Clingmans Dome, the highest point on the AT and in Tennessee.

Towards the end of a long ascent, in the vicinity of Mount Buckley, I spotted something in the woods from the corner of my eye. The unidentified object stood out because it was aqua colored and only 15 feet off the trail. As I got closer, I realized, to my horror, exactly what it was. Princess Elle had embraced a thin tree, assumed the 90-degree position, and was doing her morning business! Yikes! Gracious sakes alive! Katy, bar the door! I looked away, following the lead of a nearby squirrel, and hiked on.

Still, the scene kept re-playing in my mind, haunting me with each step. First of all, I didn't even know princesses pooped. Cinderella? No. Snow White? Absolutely not. Ariel, Princess Jasmine, and Sleeping Beauty? No, no, and no. Peach? Technically no; she only drops bananas from her Kart to slow down Bowser. Middleton? Unlikely...she's not the Duke of Earl. Fiona? Okay, I'll give you that one, but she's an ogre. And why so close to the trail, Elle? So many unanswered questions.

As I approached a fork in the trail near Clingmans Dome, I misread the poorly worded and positioned sign. I also entirely missed the single white blaze down low and off to the left on a rock. I learned later that half the hikers in our group would also wrongly veer to the right, adding an unnecessary quarter mile down to the parking lot. I eventually realized my mistake and returned to the AT and shortly thereafter summited Clingmans Dome.

The observation tower at Clingmans Dome is always impressive, but I was glad I had been there before. With the fog and wintry weather, visibility was poor. Atop the tower, I saw Booknboot walking around with a friend who had met her. They planned to spend some time in Gatlinburg and then she would return to the trail.

To my dismay, this would be my last time seeing my hiking buddy and favorite Aussie, Booknboot, a key inspiration for this book. Upon returning to the trail, she would fall and break her wrist. The injury required surgery back in Australia, effectively ending her thru-hike attempt. However, to her credit, she returned to the AT to hike (and sometimes drive) her way to Maine. I will forever be thankful for our wonderful, though limited, time together and the powerful impact she had on my life. I hope our paths will cross again in the future.

Eventually, Princess Elle arrived, smiling, as if a heavy load had been shed. I should have pretended like the embarrassing thing I witnessed had never happened. A better man would have done that. I'm not that better man. As Princess Elle talked to her dad on the phone, I walked by, interrupted, and teased her for what she had done to that poor tree so close to the trail. I told her I planned to send her the bill from the therapy sessions I would need. In fairness, she could have called me out for being the father of a boy who pooped right on the trail.

With the ice having been shattered in a most unfortunate way between Sir Fob and Princess Elle, we decided to hike together for the next few hours. Elle was planning to meet her boyfriend at Newfound Gap in order to spend a few days together in Gatlinburg. We brainstormed April Fool's jokes we could play on him, like having me arrive first to tell him she had met another guy and decided to stay at the last shelter.

As the day wore on, Princess Elle sensed that my 50-year-old body was starting to tire. She began singing a series of Jack Black songs to motivate me. I wasn't familiar with any of them but appreciated her company and vocal efforts. At the Road Prong Trail parking lot, we stopped with Master Wayne to rest and dry our socks on a grassy slope.

We eventually arrived at the popular, touristy Newfound Gap, a mountain pass dedicated by President Franklin Roosevelt in 1940. After multiple days of solitude in the wilderness, it was odd seeing so many cars and people. Noticeably absent was Princess Elle's boyfriend, but I defended him and assured her that he was probably in town making preparations for their reunion.

Several AT books I've read talk about the "rock star" treatment that aspiring thru-hikers receive at points along the trail. I hadn't experienced any of that until Newfound Gap. As we organized our backpacks, dumped trash, and ate snacks, several individuals and families approached us like you might approach a wild, smelly emu. Interested, but cautious.

"That's a thru-hiker, dear," whispered one mother to her young daughter, as she held on to her to keep her from getting too close. "Aspiring thru-hiker," I clarified. "Some people disagree with me, but I don't believe you earn the thru-hiker title until the final summit in Maine." From a variety of folks young and old, we got the usual questions about where we began, how far we had gone, and whether we had seen any bears. On that last question, I wanted to answer, "No, but I saw a princess poop in the woods this morning." I showed restraint, not wanting to cause confusion for the young tourists and aspiring princesses listening and staring. Besides, what Elle had done was a private matter—one that shouldn't be shared.

Honestly, after hiking 207 miles, recently in miserable conditions, I appreciated the rock star treatment, even though I was just a smelly hiker. The experience brought back memories of the last time I had felt that way. I was on a plane full of troops on our way to Afghanistan in January, 2007. We stopped to refuel at 1:00 a.m. at Bangor International Airport in Maine.

As we exited the plane and walked down the ramp for a two-hour layover, we saw rows of 15 to 20 elderly people lined up on both sides. They clapped enthusiastically and patted us on the back. I was stunned. It was the middle of the night and we had not yet stepped foot in a combat zone. But there they were, serving refreshments and handing out cell phones so we could call home.

These sweet elderly people made us feel like rock stars, even though we were still on American soil. I felt so honored to be among these troops. Some had been on multiple deployments. Perhaps others would never return home, having given their last full measure of devotion. I truly appreciated the kindness and appreciation of my fellow Americans that night.

I also appreciated the kindness and interest shown in my hike by these tourists at Newfound Gap. Even though I wasn't a rock star or anything close, the rock star treatment felt good and lifted my spirits. With so many friends and family back home pulling for us, and now all these strangers cheering us on, how could we do anything less than finish the trail?

Fob Fundamental #15 – Do as much as you can, as often as you can, to make those around you feel like rock stars.

I said farewell to Princess Elle whose boyfriend arrived just after I left. I hiked uphill a few more miles and settled in at Icewater Spring Shelter along with the remainder of the Great Smoky Mountains Bubble. As is often the case, we were joined by some new faces.

John Just from Peoria, Illinois was attempting a thru-hike to draw attention to his rare, genetic Fabry disease. The illness affects one in 40,000 people, including six in his family. To stay alive, he must get an IV transfusion every two weeks for the rest of his life. And he was hiking the AT! After each transfusion, he began working the logistics for the next one. Meanwhile, I complained about a sore knee! He said, "Fob, I hope my hike sends a message to people with this disease and others that you can still get out and do things and enjoy life. I want to raise awareness." I didn't know whether he would successfully complete a thru-hike, but in my opinion, his hike was already a success.

A couple and their 9-year-old daughter joined us at the shelter. More accurately, we joined them. The mom had reserved the shelter, and thought that meant they would have it all to themselves. She planned a big family weekend getaway there, complete with a guitar, telescope, and canned goods, but no sleeping pads. Upon arrival, she was shocked to learn they would be sharing the shelter and camping area with a dozen stinky hikers. She was not a happy camper, but they ended up having a good time interacting with our bubble.

Despite more adversity in the form of dismal weather, the day had been simply wonderful. As AT thru-hiker and author Kyle Rohrig once wrote, "Your attitude and frame of mind determined everything."

Day 22 – Icewater Spring Shelter to Tri-Corner Knob Shelter
12.1 miles, 222.2 cumulative miles

"Can you think of a single situation, no matter how grave, where the atmosphere would not be instantly shattered with a loud fart - or a drawing of a butt? There is no faster way to create universal common ground."
- Euny Hong

The weather was slightly better for today's hike, which would take us through arguably the most scenic part of the Smokies. We enjoyed stunning mountaintop views from places like Charlies Bunion, The Sawteeth, Bradley's View, and Eagle Rocks. At Copper Gap, mile 218.9, I stopped and reflected on having completed 10 percent of my AT journey. That seemed like an awfully low percentage for all that I had seen and experienced so far.

The Bubble and I eventually arrived at the Tri-Corner Knob Shelter, coming in at 5,897 feet. Deadwood and Nesquick wasted little time in doing spot-on *Monty Python* movie impressions. Before long, everyone was saying their own favorite lines from the movie and continued with those accents for the rest of the evening. As the wind picked up and temperature dropped, we worked our way inside the three-sided shelter to share stories and eat second dinner. Oddly, almost everyone had some form of potato, including the highly popular Ramen Bomb (Ramen noodles + instant potatoes + the meat of your choice + hot sauce).

As we wrapped up supper, the kind, sweet, mild-mannered section hiker known as Master Wayne excused himself and stepped just outside the hand-hung tarp which comprised the shelter's makeshift fourth wall. Seconds later, during a lull in the conversation, he ripped the loudest, bat cave-shaking fart in human history.

We all laughed hysterically and applauded Master Wayne for his masterpiece, even while the embarrassed caped crusader remained outside to compose himself and check for trouser damage. It was unclear why he felt the need to step outside, since we were in a hiking environment where such grand noises are not only allowed, but celebrated. And yet, if you listened closely, you could almost hear *Monty Python's* Sir Bedevere declare, "The tarp is designed to protect the shelter from wind, is it not? That's what happened here. Nothing to see. Run along."

Day 23 – Tri-Corner Knob Shelter to Standing Bear Farm
18.4 miles, 240.6 cumulative miles

"If you wash your entire wardrobe in the wilderness using a rusty washboard…
you might be a redneck."
- Sir Fob W. Pot

On the morning of Day 23, the only warm spots within 20 miles of us were inside our sleeping bags, and that's where we wanted to stay. But it was time to break up with the Smokies and move northward toward greener, and hopefully warmer, pastures.

To stay focused and motivated, I always had to have a next big target, be that a trail town, hostel, or swimming hole. Today, my next big target was Standing Bear Farm Hostel, just 18.4 miles away. After an initial climb, I began a long descent to Camel Gap. At mile 225.9, I passed the barely visible wreckage of an F-4 Phantom fighter jet that crashed in 1984. To date, there have been 54 recorded plane crashes within the Great Smoky Mountains National Park. They are usually private planes flying in bad weather. A pilot becomes spatially disoriented, not knowing up from down, and hits the side of the mountain or trees.

As I hiked that afternoon, the weather continued to improve, but I was growing weary. My feet ached and pain shot across my left knee about every three paces. At mile 236, I sat down on a log next to Master Wayne for a much-needed rest. He was preparing to take a side trail to a parking lot, as his section hike was over. Physically, I had bottomed out and wasn't in a good place. I was sad that our Smoky Mountain bubble was about to break up.

After a long break and with two hours of daylight remaining, I said a quick prayer, popped three Advil, and stood up. While struggling to put my backpack on, I wondered who had filled it with bricks. I slowly put one foot in front of the other and continued my descent, eventually walking under Interstate 40. After a tough, painful final mile, including some killer stairs, I staggered into Standing Bear Hostel just before sunset.

Standing Bear Hostel, by any definition, is a really odd place. The wilderness campus was managed by Lumpy, a legitimate mountain man who was a mix between *Swamp People*, *Duck Dynasty*, and *Deliverance*. I wondered why there wasn't already a reality television series based on Lumpy and this hostel. With a long beard and slow, drawn out speaking style, it seemed like he was playing a movie character. But he was not—he was the real deal.

After a brief campus tour, Lumpy and I sat down on the porch of the old wooden bunkhouse for a chat. He said he got his nickname because he once was a "fat kid." It's interesting how some nicknames stick to a person for life, even though he ended up quite skinny. I told him I really liked his beard, and hoped that one day the mangy crop of Spanish moss on my chin would grow into something that impressive.

Lumpy proceeded to tell me a true story about his beard. Years ago, he agreed to let a local organization use his famous beard for a fundraiser to raise money to pay the hospital bills of a sick child. The organizers used an auction format, and the highest bidder got to decide whether to cut Lumpy's beard or preserve it. After several minutes of competitive bidding, a local businessman ultimately won with a bid of $2,800, and chose to have Lumpy's beard cut off.

As Lumpy told this tale in his slow, Lumpy voice, I thought it was such a cool, heartwarming story of rural compassion. I loved how he willingly used one of his greatest assets, his beard, to help a sick child in need. But Lumpy wasn't through yet—not by a long shot. In fact, he was just getting started.

He continued... "I got up on the stage. Then they brung me and my beard over to the gal with the scissors who would do the cuttin'." He paused for a moment and grinned from ear to ear. Then, in a higher, excited voice, he declared, "and that gal had the biggest hooters I've ever seen!" (He gestured just how large so I could get a sense of their magnitude and longitude.)

I was speechless. We had reached the purpose for the story—the main take-a-way, the apex, the reason it was being told. Lumpy's tale didn't end with a sick boy in a wheelchair being wheeled across the stage to hug and thank a teary-eyed Lumpy. Nor did it end with a beardless Lumpy being lifted on the town's collective shoulders and celebrated as the high school band played. Rather, it ended with an extremely well-endowed country gal taking Lumpy's magnificent beard from him, but giving him an even more thrilling gift in return.

As for the hostel, $20 got me a bunk bed with a foam mattress and linens. I passed on the option to tent camp for a lesser rate. At least two of the tent campers were drinking, smoking pot, and had taken six consecutive zero days in Gatlinburg to party, recover, and party some more. I located the hostel's resupply store with reasonably priced, mostly not expired food and other hiker amenities. Across from the store were laundry facilities—sort of. Next to a standard dryer, there were two wash tubs, a hose, a washboard, and soap.

I soon learned of two downsides to this place. First, the hot water was out, so my only option was an ice-cold shower that took my breath and other things away. That's right, a hot shower, the very thing I had hiked a personal best 18.4 miles for, simply wasn't there at the finish line.

Second, the port-a-john had not been emptied since Nixon was President, and was literally filled to the brim. The outhouse scene was truly disgusting, and there aren't many things that truly disgust long-distance hikers. Thankfully, there was another privy by the camping area that offered an alternative. In fairness, I should add that as I exited the hostel the following day, the new port-a-john was being delivered.

After showering, I got ready to do some old-school laundry. I examined the old washboard, too clueless to know how to use it and too proud to ask for help. The contraption looked like something that would be used in a hillbilly band or to decorate a wall at the neighborhood Cracker Barrel. Noticing my incompetency, Stitch mercifully came over and gave me a short tutorial. I'm not sure my clothes ever really got clean, but I had learned a new, non-marketable skill.

For first dinner, I consumed a large supreme pizza, Gatorade, and Diet Coke. I set aside two packages of string cheese, two cherry pie packets, and a Mountain Dew for second dinner to be enjoyed an hour later. I then shot and posted a video clip on Facebook of Lumpy and my hiking buddies quoting lines from various *Monty Python* movies.

Before retiring for the evening, I decided to weigh myself on the hostel's scales. I discovered that I had lost a whopping 31.6 pounds! Amazingly, I had exceeded my weight loss goal for the entire journey in just 23 days! This realization was also a psychological boost, knowing I was no longer carrying around a "front pack," the equivalent of two bowling balls.

As we laid in our bunks and started to doze off, a nearby rooster crowed. From somewhere outside our bunkroom, Lumpy yelled, "Sorry y'all...the bird gits his nights and days confused sometimes." His comment was the perfect way to close a peculiar evening at a peculiar place. In fact, we may use his exact words each time we close an episode of the new reality television show, *Lumpy at Standing Bear*.

Day 24 – Standing Bear Farm to Groundhog Creek Shelter
6.9 miles, 247.5 cumulative miles

I began the day with the weird sensation of being in a bed—because I was! My next sensation was my tibial collateral ligament telling me to take the morning off. On the AT, I had already learned to listen to my body. I had to be able to hike with a certain amount of pain, but I also needed downtime to rest my body and mind and regroup for the next section ahead. I realized that over the long-haul, I would not be able to out-tough or out-ego the AT. It was far superior on the toughness scale. With 50 years' worth of life experiences under my belt, my only chance against the AT was to make wise choices related to rest, nutrition, hydration, mileage, and weather.

As I finally rolled out of bed around 10:00 a.m., I realized we were out of the Smokies and our Great Smoky Mountains Bubble had burst. Orbit, Mom, Stitch, and Deadwood were already on the trail. I planned to leave mid-afternoon. Nesquick was taking a zero day to enjoy additional bonding time with Lumpy. Princess Elle and Booknboot had been sucked into the great Gatlinburg vortex, and Master Wayne was at home eating Cheetos and watching Netflix.

Such was the nature of hiking bubbles—you love them, appreciate them, and ride them for as long as you can. I hoped to cross paths with one or more of my friends further down the trail, but there were no guarantees. I found it interesting that in five days in the Smokies, under tough conditions, I had learned more about these people than many of my casual acquaintances back in the real world. I was amazed at how much I could learn about a person from talking with them during a five-hour, uninterrupted hike.

Fob Fundamental #16 – It's possible to get to know and become friends with someone through many short, casual conversations over the course of several years. To short-circuit that process, have a five-hour uninterrupted conversation with them.

I gave Lumpy a final fist pump, thanked him for his hospitality, and coveted his beard one final time. His parting words were, "In case anyone hasn't told you lately, I'm proud of you." While I suspect those are his parting words to all his customers, he sounded sincere and I appreciated them. In fact, I may have gotten a little lumpy in my throat.

I got back on the trail around 2:30 p.m. After a five mile, 2,500-foot climb, I was standing on the beautiful, grassy bald of Snowbird Mountain. I looked up and saw an interesting, seemingly misplaced facility. The building looked like the kind one would enter to solve a puzzle and unlock a new world in the popular 1990s computer game, *Myst*. I was tempted to enter, throw some switches, and be instantly transported to Katahdin. Unfortunately, it was just a Federal Aviation Administration Control Tower, with a warning sign that if one messes with anything, people could die. Valuing life, I heeded it's warning.

By late afternoon, I arrived at Groundhog Creek Shelter and set up my tent nearby. As I cooked my 2.5 servings of New Orleans-style Rice with Shrimp and Ham, I became acquainted with a whole new cast of characters, including...

- Lindsay and Patrice – These two ladies were making a movie about women thru-hikers entitled *Thru*. I told them I would check out the trailer for the film at thruatdoc.com. I also told them if they changed their minds and decided to include a token man in the film, I would like for Fob to be played by Bear Grylls.
- Little Bear – This short, blond, female hiker hailed from Pulaski, Tennessee. She had a great smile, a sweet disposition, and was the best smelling person on the trail that week.
- Tyler and Tyler – The two friends of the same name were fairly quiet, but worked tirelessly to build and maintain the campfire.
- Squirrel Nut – His trail name was allegedly based on some physical deformity, but no one pursued that line of questioning.
- Tree Hugger – A man about my age who wore the same blazed hiking shirt as me, along with a kilt. He literally stopped and hugged every tree with a white blaze on it, and said a short prayer asking God to protect him and keep him on the right path. His approach would involve a lot of tree hugging...and a lot of prayers. I had said many prayers, but could only remember hugging one tree—just off the trail at Quesalupa Gap.

Day 25 – Groundhog Creek Shelter to Old Road
18.4 miles, 265.9 cumulative miles

"The reward of a thing well done is having done it."
- Ralph Waldo Emerson

I got an early start this morning and was thankful the pain in my left knee had subsided. As I began the descent into Brown Gap, I came across an old man with a long white beard wandering along the trail. He had no pack or gear and we were several miles from civilization. We exchanged hellos and I asked if everything was okay. He smiled and told me everything was fine. I found the encounter odd but wished him well and hiked on.

Five minutes later, I caught Lindsay and we discovered trail magic right along the side of the trail. Someone had left a case of cold Cokes beside a tree. My theory: The bearded man I had just recently passed was the trail angel responsible for the Cokes. Unencumbered by a backpack full of gear, he would have been able to transport the drinks to this section of trail.

Theory #2: The man wasn't looking for praise, which is why he walked southbound from the drinks. He wanted us to discover the drinks *after* passing him. He smiled at me because he knew of the magic I was about to receive—magic that he was responsible for. Regardless of the validity of my theories, Lindsay and I enjoyed a Coke and a smile together. Had I been born with ovaries, this lovely scene might have even made her documentary!

The highlight of the day came when I summited Max Patch Bald. Several years ago, my extended family decided on a Christmas vacation in the mountains. I insisted we take a day trip to Max Patch, a place I had read about in various AT books. The family was reluctant, to say the least, but I told them the view would be well worth the "30 or so" minute trip to get there. The journey ended up taking 90 minutes due to winding roads and blustery snowfall.

When we arrived at the Max Patch parking lot, the temperature had dropped to 20 degrees with a wind chill factor closer to zero. Between the cold and several inches of snow on the ground, half of those in our group (the pansies), refused to exit their cars. The other half begrudgingly followed me up the bald. With each step, the temperature decreased, along with any hope of me getting any Christmas presents.

At the summit, we were frozen to our core, like the frozen Jack Nicholson in the maze at the end of *The Shining*. We took a two-second look at the spectacular view, wiped our snotty noses with our sleeves, and rushed down the mountain toward the warmth of our cars. The entire family was not happy with me. I knew this because they told me so. In fact, they later presented me with a Christmas present, a coaster that read, "The voices in my head don't like you," to reinforce the group's disdain for my choice of the day's activity.

I was the butt of jokes for the rest of the vacation and still get grief over Max Patch. In fact, whenever we are on vacation and there is a lull in activities, someone will usually look over at me and say, "Hey, we should go to Max Patch Bald." With that history, it was great for me to return to this spot—alone—on a somewhat warmer, low 40s day and think about my sweet family. The voices in my head told me I missed them!

As I descended toward Lemon Gap, I entered an engaging stretch of trail featuring rolling hills, stream crossings, birds chirping, and mountain laurels in every direction. The place was how I imagined the Garden of Eden. Five minutes after thinking that, I ironically came across my second AT snake. He was a little fellow, slithering across the trail in front of me. Had he offered me an apple, I would have been really tempted to bite it.

After a personal best-tying 18.4-mile day, I stopped at a stealth camping site on a steep ledge by a stream. The location would have been a perfect spot for an REI camping advertisement. I was alone, but fortunately Rocky, a friendly section hiker, strolled by to snap a photo of me and the site, and then e-mailed it to me. I dozed off to the sound of the stream, with visions of Hot Springs dancing in my head.

Days 26 & 27 – Old Road to Hot Springs
7.8 & 0 miles, 273.7 cumulative miles

While a woodpecker tapped Morse code on a trunk high above me, I packed up and began a 7.8-mile descent into Hot Springs. Like Franklin, Hot Springs is another classic trail town with a reputation for catering to hikers. I arrived at the Hostel at Laughing Heart Lodge just after noon. Tie, the amazing caretaker, welcomed me and gave me a tour of the place. There is an upscale lodge, perfect for romantic getaways, along with a hostel, perfect for hikers who just need a non-romantic getaway from the trail.

The first order of business was to get my mail. Janet and my sister, Ellen, had both sent me care packages! Among other things, I was blessed with homemade peanut butter cookies with Hershey kisses on them, beef jerky, gummy bears, cards, and notes. After reading Janet's encouraging card, I kept hoping Jeff Probst, the television host from the show *Survivor*, would pop his head in and tell me I had a special visit from a loved one. Then Janet would walk in and whisk me away to the romantic upscale lodge instead of the hiker hostel. The dream reunion didn't happen, but I looked forward to when it would.

After showering, I walked a half mile to take care of the usual trail town business—doing laundry at the Wash Tub and resupplying food at Bluff Mountain Outfitter. Stitch, Orbit, Mom, Moses, Fisherman, Deadwood, Deadwood's parents, and I gathered at the Spring Creek Tavern for some food, fun, and storytelling. Oddly, it felt like a family reunion of at least some of our Bubble members.

I devoured a giant cheeseburger with jalapeños and French fries in an attempt to slow my weight loss. I learned that Moses had melted his insoles while drying them by a campfire, and that Jenga (who wasn't with us) earned his trail name after getting drunk in Franklin and toppling over. I also learned that, sadly, a sight-seeing helicopter had crashed in the Smokies on April 4th, killing all five people on board.

I was especially glad at dinner to sit next to Fisherman, aka Fernando, one of the Hikers Formerly Known as ABBA. He got delayed in Hot Springs waiting on a late-arriving hammock he ordered, and planned some big mileage days to catch his Swiss hiking partners. He confirmed for me what I had suspected—Switzerland, Sweden, and Swaziland are, in fact, entirely different countries.

Fisherman is a Swiss architect specializing in mountain chalets, and said he'd hook me and Janet up in one next time we're in Gothenburg. I'm holding him to that. He also loves to fly fish and ties his own flies, thus the trail name. His favorite Swiss food is fondue and his favorite American food is steak, which costs $60 and up in Switzerland for 12 ounces. I almost confessed to him that I had crab-walked over his sleeping face in the middle of the night in the Wayah Bald Shelter, but couldn't muster the courage. Still, by the end of the night, he was my best Swiss friend ever.

I had three priorities on my zero day in Hot Springs. First, I made several phone calls to the family to let them know I was alive and well. Once again, I enjoyed hearing familiar voices and getting caught up on family matters. Talking to my wife is like Ramen Bomb for the soul. My dad was continuing to adjust to life without my mom, who had passed away the previous summer, and I was proud of him. I also got to FaceTime with Mrs. Wilkinson's class at Foundation Christian Academy, where I used to teach. They are one of two classes following my journey and doing various assignments related to it. I enjoyed fielding their questions and listening to them giggle at my stories.

Second, I decided to invest $20 for a 1-hour soak in a hot spring-fed hot tub/whirlpool at the Hot Springs Resort. After walking there for my 3:00 p.m. appointment, I realized I had no swim trunks and none were available at the front desk. The lady told me, "You won't need any swim trunks. You'll be alone and the tub has three sides to it, with the open side right on the river." I looked at her and in my best Austin Powers voice said, "Oh, behave!" Based on her reaction, either I did a bad impression, she was extremely creeped out, or she had not seen the movie.

The attendant then led me to the river, turned the jets on, and handed me a towel. As I stripped down and lowered myself into the wondrous tub of healing waters, I got that feeling you get when you're naked in a hot tub in the woods. As my bare behind submerged and then floated to the top, I wondered if the local Boy Scouts ever canoe down this river, or even worse, the Girl Scouts. I could hear them now... "Look away, Sarah! That's not a rare albino manatee, that's Fob's behind!"

I decided to send a hot tub selfie to Janet, but only from the shoulders up. In light of FCC Rule 438-09-b, *Obscenity on Commercial Airwaves*, and National Forest Service Pamphlet 10-8, *Sexting from the AT*, I had to be very careful what I sent. Even my chosen pose was arguably fobscene and in violation of federal law.

After my 1-hour relaxing soak, I got dressed and walked to the Smoky Mountain Diner for a large, supreme pizza, my third priority for the day. For the first time on my AT journey, I was unable to finish a meal. Not wanting to be wasteful, I took a to-go box with the leftovers. Not finishing any meal is an embarrassing, shameful thing for a long-distance hiker;

wasting food is a punishable offense.

As I returned to the hostel with half a pizza, I saw two tired, weary young hikers descend from the mountain and approach the hostel like I had done the previous day. I asked if they wanted half a large, still warm supreme pizza. Their faces lit up and they said, "Are you serious? Absolutely!"

Watching them close their eyes in ecstasy and gobble down the pizza in under three minutes, I realized how good it feels to be on the giving end of trail magic for a change. In fact, as awesome as it was to get the two care packages, I felt an even deeper satisfaction watching those two guys smile and devour that pizza. I was reminded once again of the words of Jesus, *"It's more blessed to give than to receive."*

Fob Fundamental #17 – To really understand the joy of giving…while a present is being opened, focus not on the face of the recipient, but on the face of the giver.

Day 28 – Hot Springs to Allen Gap
14.8 miles, 288.5 cumulative miles

"By doing periodic 'controlled burns' on the undesirable influences in your life—mindless television shows, social media arguments, and similar time wasters—you free up your mind for spiritual germination and renewal."
- Sir Fob W. Pot

After showering, I finished off a box of trail magic donuts, courtesy of Deadwood's parents. Refreshed and recharged, I crossed the French Broad River, hiked along it for a few hundred yards, and then climbed the mountain out of Hot Springs. At mile 278.5, I reached Dammed Pond, the first mountain pond on my journey. If you live near Hot Springs and need to catch a fish, read a book, or get engaged, Dammed Pond is truly a place of beauty.

At Tanyard Gap, I passed Tree Hugger as he stopped to pray and hug a white-blazed tree. If he completed his thru-hike, I estimated he will have hugged 165,000 trees and offered 165,000 prayers. Let that sink in for a moment. Based on a six-month hike, he would average thirty-eight prayers and trees hugged every single day.

Later, I came across several miles of a controlled burn area on the west side of the trail. A controlled burn is a technique used in forest management to reduce fuel buildup (e.g., leaves, brush, dead trees, etc.) and the likelihood of serious hotter fires. The fires also stimulate germination of some desirable trees, thus renewing the forest. I was impressed by the hundreds of square miles of burned forest to the left or west of the trail, while the right side was untouched.

As the day progressed, the temperature dropped and light snow began to fall. At Allen Gap, I headed .2 miles west to get water under a bridge at Paint Creek. I was concerned about the water's quality, but that's all water under the bridge now. I found a campsite nearby and checked the forecast. The snow had stopped but, here at lower elevation, rain was expected in 15 minutes. Three minutes later, as I was unpacking my backpack, rain began to fall.

Quickly setting up a tent in the rain, while keeping my gear as dry as possible, took practice and precision. The goal was to get my tent, gear, and self under the rain fly as soon as possible. I performed fairly well but knew I'd become more proficient with practice. I sat there in my tent, feeling cold, wet, and alone.

I realized I forgot to hang my bear bag line and was sitting next to my food bag, a special invitation for local bears to come eat me. I gobbled down three flour tortillas filled with sharp cheddar cheese and hard salami, then went back out in the rain to hang my food. Upon returning to the tent, I was happy to have warm, dry clothes to put on and a warm sleeping bag to crawl into. I would have been even happier had I known that just a few hundred yards away, trail magic awaited me.

Day 29 – Allen Gap to Flint Mountain Shelter
17.9 miles, 306.4 cumulative miles

"We are told to let our light shine, and if it does, we won't need to tell anybody it does. Lighthouses don't fire cannons to call attention to their shining - they just shine."
- Dwight L. Moody

My breath was once again visible on this chilly April morning. Just a few minutes into my climb out of Allen Gap, I stumbled upon some timely trail magic. The good people of Chuckey (Tennessee) United Methodist Church had placed a cooler of ice-cold Gatorade along the trail which gave me a much-needed morale and electrolyte boost. Less than a mile later, I discovered even more trail magic. Someone had stacked a dozen or so fresh oranges on the trail. With the cold temperatures, I wasn't quite ready to take my gloves off and peel an orange, so I saved the citrusy snack for later.

I hiked along Blackstack Cliffs and Big Firescald Knob, a stretch of scenic, rocky, and strenuous cliffs. I took a quick break on Howard's Rock and read the plaque honoring Howard McDonald, a trail builder who had dedicated countless hours to creating and maintaining this magnificent trail. The section along Firescald involved a brief hand over hand scramble, the first since Albert Mountain.

81

After celebrating the AT mile 300 marker with a Snickers candy bar, I climbed over Big Butt Mountain. (I liked Big Butt, I cannot lie.) Shortly after, I met two section hikers from Alabama: Hiccup, who does so after eating trail mix, and his unnamed friend who works for NASA. They were joined by their dog, Blaze, who was happy to help me finish off a granola bar.

As the afternoon progressed, the temperature dropped and light snow blanketed the ground. To pass the time and keep my brain from freezing, I began brainstorming what the *Pisgah* in Pisgah National Forest could possibly stand for. I came up with...

- Perhaps I Should Garner a Heater
- Place I Should Generally Avoid, Honey
- Peasants in Scotland Get Awful Hernias
- Pastor in Skivvies? Gross! Avoid Him
- People in Straight-jackets...Great AT Hikers

In addition to playing mind games, I pondered...

- Is there a Guinness World Record for "Longest Runny Nose"? (By that, I mean duration of drip, not length of proboscis.) Mine had been running virtually non-stop for 29 days.
- Given the popularity of the movies/books *Wild* and *A Walk in the Woods*, what percentage increase (if any) will there be in attempted AT thru-hikes this year? Also, will the 20-25% success rate remain the same? (I predicted a 15% increase in attempts and a similar success rate.)
- Percentage-wise, how much of a successful AT thru-hike is physical and how much is mental? (For me, so far: 70% physical, 30% mental.) How much does that vary between hikers, and does it vary by month on the trail? (I'd say wide variance between hikers, with the physical percentage increasing with a hiker's age. I would guess the mental percentage increases during the middle third of the trail, then back to more physical for New Hampshire and Maine. Only time would tell.)

After a long, bone-chilling 17.9-mile day, I arrived at Flint Mountain Shelter with several other hikers. We built a huge campfire and gazed at constellations in the clear night sky. Just before dozing off inside the shelter, I pulled the orange from my pocket, peeled, and ate it. Because nothing took my mind off the cold better than sticky hands that smelled of citrus.

Day 30 – Flint Mountain Shelter to Low Gap
14.9 miles, 321.3 cumulative miles

"We can't expect people to act like Jesus when they don't know him."
- Rachel Elizabeth Johnson

On the morning of Day 30, I recalled a comment from a fellow hiker, who heard from a foot guy at an outfitter, who probably heard from an African witch doctor, that it took 300 miles of hiking for one's "hiking muscles" to form, and 600 miles for one's "hiking tendons" to do the same. Having just hiked 300 miles, I was anxious to see if I would begin to notice any difference in my hiking stamina.

After a few downhill miles, I saw a sign posted on a tree warning hikers not to befriend or feed any dogs they were about to see. If necessary, hikers were to even throw rocks at these canines. Apparently, dogs that once lived there followed some friendly hikers northward and never returned.

Five minutes later, as I approached a foot bridge over a creek, I saw a pack of dogs barking and charging toward me from a distance. I have been bitten twice by dogs, while jogging in Alabama and Illinois. I wasn't about to be bitten again. Testing my new 300-mile hiking muscles, I made an adrenaline-fueled, 50-yard sprint for the footbridge, crossed over it, and spun around in a defensive position with my hiking poles extended. My former colleagues at the National War College would have approved of this rarely used, single troop phalanx formation.

As the sound of the pack of dogs drew near, the voice in my head shouted, "Spartans, prepare for glory!" The pack of six dogs arrived seconds later, barking ferociously at me from across the narrow creek. The pack appeared to be led by a dirty poodle, flanked by a couple of schnauzers, an old hound dog with a limp, and two ugly mutts. I ran from these sorry misfits? Not a single Pitbull or German Shepherd or Doberman. I stood up, stared at my adversaries, and unnecessarily shouted, "Shut your pie holes, you sorry bunch of losers!"

I climbed 4,541-foot Lick Rock with Orange Pacer, who got that name due to a tendency to mix in a little vodka with his orange Gatorade. He said it helped him "set just the right pace" on hikes. I didn't doubt him. Later, I met two sweet ladies from North Carolina on a section hike. They dreamed of thru-hiking the AT someday and I told them to make that a reality. At Sams Gap, one of those ladies gave Orange Pacer and me her last two homemade chocolate chip cookies. She said, "You need these more than I do."

As I climbed out of Sams Gap, I was feeling pretty good about my stamina and 300-mile leg muscles. Just then, a young, blond, highly attractive gal zoomed passed me with a wiener dog in tow. I didn't mind being passed by a woman, especially one half my age wearing amazing, woman-smelling deodorant. But watching a wiener dog with four 3-inch legs blow by me was beyond demoralizing! If I had been carrying a bottle of mustard, I'd have squirted him down the length of his back as he went by. So much for having my trail legs.

After a 14.9-mile day, I tented with about 15 others at Low Gap. There was good and bad around the campfire that night. The good was the personable Cambria, who not only is from my birth state, Delaware, but was born in the same hospital at Dover Air Force Base! Since leaving Delaware at age 12, I had never met anyone from Delaware, much less from the same hospital where I was born. We shared a few stories and she brought me up to date on important matters around town, including the football rivalry between Caesar Rodney and Dover High Schools. I have fond memories of playing for the undefeated Caesar Rodney Junior High football team and watching my sisters cheer for the high school team.

The not so good around the campfire was the pot smoking, which was accompanied by heavy cursing. Several in this group were dropping F-bombs like a common adjective, with the frequency that most people would use the word *the*. Drug use and cursing are simply not compatible with my Christian faith. I don't do those things and I don't enjoy being around those who do. In fact, eating in the midst of excessive cussing is like watching a sunset in the midst of someone juggling globs of manure.

I found it interesting, and a bit sad, that in an environment like the AT, with amazing sights, sounds, and sensations in every direction, some would find that wasn't enough to enjoy the day. Some needed additional artificial stimulation to enhance the experience, to be cool, or perhaps to escape something. If the AT environment wasn't thrilling enough, I was concerned how these young folks would fare back in society.

While I have strong opinions on this behavior, I wasn't judging them. God handles that and I needed to focus on the planks in my own eyes. However, I do believe that the apparent empty space in their lives they are trying to fill with drugs can only be filled by a relationship with Jesus Christ. A relationship of that nature would likely also do wonders for their vocabulary. I didn't make a scene or go all "campfire preacher" on them. I simply declined their offer of drugs and retired early to my tent. I prayed for them. I also prayed my hike, and my life, would be more Christ-like, and thus serve as an example of a better way to live.

**Fob Fundamental #18 – As Christians, we're called
to change the world by being salt and light.
We're not called to judge—to bring fire and
brimstone, as that is God's domain.**

Like the rest of society, the AT had its good and bad aspects. Fortunately, my experience to date, including interactions with other hikers, had been overwhelmingly positive. Positive interactions with attacking dogs—not so much.

Days 31 & 32 – Low Gap to Erwin
20.8 & 0 miles, 342.1 cumulative miles

I began this thankfully warmer day with a 1,200-foot climb to the incredible Big Bald, every bit as scenic as Max Patch. After taking a few photos, I descended toward Bald Mountain Shelter and felt nature's call. As I approached the shelter, I asked a fellow hiker if there was a privy nearby. He told me there wasn't. Bummer. So, for just the 3rd time on my AT journey, I found a suitable, secluded spot and assumed the position behind a tree. Upon returning to the shelter, that same hiker said, "Oh yeah, there is a privy...just found out. My bad." Seriously?! Before departing, I renamed the area Mount Unnecessary 90-Degree Angle.

Just after noon, I descended into Spivey Gap and discovered some trail magic. Yes, trail angel Bob's Twinkie and Coke hit the spot. A couple of hours later, I arrived at No Business Knob Shelter and visited with Pop tart, SpongeBob, and Gunga Dan, who had stopped for the night. Pop tart, a fellow Air Force retiree, was having the common hiker problem of too much food based on unnecessary or poorly timed food mailings. I ended up trading some of my tortillas and pepperoni to him for some of his excess electrolyte tablets and Gatorade mix. Lewis and Clark would have been proud of our trail bartering skills.

With my legs feeling good and a trail town just ahead, I decided to push on. After hiking a personal best 20.8 miles, I arrived in Erwin, Tennessee and took a shuttle to the Super 8. This economy hotel beat camping by the river or staying at a hostel, because rain was in the forecast and I longed for a hot bath.

As I was doing laundry, I noticed a hiker box—a container in which hikers leave unwanted items for others to take for free. In retrospect, I made one really good selection from the box...and one terrible one. The good one was an unopened bag of Epsom salt, which I would use in three hot baths over the next 36 hours, much to the pleasure of my aching feet. The bad choice was the package of Bear Creek Country Kitchen's Darn Good Chili Mix—eight servings coming in at 9.8 ounces. I'll come back to that later.

After doing laundry, cleaning (back-flushing) my Sawyer Squeeze water filter, taking a shower and bath, and cleaning my cookware, I walked to Erwin's Huddle House restaurant, adjacent to a gas station. I feasted on a rib eye steak, two eggs, hash browns, bread, water, and Mountain Dew. Simply marvelous!

Not wanting to walk farther to the grocery store, I purchased the few crackers, energy bars, and Ibuprofen I needed at the gas station, then returned to the hotel. I called my wife and sons to check in and get updated on their lives. Satisfied that they were alive and well, I got a Super 8 hours of sleep.

I began my zero day with the hotel breakfast, specifically a waffle, cereal, and several cups of coffee, milk, and orange juice. After another Epsom salt bath, I caught some of a news broadcast. As a bit of a news junkie, I was surprised I hadn't missed daily dosages of news. I certainly didn't miss all the politics and election coverage. I care about those events, but found that hiking the AT consumed most of my physical and mental energy.

Television wise, I only missed watching some March Madness basketball games and watching *Survivor* with my wife while eating a big bowl of buttered popcorn. Oh, I also missed watching sappy Hallmark movies with our friends, Ken and Syndi Butler, and saying, "See, I told you so," when the lead characters invariably kiss at the end of the movie.

I finished off my day at McDonalds, where I consumed a high calorie, large double quarter pounder with cheese meal, 10-piece McNuggets, and a hot fudge Sundae. Janet told me I needed to eat more. I was just following her orders.

Day 33 – Erwin to Unaka Mountain
12.3 & 0 miles, 354.4 cumulative miles

I packed up, caught a shuttle to the trailhead, and began the long climb out of Erwin. The first few miles featured several streams, springs, and footbridges surrounded by mountain laurels and rhododendrons—a peaceful section. As I continued the climb, a 2,700-foot elevation gain, I felt the heat and weight of my fully loaded, post-trail town backpack. Sweat poured off me and I was drinking a liter of water with electrolytes every two hours.

At Beauty Spot Gap, Tetris, Mumbles and I stopped for some coffee, lemonade, and snacks, courtesy of a trail angel named Brother Tom. Tetris is a 20-something former auditor for New York's Department of Education. Mumbles, also in his twenties, hails from Lexington, Kentucky. After a mostly uphill day, the three of us tented at the base of Unaka Mountain.

Given the exhausting day and my belief that my pack was too heavy, I decided to eat the heaviest food item I had, regardless of what it was. After reviewing each item, the winning contestant was the previously mentioned Bear Creek Country Kitchen's Darn Good Chili Mix, taken from the hiker box at Erwin's Super 8. Weighing a whopping 9.8 ounces, and featuring three kinds of beans and a blend of spices, it seemed like a perfect choice.

Folks, the devil is in the details. Fine print matters. As I sat there on a log, at the base of Unaka Mountain, starving and licking my salty face, I read the instructions. I noticed it called for seven cups of water, a six-ounce can of tomato paste, and a simmer time of 20 to 25 minutes. Realistically, none of that was going to happen, which may explain why this item was comfortably resting in the hiker box.

If I could live Day 33 over, I would have violated Leave No Trace principles and chucked the Darn Good Chili Mix into the forest for the ants and squirrels to deal with. But no, not Fob! I was going to be creative and adaptive, and take matters into my own hands. I intended to eat those eight servings of chili on my own terms, following my own instructions. Translation: all 9.8 ounces of the Darn Good mix, only 2.5 cups of water, no tomato paste, and just eight minutes of simmer time. For you cooks out there, warning sirens are now going off.

I had no clue. I was a stupid, exhausted, hungry hiker, and I was about to create what Hispanics call *Chile Bola De Fuego Nuclear*, the highly toxic Nuclear Fireball Chili! My creation smelled terrific, but was thicker than a Dairy Queen Blizzard made with 10W-40 motor oil and the brown sugar cinnamon pop tart sawdust at the bottom of my food bag. One could set fence posts with this stuff. To make it just juicy enough to swallow, I added my final three packets of tabasco sauce. If this were a movie, the scary music would have started then.

As I slowly ate, a process that took 40 minutes (five minutes per serving), I ignored the warning signs, including a mountain-shaking belch after every third or fourth bite. I was a hungry, long-distance hiker, this was my own recipe, and I was going to eat it—all of it. In retrospect, I was being fobstinate. As Tetris looked on from opposite the campfire, he remained silent, but had a concerned, "Is he really going to eat all that?" look on his face. A closer friend would have intervened.

I finished off the last of the eight Darn Good servings, said good night, and crawled into my tent just after 9:00 p.m. At 9:05, my stomach made the sound of a mother grizzly bear mourning the loss of her cubs. My opening salvo was a burst of a dozen trouser clouds, as if to announce the arrival of royalty. I heard giggles outside and laughed myself. Next came a seven-second long, high pitched squealer that sounded like someone slowly letting air out of a balloon. I had become a human fart app! I could fart at will, but much more so when not willed.

Moments later, the partially cooked, partially digested, tabasco-coated beans in my large intestine began colliding at high speeds, like atomic nuclei. My bowel matter was fusing quicker than I could say Darn Good Chili, and the highly charged particles were converted to photon energy. In other words, I had inadvertently created a nuclear fusion-powered wind tunnel in my digestive track. If I hadn't donned my emergency travel Depends, escaping Darn Good beans would have been ricocheting all over the inside of my tent. By 10:30 p.m., when I stopped counting, I had farted more than 220 times. Not just any farts—Darn Good ones.

As embarrassing as the noises were, that wasn't the real issue. Pungent doesn't begin to describe the smell in my tent. I was nesting in a Chernobyl I had created. Each time I raised my behind, I buried my nose further into my clothes bag. It didn't work. Do I suffocate in my clothes bag, or die from toxic fumes? What would they write in my fobituary?

I considered opening the tent's zipper to create a backdraft, but that could invite mosquitos, mice, and other creepy crawlies. (Although, technically, only the American cockroach could survive in such a toxic environment.) As the minutes passed and the salvos increased in frequency, intensity, and pungency, I became desperate. I didn't want my thru-hike attempt to end this way.

Desperate times call for desperate measures. In times like these, I asked myself, "What would Larry Alexander, my AT mentor, do?" And that's when it came to me! I reached up with two hands, pulled both earplugs out of my ears, reversed them, and jammed them up my nostrils! Problem solved! Bear Grylls ain't got nothin' on Fob!

Day 34 – Unaka Mountain to Clyde Smith Shelter
13.9 miles, 368.3 cumulative miles

After a long, miserable night, I crawled out of my pungent tent, removed my nose plugs, and took a deep cleansing breath. I had survived and had learned valuable lessons about hiker boxes, serving sizes, and following recipes.

Powered by Darn Good Chili aftershocks, I began the climb up the enchanting, extremely cool Unaka Mountain, which would become my favorite forested summit hike of the first 400 miles. Half in Tennessee and half in North Carolina, it features dense spruce and hemlock forests, grassy patches, fog and mist. I expected Frodo Baggins to emerge from behind a tree, on his way to destroy the One Ring in the fires of Mount Doom. Near a campsite at the summit, I stopped to take care of some personal business, at the recently named Darn Good Patch. My desire to maintain privacy does not permit me to share the details of the dozen or so similar stops that I made that day.

I descended Unaka Mountain and began a series of ups and downs, including the picturesque Little Bald Knob. By late afternoon, I rolled into Clyde Smith Shelter with Tetris, Mumbles, and Old School. After the noises coming from my tent last night, I was surprised Tetris and Mumbles let me stay in the shelter with them.

Old School is a dentist from North Carolina who recently moved to Tulsa, Oklahoma. He began a thru-hike attempt in 2015, going from Harpers Ferry to Maine, and then headed southward from Harpers Ferry. Unfortunately, severe winter weather ended his bid, so he was back this year to finish his hike to Springer.

He got the trail name Old School because most of his hiking gear is from the late 70s and early 80s. In fact, he said he went into some museum along the AT that showed a sampling of hiking gear by decade, and several of his items were in the 70s and 80s cases. Around the campfire, he not only answered questions about brushing and flossing, but a series of questions about what we should expect in New Hampshire and Maine. He said the AT in those final two states is every bit as tough as hikers make it out to be.

Day 35 – Clyde Smith Shelter to Overmountain Shelter
15.6 miles, 383.9 cumulative miles

Feeling creative, I added a Little Debbie Oatmeal Cream Pie to my usual pop tart breakfast lineup. Sufficient caloric intake would be key for today's climb of the highly popular Roan Mountain. This massive, 6,285-foot mountain can be divided into two sections, with Carvers Gap in the middle. Hiking from the south, the first section features Roan High Knob Shelter (the highest backcountry shelter on the entire AT) and the peaks Roan High Bluff and Roan High Knob, which are blanketed by a dense spruce-fir forest. Tollhouse Gap lies between these two peaks and features the Rhododendron Gardens, the largest of its kind in the world. The climb to the summit was long, hot, and taxing, and the hike down was covered in foot-jarring rocks.

Descending the mountain towards Carvers Gap, I was tired, hungry, thirsty and my feet and left knee had begun to ache again. It had been a beautiful, but rugged, several hours of hiking. I thought maybe, just maybe, there would be some magic at the Gap. And there it was!

Like angels sent from heaven, Haynes and Janice Miller from Bluff City and the Tri-County Church of God had set up a magnificent trail magic stop. Janice had been a life-long blood donor which was an important part of her Christian faith and community service. Unfortunately, she had suffered a stroke the previous Fall and her doctor told her she could no longer donate blood. He said she could find new ways to give of her time and money, so long as she didn't donate blood.

After researching and thinking about needs in their community, Haynes and Janice considered serving the AT community as trail angels. They researched things hikers crave, and today was their first day as trail angels. They nailed it! Comfortable chairs for multiple hikers...check. A variety of ice cold drinks to wash down grilled hot dogs with homemade chili (cooked according to package instructions) and mustard...check. Homemade brownies, chips, and other sweets, including Ding Dongs...check. Hand sanitizer, napkins, and trash bags for hikers to unload their trash...check. Good conversation, knowledge and advice about the upcoming towns and section of trail...check. Sufficient cold water for hikers to drink and fill their bottles...check.

The trail magic station was pure bliss and entirely changed my attitude and disposition for the day. The only thing missing was Haynes offering to give me a foot bath and pedicure. If you've seen my feet, you know that was a bridge too far.

With a full belly and a smile on my face, I continued on toward the second section of Roan Mountain known as Grassy Ridge. At seven miles, it is the longest stretch of grassy balds in the Appalachian Mountains, featuring balds known as Round, Jane, and Grassy Ridge. I designated this stretch my favorite section of the AT thus far, surpassing even the section north of Spence Field Shelter in the Smokies. If you ever want to take the family on a day hike of the AT, park at Carvers Gap, head north toward the Balds, and thank me later.

On Grassy Ridge Bald, I stopped and visited with day hikers Erik and Belle from Milwaukee along with their dogs, Bo and Gabe. We discussed my thru-hike attempt, and they suggested I pose for an "REI photo" on a rock ledge—so I did. Even though the photo never appeared as an REI magazine cover, it does appear on the cover of this book. I then returned the favor and took photos of them and their dogs striking similar poses.

As I descended the Balds, a fellow hiker asked if I had heard the rumor at Carvers Gap that a section hiker was bringing PBR (Pabst Blue Ribbon) to the Overmountain Shelter that night, and whether I drank alcohol. I told him I had heard the rumor but didn't drink alcohol. He asked, "Why not?"

I told him my decision not to drink alcohol was for a variety of reasons related to my faith, family history, and really just wanting to set a good example and have credibility with the many youth groups I've led over the past 2+ decades. I have many friends and family members who drink socially, I just think my life will be better off in the long run without alcohol and the baggage that often comes with it. In short, I don't need it. I get enough of a buzz hiking the AT, living in an RV, and being married to Janet!

He then asked how long I'd been a Christian. I told him I had confessed my belief in Christ and been baptized in frigid baptismal waters at the Dover (Delaware) Church of Christ on Christmas morning, 1977, at the age of eleven. He asked if I had been raised going to church and I told him I had. He told me he had an interesting story to share with me about his faith, but would save that for tonight's campfire (as a much faster hiker, he was ready to accelerate). Sadly, that conversation never took place, and I never saw him again.

I ended my day at Overmountain Shelter, an AT classic. The shelter is a converted barn with a stunning view, the best shelter view on the entire AT. The barn appeared in the 1989 movie, *Winter People,* starring widower Kurt Russell and Kelly McGillis, the unwed mother he loves. The area also has historical significance, as it was traveled by the Overmountain Men, frontiersmen who took part in the Revolutionary War. They are best known for their role in the American victory at the Battle of Kings Mountain in 1780.

I chose to sleep in the barn's loft out of the wind, rather than down below to view the sunrise. Just when I thought there would only be a few of us in the loft, 10 college students arrived, members of a recreation and hiking club from the University of Florida. I explained that I was a Tennessee Volunteer fan, an aspiring thru-hiker, and an Overmountain Man, and there would be no Gator chomps or Florida fight songs in the loft or by the campfire that night. They agreed.

Between conquering Roan High Knob, hiking the stunning Balds, devouring the fantastic trail magic, conversing with hikers and trail angels, and sleeping at the famous Overmountain Shelter, Day 35 was my all-around favorite day on the trail so far.

Day 36 – Overmountain Shelter to Roan Mountain
9.2 miles, 393.1 cumulative miles

I rolled over and quietly got ready in the loft as the University of Florida students snoozed nearby. On the other side of them was Lost Gear, an African-American, retired Marine. He was doing a 3-day section hike with an eye toward an eventual thru-hike with some of his fellow Marines. He was out of water and didn't have a filter, so I hooked him up with some of my filtered water and enjoyed our conversation on the military and his future hiking plans.

I climbed the incredibly scenic Little Hump and Hump Mountains. Along the way, I started channeling my inner *Secret Life of Walter Mitty.* I imagined being Mitty, played by Ben Stiller, as he climbs the Himalayas in search of Sean O'Connell, played by Sean Penn, who is on a summit photographing a rare snow leopard. Halfway up Hump Mountain, I stopped and looked around for a snow leopard. Finding none, I did the next best thing…I took a selfie. I looked at the picture and couldn't decide whether I looked more like a ninja warrior or a member of the Taliban.

Later on, I met Chopper who got that name from having to be medically airlifted to a hospital while hiking. Doctors told him he had drank plenty of water, but not enough electrolytes. He was a huge proponent of putting electrolyte tablets in drinking water while hiking. It was a good reminder and I regularly did so from that point on. Near Doll Flats, after going back and forth between Tennessee and North Carolina multiple times, I left North Carolina for the final time on my AT journey.

I eventually arrived at US 19E near the town of Roan Mountain and hiked .3 miles west to the Mountain Harbour Bed and Breakfast and Hiker Hostel. Upon arrival at the hostel, Hightop and his dog were kind enough to share their pizza with me. Sharing the hostel with us were Bevo (from Austin, Texas), Not a Bear (has a black backpack that other hikers mistake for a bear), Ptarmigan (named after a Colorado hiking club, and a bird), Morning Lori (from Maine), and Cactus (from Dallas).

Cactus earned his name by falling on a prickly pear cactus while hiking in Texas Hill Country. The cactus needles stuck into him all over his rear end and thighs. In severe pain, he dropped his shorts and underwear and bent over so a friend and fellow hiker could pull out the embedded cactus needles. With each pull of a cactus needle, Cactus would cry out in pain. Unbeknownst to him, once all the needles were gone, the "friend" began pulling out his butt hairs for several minutes, as others looked on smiling. That's just wrong.

At the hostel parking lot, I ran into Lost Gear, the Marine with whom I had shared a loft and water. He offered me a ride into town, where I picked up some groceries at Redi Mart and had a filling steak supper and peanut butter milkshake dessert across the street at Bob's Dairyland. Needing a way back to the hostel, I approached a young local guy putting gas in his pickup truck and asked for a ride. He agreed but said he'd need to clear a spot for me.

We walked to the passenger side and the seat was filled with what appeared to be his life's possessions—pictures, glasses, clothes, a thermos, lampshade, etc. I helped him move the stuff to the bed of his truck with his other possessions, and felt bad that he was going to all this trouble for me. During our 5-minute drive, I learned that he and his girlfriend had just had a fight and that she had kicked him out, along with his stuff. He said, "It was all my fault," to which I thoughtlessly responded, "Probably so."

Day 37 – Roan Mountain to Mountaineer Shelter
8.8 miles, 401.9 cumulative miles

By far the best thing about the Mountain Harbour Hostel was the optional, $12, all-you-can-eat breakfast buffet. That was six times what I normally spent on breakfast, but I'd have to say it was the most satisfying breakfast I had eaten in 50 years. Watching ravenous, hairy, rough-looking hikers walk up the stairs from the hostel to the up-scale B&B to line-up for breakfast was quite the sight. Like ornery, 7th grade boys lined up outside the principal's office, we were anxious, fidgety, and drooling just a tad. We finally were allowed in where we devoured a simply magnificent breakfast. I ate and ate and ate some more, and drank at least 20 cups of orange juice, cranapple juice, and coffee.

With the help of Google, I located Tom and Sandra Johnson from Roan Mountain, Tennessee and the Centerview Church of Christ of Elizabethton. After explaining my situation to them, they graciously agreed to pick me up at the hostel, take me to church services, and then deliver me back to the trailhead. That's what you call a very sweet couple, a very successful phone call, and God's providence at work.

My brothers and sisters in Christ were so kind. The services were uplifting and they invited me to the front of the line at their potluck luncheon. While Catholics are known for rosary beads and Jews for the menorah, members of the church of Christ can do casseroles better than anyone! Romans 12:13 reads, *"Share with the Lord's people who are in need. Practice hospitality."* I truly appreciated the hospitality of Tom and Sandra and the other church members in Elizabethton.

I got back on the trail at 2:20 p.m. and was able to get in 9.2 miles of hiking. At mile 396, I passed a scenic wilderness cemetery and regretted no other hikers were nearby to hear my only cemetery joke. Do you know why none of the locals are buried in this cemetery? Because they're not dead yet!

Later, I took a short blue blazed trail to get a picture of Jones Falls, and then began a pretty section along the Elk River, the longest riverside hike to date. I stopped for a moment and pulled my first ramp out of the ground, wiped the dirt off, and ate it. Ramps are delicious wild onions that can be eaten raw or cooked with Ramen noodles or pretty much anything. They trashed my mouth out, but that's not really an issue in the wilderness. While still digesting the ramp, I stopped and took a picture of some sticks that spelled "400" to mark mile 400 on the AT. I congratulated myself, but then, being the math nerd I am, realized I had only completed 19 percent of the trail. There was still much work left to do.

That night I decided to sleep in the Mountaineer Shelter, a rare 3-level shelter. I was joined in and around the shelter by Black Bear (from Maine), SpongeBob, Sunshine, and Outstanding. Outstanding was so named because it reflected the high standards with which she tried to live her life. I liked that. While heading to bed on the second level, I noticed shelter graffiti which read, "Brooks was here. So was Red." Just for the record, so was Fob.

Day 38 – Mountaineer Shelter to Dennis Cove Road
16.3 miles, 418.2 cumulative miles

I got an early start on our warmest day yet. As I crossed a footbridge near mile 404, I saw my first AT rabbit. He glanced at me and hopped away, not wanting to be spork-shanked, field dressed, and eaten by Sir Fob. At mile 406.7, I crossed U.S. Forest Service Road 293. Little did I know that just 24 hours later, hikers would be diverted down this road to avoid a forest fire in the area. I had cleared this section of trail just in time.

By late morning, I caught up with SpongeBob and we hiked together for an hour. He is a recently retired doctor from Hawaii living his bucket list dream. He wants to transition from working with humans to working with animals as a biologist. A friend of his has a job that includes doing autopsies on dead whales to determine the cause of death. He's helped her with that and wants to do more of that kind of thing. At my request, he also gave me a rundown on the pros and cons and touristy things to do at each of the major Hawaiian Islands. Now I just have to figure out how to get my RV across the big pond.

As I descended White Rocks Mountain, I saw my third AT snake slithering across the trail. From that point on, snake sightings would become an almost daily occurrence. After a warm, muggy, 16.3-mile day, I headed .3 miles west on Dennis Cove Road to the popular Kinkora Hostel, operated by the legendary Bob Peoples. As hostels go, it's pretty primitive. The suggested $5 donation gets a hiker a bunk to sleep on, hot shower, shuttle to town, and access to a kitchen.

What sets this hostel apart, though, is Bob Peoples, one of the most interesting people I met on my AT journey. In addition to running the hostel for the past 20 years, he is an avid trail maintainer who takes hikers (on their days off) and other groups to repair sections of trail. He loves the AT like few others, and loves interacting and sharing his experiences with hikers. While eating a large pizza, which Stitch graciously picked up in town for me, I sat listening to Bob with my fellow hikers. Here is just a sampling of some of his tales...

- The worst hiking injury he has seen was a woman who broke her femur so badly it dislodged her artificial knee. She was airlifted out.
- Bob explained how decisions are made regarding the building of shelters and privies. There are plants and animals that are considered endangered by one state (like North Carolina) but not another (like Tennessee). So, at the top of a mountain shared by both states, that might affect where a privy or shelter gets placed.
- He confirmed rumors of two-foot-long earthworms that live atop Roan Mountain. That's longer than most of the fish I've caught.
- Bob explained the detailed, three-year, multi-agency process to re-route a section of trail, and some of the rules involved, like not exceeding the maximum slope. (The folks at Jacob's Ladder apparently didn't get the memo!)

- He advised that when we departed Kinkora Hostel and got back on the AT northbound, we would come to a Pond Mountain Wilderness sign. If we traveled six more white blazes, near mile 418.8, an unmarked trail would break off to the left, opposite the river. That trail leads to a "private, secluded swimming hole…perfect for you and your honey." (Being without my honey, I passed on this opportunity.)

- Some trail privies have worms in the drop zone (my term, not his) to aid in the breakdown of solid matter. The reason hikers are asked to poop, but not pee, in said privies is because too much urine will drown the worms. I can't think of a worse way to die for a worm than by urine-drowning in a poop-filled privy. I started to explain that when I do #2 in a privy, there's no way to stop #1 from happening, but thought better of it.

- Bob explained how wood used to build shelters and footbridges is carried up and down mountains. In situations where it's necessary and feasible to use a 4-wheeler, they will do construction in the winter on snow, so as not to tear up the trail.

- He cautioned us about the upcoming Laurel Falls, the biggest and best waterfall on the entire AT. We were warned not to swim at the base of the falls, to the left as you look at them. Several have died doing so, including a father and son on July 4th, 2012. There is a whirlpool there that will submerge any and everything in its path for about four minutes. (Bob has tested it with a backpack.) Authorities believe the dad went in to try to save his son, because the dad was recovered with hiking socks on. Really tragic.

- Bob met one hiker who was attempting a thru-hike despite having stage-4 cancer and a dim prognosis. On his day off, the hiker volunteered to deliver a toilet seat to a privy that had just been built. On his way to the privy, he convinced several other hikers that the toilet seat he was carrying was his luxury item!

- He gave updates on the forest fires that were burning, or had been burning, at locations both north and south of our present position. We had inadvertently timed our hike almost perfectly to avoid any fire-related detours.

- Bob explained the back story on the closing of the Watauga Lake Shelter (in 2014, 2015, and recently) due to aggressive bear activity. It seems a local hunter (and jerk) began placing food at the shelter to bait a bear. During hunting season, the hunter returned and killed the mother bear. However, her two male cubs survived and associated that shelter with food. Recently, some section hikers tented there and hung food bags, but kept a few snacks in their tents and were harassed throughout the night by the bear brothers. So, due to the actions of a thoughtless hunter, none of us got to camp on the portion of the AT that runs along Watauga Lake.

- Bob's wife returned from a horse show several years ago and wasn't feeling well. She died from cancer just nine months later. She was the love of his life. The experience taught him to do the things he wants to do in life, because a life can end unexpectedly.

Finally, Bob told a story about "Hike Naked Day" which occurs every year on the AT on the summer solstice, the first day of summer in the Northern Hemisphere. The AT tradition is to hike at least a portion of the day in the nude, although compliance varies. A few years ago, a group of four young, male 20-something hikers were cruising along on Hike Naked Day. They wore nothing but boots, their backpacks, and a bandana hanging from the front of their hip belt to at least partially fobscure their manhood. Their butts were exposed.

Hike Naked Day that year fell on the same weekend as the local town's Rhododendron Festival. This festival brings together hundreds of mostly geriatric women from around the country to celebrate Rhododendrons, however one goes about doing that. Among the activities was a few-mile hike on a Rhododendron-heavy section of the Appalachian Trail. You can see where this is going.

Yes, reportedly there were several "interactions" between these nude hikers (and probably other naked hikers) and the sweet little old ladies who hadn't signed up for the Dangling Pear Festival. Word of these encounters caused Bob, the mayor, festival planners, and AT officials to worry these interactions might harm the festival and cause hard feelings toward the AT community. Those concerns turned out to be unfounded, as Rhododendron Festival attendance tripled the following year!

After story time ended, I went to sleep upstairs. At midnight, I woke up tossing and turning, with Bob Peoples' trail stories still stirring in my head. With sleeping hikers in the bunks all around, I turned on my headlamp and wrote a song, entitled "My Favorite Trail Things." With that off my mind, I turned off my headlamp and went back to sleep. With apologies to Julie Andrews, the following is dedicated to my fellow 2016 AT thru-hikers…

My Favorite Trail Things

Switchbacks and privies and gaps with Trail Magic
Hitchhiking, hostels, Gold Bond for butt rashes
A trail town buffet that is all you can eat
These are a few of my favorite trail things…

Tortillas for dinner, with oatmeal cream pies
Nose ran so much that it drowned two black flies
Took Vitamin I for the pain in my knee
These are a few of my favorite trail things...

'Twas cold in the Smokies, could not feel my fingers
Eight servings of chili, the pungency lingers
Met Lumpy, Ron Haven, and Bob Peoples too
These are a few of my favorite trail things...

Chorus:
When the bears bite, when my tent leaks,
When I'm feeling sad
I simply remember my favorite trail things
And then I don't feel so bad.

Hiked 400 miles, every blaze, not a cheater
Map must be wrong, I've gone one centimeter
A family of field mice now live in my beard
These are a few of my favorite trail things...

Read Dave Miller's AWOL, like it was the Bible
Slept in a barn's loft, and it all felt so tribal
When I need water, I give Sawyer a squeeze
These are a few of my favorite trail things...

I pee in a bottle, at midnight and later
Eat spuds with my Ramen, and poop 'em out later
Katahdin is calling, I'll hike till I'm thru
The AT is one of my favorite things...

Chorus:
When the bears bite, when my tent leaks,
When I'm feeling sad
I simply remember my favorite trail things
And then I don't feel so bad.

Day 39 – Dennis Cove Road to Stealth Campsite
8.2 miles, 426.4 cumulative miles

"Come, follow me," Jesus said, "and I will send you out to fish for people."
- Matthew 4:19

I slept in because I had only 8.2 miles to hike to put me in striking distance of the rendezvous pick-up point with Janet the following day. By the time I rolled out of bed, all but two of the other hostel dwellers were long gone.

As I relaxed and ate breakfast, I got into an interesting discussion on religion with a fellow hiker taking a zero day to rest his feet. Like a few of my former students, and more than a few of the hikers I had encountered, he was somewhat skeptical on matters of faith. He was big into science and looked more for scientific explanations for things, rather than to a Creator-God. I told him I was a believer and that the things I'd seen on the trail had only strengthened my faith. I shared a story with him that I have found helpful on my faith journey.

A man hikes way out into the woods, far from civilization, and stumbles upon the most magnificent, million-dollar cabin he's ever seen. The perfectly manicured lawn and landscaping draw him closer and he discovers the cabin is unlocked. Curious, he steps inside to an immaculate interior with all the latest furnishings, expensive hand-crafted furniture, a marble hot tub, computer-operated controls for heating and lighting, a big screen television with theater seating, several state-of-the-art appliances, and more.

He's never seen such an incredible place where clearly no expense has been spared. He steps outside, sees a man pass by, and asks him about the cabin. The man tells him there was a massive explosion in the woods, a Big Bang, with wood and rock flying in every direction. The cabin, and everything in and around it, just happened to land that way—nothing but pure chance. (Or, if you prefer, the cabin favorably "evolved" into its current configuration through lucky breaks over millions of years.) Either way, the scene was a random freak of nature and no one designed any of it. As crazy as that sounds, imagine a universe, or just a human body, or just an eyeball, that is infinitely more complex than that cabin. Wherever there is design—a cabin, a laptop, or even a spider's web—there is a designer behind it.

I told my fellow hiker that, in my view, the AT had simply presented more evidence that there is a Creator-God behind our magnificent universe. I think it actually is more of a stretch to believe this universe all came about by chance, that we are the result of a big bang, and that we evolved from single-celled organisms.

He got my point, but was still working through what he believed. I enjoyed the discussion immensely. There was no judging, condemning, or name-calling. We were just two hikers processing all we had seen and were respectfully sharing our thoughts. As we each continued to work out our salvation with fear and trembling (Philippians 2:12), I hope I had given him some things to ponder.

Early into the day's hike, I descended upon the mesmerizing Laurel Falls, which lived up to its hype. I saw the dangerous whirlpool and a nearby plaque on a tree honoring Dwight and Dagan Cope, the father and son adventurers who died there.

Rather than swim, I hiked 100 yards or so downstream to try to catch a fish. Catching a fish while hiking the AT, without using a rod and reel, was on my AT bucket list. Using a spool of string, lead weight, hook, bobber, and tiny piece of Snickers, I tossed the hook into some rapids that had water pooling at their base. No luck. After a few more unsuccessful tosses, I switched to a tiny piece of Slim Jim for bait. Bam! On the first toss, I landed a small trout! I felt like a Hunter-Gatherer who had saved his tribe from starvation, despite the three days' worth of food in my food bag. Figuring I had probably broken the law by fishing without a license, I let the fish go and hiked on.

After climbing one final mountain in hot, humid conditions, I tented at a campsite with Gentle Ben from Idaho. I enjoyed talking to this friendly young man, but I was distracted. I kept thinking about Janet and our upcoming rendezvous. She was going to drive three hours in the morning to pick me up at the Shook Branch Recreation Area on Watauga Lake for our first getaway. I was beyond excited. I was like a kid trying to go to sleep the night before Christmas, knowing he had been a (mostly) good boy and Santa was about to deliver the goods!

Days 40-42 – Stealth Campsite to Watauga Lake
.4, 0, & 0 miles, 426.8 cumulative miles

The day promised thrills; my wife and I were about to be reunited! Although I had only been in the wilderness 40 days, I missed her even more than I did while I was deployed to Afghanistan for nearly six months. Was it because there was more solitude on the trail? Was I more in love with her now than in 2007? Or could it be that I was ready to have some one-on-one time with someone who didn't smell like rancid socks?

At the bottom of the hill, I discovered trail magic sodas, courtesy of a group of 2015 thru-hikers. I helped myself to a 7-Up and then covered a whopping .4 miles in 10 minutes. I sat at a picnic table near the swimming area at the scenic Shook Branch Recreation Area on Watauga Lake. While waiting on Janet, I fed crackers to ducks and geese, inventoried my food, and anticipated the arrival of my gorgeous wife!

After two hours and 27 minutes (not that I was keeping track), Janet drove up! I was curious to see if she would be wearing a yellow springy dress like I had requested. (I have a thing for yellow springy dresses even though she told me yellow's really not her color.) Like a heavenly angel, she jumped out of the car, wearing a stunning yellow springy dress! She came running toward me singing the "Hallelujah Chorus." Wow! Just wow!

We embraced and kissed and my heart melted. One of the geese teared up. Janet looked amazing! I felt bad that I was a stinky, nasty hiker who hadn't showered in days. If that bothered her, she didn't let on. Before heading to the lakeside cottage she had rented for three nights, we went into Hampton to grab lunch and then to a small country grocery store. She was getting our food for the cottage and I was re-stocking my trail food.

As she perused the food options from aisle to aisle, I couldn't take my eyes off her. I was stalking her without her knowing. It was going to be a great three days. Someone once said, "Life is not measured by the number of breaths you take, but by the moments that take your breath away." I had four such moments just watching her check the expiration dates on sandwich meat an aisle over. Her yellow dress was the brightest thing in the store, maybe even the town, and I was the luckiest man alive.

As we drove toward the cottage, we stopped by our pickup point and gave ice cream sandwiches to Brief Thief (who got the name by claiming the wrong underwear from a hiker clothes dryer) and Bevo (named after the University of Texas mascot). The 30-minute drive to the cottage seemed to take three hours. I was torn between wanting her to drive safely on the curvy mountain roads and wanting her to go all *Crazy Taxi*.

We finally arrived to an adorable cottage overlooking Watauga Lake. The mountain getaway had everything we needed, including a secluded hot tub with a view of the lake. I had planned to pick her up and carry her across the threshold, but was too exhausted after lugging her 90-pound suitcase up the stairs. Once inside, my mind raced as I processed so many competing priorities—close the sliding door I had just opened, put the ice cream sandwiches in the freezer, take a hot shower, drink a quart of milk, and get caught up on family news.

The next three days would be the most relaxing and satisfying I had ever had. Janet fed me my special food requests, pampered me, massaged me (even my feet!), and stretched my sore body. The hot tub was piping hot and refreshing for my aching joints. As for the conversation, it was exhilarating and breathtaking, even for a long-distance hiker. She caught me up on family news like never before.

I realize I am richly blessed being married to Janet. We met at the Freshmen mixer on our first day at Lipscomb University in Nashville, Tennessee. In the three decades we've been together, she has been a constant source of strength and encouragement. The three incredible days and nights on Watauga Lake were just the latest example. She is a wonderful Christian mom who raised two outstanding young men. She is the kind of friend that everyone deserves to have at least one of in their lifetime. She is a nurturer, a giver, and a leader. She is sexy, funny, and a talented singer and speaker.

Janet is the only person on the planet I could live with in a 32-foot house on wheels and never grow tired of it. It is a cliché, but without a doubt she makes me want to be a better man. She dazzled me the first time I met her and has only grown more beautiful through the years. If you are wondering whether six months on the AT can hurt a relationship, I say, "Not this one." We are in it for the long haul—till death do us part.

(Later that night, I put the ice cream sandwiches away.)

Day 43 – Watauga Lake to Vandeventer Shelter
9.1 miles, 435.9 cumulative miles

"Bad times have a scientific value. These are occasions a good learner would not miss."
- Ralph Waldo Emerson

Sadly, my reunion with Janet had come to an end, and she drove me back to the Shook Branch Recreation Area. Her parents, sister, and brother-in-law were in the area and wanted to stop by and hug my neck. I enjoyed seeing them and having my neck hugged. It was nice to have a little shot in the arm of family love. We said our goodbyes, I gave Janet a final kiss, and they drove off. Janet was headed to Birmingham to visit friends and to finalize wedding plans for our son—the one who pooped on a trail.

The one thing that can take the sting out of saying goodbye is a bit of trail magic—and there it was! Yes, near the recreation area's beach, a group of 2015 AT thru-hikers had reunited from different parts of the country to set up a wonderful cookout. I knew it would be special because those who have hiked the trail know just what hikers want.

Among many possible options, I went with a bacon cheeseburger, chips, soda, and dessert. I sat there for 30 minutes picking the brains of Rock Boat, Forward, Jeopardy, Doc, Klank, and Poboy. They shared their experiences and told me what to expect heading northward.

One of the last things Rock Boat said was, "Fob, there were lots of good and bad things that happened on the trail, but I only remember the good stuff." His comment gave me something to think about as I headed for the beautiful, several-mile-long hike along Watauga Lake.

Had Rock Boat actually forgotten the bad stuff that happened on his thru-hike? Was that possible? Or, was the bad stuff, in the context of the overall hike, eventually considered to be part of the good stuff? For example, was the hike through a thunderstorm (considered bad at the time) ultimately considered good because he had survived and, as a result, developed a closer bond with other survivors?

Looking at supposed negative events in a positive light seems to be what James had in mind in James 1:2-4. He writes, *"Consider it pure joy, my brothers and sisters, whenever you face trials of many kinds, because you know that the testing of your faith produces perseverance. Let perseverance finish its work so that you may be mature and complete, not lacking anything."*

I tried to take these verses to heart and apply them on the trail. I wanted to find joy in the thunderstorm, the foot numbness, the homesickness, and other trail trials, knowing God would somehow use them to make me a more mature and complete person and Christian. Overcoming bad stuff had already increased my trail perseverance, resolve, and "bad" tolerance levels, and a new goal was to have that translate back in the real world.

I wanted to more consistently find joy in the seemingly good and bad, knowing God would use both to mold me into the man He wants me to be. I also wanted to have a much higher percentage of bad stuff—daily annoyances, perceived slights, inconveniences, traffic jams, cold showers, and the like—be small stuff I don't sweat.

> **Fob Fundamental #19 – An experience initially considered difficult, painful, or bad, might ultimately be considered good if it draws one closer to God, develops one's perseverance, or strengthens one's resolve.**

As I hiked along the lake, I saw Watauga Lake Shelter which had been closed due to bear activity. I also passed a .5-mile-long section of trail which had burned in the recent forest fire. Later, a group from the Centerview Church of Christ, where I had worshipped the preceding Sunday, passed me from the other direction. I enjoyed seeing David Irick, one of their ministers, and other familiar faces, out on a day hike. We spoke for a few moments and David was kind enough to give me my first Yoo-hoo chocolate drink. Later, near Wilbur Dam Road, I enjoyed one final parting gift from the Centerview congregation—a cooler full of Throwback Mountain Dew!

After a fairly easy 9.1-mile day, I stayed at the Vandeventer Shelter with a gorgeous view of the valley behind it. The shelter and surrounding tent sites were full that night, with a cast of characters including 5-Star, Odysseus, and Nesquick, my hiking buddy from the Great Smoky Mountains Bubble.

There was also a rather odd fellow who said he and his fiancé had been robbed of their food and money while getting water at a shelter a few days prior. They subsequently had a big fight and were now hiking in opposite directions, even though they were "on their way to Texas." I started to tell him the AT doesn't go through Texas but decided not to.

The man had no food and no stove. His phone was dead. Throughout the evening and morning, he never got out of his sleeping bag. Something just didn't seem right. Although he didn't ask for any help, we passed around a large Ziploc bag as we sat around the campfire and filled it with snacks for him. Our gesture seemed like the right thing to do, even though we questioned the legitimacy of some of his comments.

That night, I did my best to find joy in the loud snoring of the hiker next to me in the shelter. If his snoring kept the mice away, I would consider that a good thing.

Day 44 – Vandeventer Shelter to Double Spring Gap
20.2 miles, 456.1 cumulative miles

I had two things working in my favor this morning—an early start (6:50 a.m., to get away from Sir Snores-a-Lot) and a relatively flat topography ahead. This had the potential to be a big mileage day, although that was rarely my goal.

At mile 444, I passed the Uncle Nick Grindstaff Monument. According to his tombstone, he was born December 26, 1851, and died July 22, 1953. He lived as a hermit on Iron Mountain the last 40 years of his life, and his tombstone reads, "He lived alone, suffered alone, and died alone." How sad. I wondered what led him to a life of solitude. I wondered if he was truly lonely and suffering all those years, or whether he preferred that over the company of others. I wondered how many other Nick Grindstaffs are currently living alone in the wild, and how many of them will have someone who cares enough to mark their passing with a tombstone.

As I descended Iron Mountain, I looked down at my sweaty right forearm and noticed my first AT tick walking along it. Because of the cold weather, I hadn't thought much about ticks during my first six weeks on the trail, but this encounter heightened my sensitivity. I pinched him dead, flicked his corpse into the woods, and spent the next mile running my fingers through my hair and checking various body crevices.

Later, I began a peaceful, scenic walk through a pasture. On the AT, I loved how God would just flip a switch and change mountains to pastures, windy conditions to stillness, and shady laurel valleys to sunny ridges in mere moments. If I didn't like the current scenery on the trail, I just had to hike a short while longer and it would change to something else.

Halfway across the pasture, I stopped and visited with Mountain Man, a rare southbound hiker. We exchanged trail notes and our beards posed for a selfie together. Later, I came across a metal cage full of trail magic. I had a soda and a snack, courtesy of the Girls in Action, a 4th-6th Grade mission group from the Nelson Chapel Baptist Church in Mountain City, Tennessee. I hoped my fellow hikers and I didn't just see and appreciate the magic and trail angels, but also their faith in Christ and desire to live like Him. In other words, I hoped they received not just the Mountain Dew, but ultimately the Gospel message that could really change their lives, and mine.

As I descended Locust Knob, I met a couple from Johnson City on a day hike. They have hiked local AT sections and other area trails for the past decade and have set up numerous off-trail secret campsites behind rock formations for their own use. He asked if I had noticed the two mating butterflies floating around 30 yards south of where we were standing. I told him I had, but wasn't sure if they were mating or just holding hands. He asked, "Did you notice they were two different species? That's just wrong." I suggested maybe a third species would result, but my comment didn't satisfy him.

After a 20.2-mile day, I stealth camped along a tiny stream fed by a spring. A short time later, Nesquick, who was having serious foot issues, and Dawn, also known as Slim Rim, joined me and tented nearby. As we ate supper, Dawn, who hails from Vermont, asked about my sons and I bragged on them for a few minutes. She replied, "That's really cool. I hope my dad talks that way about me when I'm not around." I hoped the same for her.

Part Three ~
The Mid-Atlantic States

"Man's rise or fall, success or failure, happiness or unhappiness depends on his attitude...a man's attitude will create the situation he imagines."

- James Lane Allen

CHAPTER 10

SOUTHERN VIRGINIA IS FOR LOVERS…
AND HIKERS

April 25 – May 16, 2016

"Long friendships are like jewels, polished over time to become beautiful and enduring."
- Celia Brayfield

Day 45 – Double Spring Gap to Damascus, Virginia
12.9 miles, 469 cumulative miles

Nesquick and I took a selfie, gathered our belongings, and headed north towards Damascus. I crossed the border into Virginia, the 4th of 14 states on the Appalachian Trail. I would be in Virginia for over 500 miles—over one fourth of the AT.

By mid-afternoon, I entered Damascus, Trail Town America, with Nesquick, Buckles, and Dirty Deed just behind me. We celebrated our arrival at arguably the best trail town on the AT by posing at the town welcome sign with our shirts off. Not wanting to scare the locals or be arrested for indecency, we put our shirts back on and headed to Pizza Plus. I devoured a medium meat lover's pizza and salad and drank eight glasses of Mountain Dew. My eyes would remain wide open for the next 12 hours.

Among many good town lodging options, Nesquick and I shared a room at Dave's Place, a cheap, basic hostel associated with and across the street from Mount Rogers Outfitter. Although I had struggled with bruised and blistered feet, my foot woes were nothing compared to those suffered by Nesquick. He hobbled over to a chair and pulled off his hiking socks, revealing infected blisters on top of other blisters on top of bruises. He was in pain and discouraged, fearing these foot issues would end his thru-hike attempt.

After a hot shower, I joined Nesquick at Mount Rogers Outfitter for a visit with the shoe and foot guy. I explained my foot pain and showed him the blisters on the edges of my feet. He listened and then examined my feet, boots, socks, liners, and insoles in detail. He said my boots were an excellent choice, still fit well, and had plenty of tread. The socks and liners were also fine, but he recommended I rotate them with my other set about mid-day, and hang the sweaty ones on the back of my pack to dry.

The real issue was my insoles. They were too soft and squishy and 468.5 miles of hiking had flattened them. He recommended I try Superfeet Green Premium Insoles. I did and felt an immediate improvement! In fact, I jumped up and down in the store with no pain, and came close to awkwardly hugging the foot guy. Nesquick also got some good foot and boot recommendations, although what he ultimately needed was rest and time off the trail for his feet to heal.

Nesquick and I re-supplied at Dollar General. Then he, Conductor, several other hikers and I went to Bobo McFarland's where I feasted on fish and chips. I was asked to tell the story behind my trail name for about the hundredth time, and folks continued to enjoy it. I was getting more mileage out of my son's trail poop than perhaps any other father in history.

Day 46 – Damascus
0 miles, 469 cumulative miles

"Do not believe that he who seeks to comfort you lives untroubled among the simple and quiet words that sometimes do you good. His life has much difficulty...
Were it otherwise he would never have been able to find those words."
- Rainer Maria Rilke

Allow me to introduce my dear friend, Jeff Battreall. When I arrived at McGuire Air Force Base, New Jersey in 1981, on Christmas week of my 10th grade year, Jeff was one of the first people I met. He is a few years older, but we formed an instant bond.

Our dads were both Air Force colonels and Jeff lived a few houses down from me on Orly Place. In addition to his incredible humor, wit, and sarcasm, he had a driver's license and a really nice Ford Mustang. We shared a similar taste in music and sports, and ultimately dated the same girl, but at different times. We spent many Friday nights having neighborhood dunk contests with our buddies on a 9-foot rim.

Jeff has a larger than life personality and an infectious positive spirit. We would spend hours driving around in his Mustang, sometimes with our ladies, listening to and singing loudly to the music of Queen, Duran Duran,

Prince, Styx and the Little River Band. We've had long-running arguments over who sounds better singing Styx' "Mr. Roboto" and the meaning of Prince's "Little Red Corvette." More than anyone else, Jeff made my high school years fun.

Beyond the fun, he is a loyal friend and we have remained in contact for the past three decades. He has been known to "photo bomb" the lives of his closest friends by showing up for big events in their lives. Jeff visited me on a few key occasions, including my Air Force retirement ceremony at MacDill Air Force Base, Florida in 2011. I don't know a civilian who loves and appreciates the military more than Jeff. It was no surprise that when Jeff heard I was hiking the AT, he said he wanted to meet me in Damascus and hang out.

Before his anticipated noon arrival, I had to take care of two priorities. First, I went to a hostel down the street to do laundry. Second, I FaceTimed with Mr. Terry Reeve's 6th grade class at Foundation Christian Academy. They were one of the two classes following my AT journey. I enjoyed talking with them and answering their questions, half of which related to bears and going to the bathroom in the woods.

While waiting for Jeff's arrival, Nesquick and I ran into my hiking buddy, Moses. He was considering hiking out, but I told him Jeff was coming and that meant we had wheels and a fun night in store. He decided to join us, so long as we promised not to forge a golden calf.

Jeff arrived, hugged me, and joked, "Here's some duct tape. See ya later, dude." I introduced him to Moses and Nesquick and the four of us walked to Hey Joes Tacos and More for lunch. Jeff treated...a cool gesture. Whether it has been five days or five years since I have last seen Jeff, we always pick up right where we left off.

I told him that in trail towns, hikers are either eating or planning the next meal. It's what we do. We decided the next stop was the grocery store to get some ice cream, so Jeff drove us there. We then went to Beaverdam Creek and, like the Little Rascals, sat on the creek bank eating Ben and Jerry's, talking, and enjoying a few moments off our feet.

We decided Jeff needed a trail name because "Jeff" as a trail name is as boring as they come. Jeff had an eye injury as a child which eventually resulted in him losing the eye as an adult. The loss was devastating to him at first but, consistent with his nature, he has learned to take it in stride and even have fun with it. He looked at us and said, "How about Cy Clops?" It never occurred to us to name him after a race of savage, one-eyed giants, but in retrospect, it was a brilliant choice. It also signaled that his one eye was fair game for some friendly banter. Eye, for One, loved the name. It's a (Stevie) wonder we hadn't thought of it sooner.

After stopping by another outfitter and then a coffee shop, Cy Clops drove us back to the center of town. Moses, appropriately focused on the next meal, suggested we drive to Abingdon for supper. That night we went into Abingdon and had fantastic BBQ at Bonefire Smokehouse. It was so good that Nesquick, a vegetarian who hadn't eaten meat in three years, ate a plate full of pig and cow! As Cy Clops discussed the menu with the waitress, she suggested he consider the 3-meat combo, to which I replied, "he's had his EYE on that ever since we got here!" Nesquick and Moses nearly spewed out water as they laughed uncontrollably. The waitress awkwardly shook her head.

On our way back to Damascus, Cy Clops reached for the radio. I just knew he was going to play "Eye of the Tiger," "Hungry Eye," "Don't It Make My Brown Eye Blue," or "For Your Eye Only." Nesquick was expecting "Brown Eyed Girl," "When You Close Your Eye," "Private Eye," or "Betty Davis Eye." Moses was holding out for "In Your Eye," "Eye Without a Face," "You Can't Hide Your Lyin' Eye," or anything from Third Eye Blind.

Instead, we returned to our roots and started rocking out to the music of Queen, Prince, and Michael Jackson. Cy Clops and I shared lead vocals, while Nesquick and Moses handled backup vocals and lead air guitar and drums from the backseat. We sang our hearts out. Prince, who had recently passed away, would have been proud. The moment felt like 1983 at McGuire Air Force Base all over again. We could have only sounded better had we been in a recording studio—and had just a little talent.

Cy Clops circled the grocery store parking lot two dozen times as we sang "Bohemian Rhapsody." As we loudly belted out, "Momma, just killed a man...put a gun against his head, pulled the trigger, now he's dead," with the windows down, three concerned young skateboarders picked up their boards and exited the parking lot. We cruised the back streets of Damascus several times singing "Billie Jean" and "Another One Bites the Dust." To Cy Clops' credit, he kept one eye on the road—for he could do no more.

Cy Clops and I returned to the hostel and talked for a couple more hours. He told me about some of the celebrities he had met and interacted with during his many years as a flight attendant. He was impressed with the size of Dr. J's hands. During a 30-minute, in flight conversation, he offered Kate Beckinsale his thoughts on a character in a television series her husband produces. He loaned his phone charger to Nelly and once told Larry Bird that he could lie down in the center aisle if his back began to hurt. He was also privileged to have met and talked to celebrities like John Glenn, Prince Andrew, Vanilla Ice, Cheap Trick, George Carlin, Darryl Dawkins (aka, Chocolate Thunder), Ron Howard, and Bo Jackson. I would say they were privileged to have met my friend, Cy Clops.

Our conversation then became a little more serious. We shared our experiences and pain related to the deaths of our mothers. Cy Clops discussed the difficulty in losing his eye and the pain he felt when his marriage ended. We had a good "bro talk" and it felt good to share some deep thoughts, something us "bros" find hard to do at times.

Cy Clops showed me the United States Special Operations Command coin I had given him at my Air Force retirement ceremony. He reciprocated by giving me a set of his flight attendant wings and an OEF (Operation Enduring Freedom) Veteran paracord survival strap bracelet. His gifts were thoughtful and heartfelt, and I would wear the bracelet proudly in honor of our friendship.

Fob Fundamental #20 – Appreciate short-term friendships and casual acquaintances, but cherish those friendships that span many miles and decades.

Hiking 2,189.1 miles and reaching Katahdin's summit was my ultimate bucket list goal. However, the AT is so much more about the journey—the interesting people, views, trail towns, and all the crazy things that happen along the way. The trail is a magnificent, 22-course meal that should be slowly savored a bite at a time. For that reason, I tried hard not to get caught up in the mentality of having big mileage days and getting the trail done quickly.

I was sure many great memories and experiences remained in store. However, I doubted there would be a more memorable night than the one had by Moses, Nesquick, Cy Clops and me, as together we cruised the Damascus roads and partied like it was 1999.

Day 47 – Damascus to Lost Mountain Shelter
15.8 miles, 484.8 cumulative miles

After rolling off my wooden platform bed, I handed Cy Clops my winter gear (base layer pants and shirt, winter gloves, and thick socks) along with my prescription sunglasses (not used) and rain pants (not used enough) to mail to Janet. This adjustment would lower my pack weight and volume until I needed these items again later up north.

We headed to Mojoe's Trailside Coffeehouse for breakfast—Cy Clops by car and me by foot, as I had not yet hiked that section of trail through town. Moses and Conductor joined us for breakfast. Conductor informed us that 25 percent of aspiring thru-hikers never make it beyond Neels Gap (mile 31.7) and another 25 percent never make it beyond Damascus (mile 469). While it felt good to have achieved that milestone, being in the "top half" wasn't my goal. Rather, my goal was to summit Katahdin and earn the Thru-Hiker title.

Moses and I took a few photos with Cy Clops, said our farewells, and headed north out of Damascus—with "Bohemian Rhapsody" still ringing in our ears. Nesquick decided to remain behind to rest his feet. A short while later, Moses, Conductor, several other hikers and I stopped for second breakfast and to ponder a warning sign. The sign told us that a bridge was out .5 miles ahead and thus, to avoid having to ford a river, an approved (and shorter) detour could be taken.

Moses, the only one among us with any chance of parting the waters, chose the detour. I had waited a lifetime to ford an AT river and, along with several others, chose not to take the shortcut. I got to the river and saw that there was a moderately risky path across on boulders, but they were slick, wet, and spaced such that trekking poles would be needed to jump from one boulder to the next. The path was a water and rock fobstacle course. I estimated I could make the journey three out of four times without falling in.

Liking those odds, and only needing to do it once, I went for it without taking off my boots. I stepped slowly and steadily from boulder to boulder, occasionally having to plant and leverage my trekking poles to reach the next boulder. Despite a couple of close calls, I made it! I would have failed 30 pounds ago. I noticed other hikers were putting on their shoes and socks, so I assumed they chose the safer approach and walked across in their water shoes.

Light rain fell off and on throughout the day. Later that afternoon, I stopped to eat the second half of my Subway Spicy Italian sub from Damascus and soak my feet in a stream. A couple of miles later, I passed the long and impressive Luther Hassinger Memorial Bridge. I eventually called it a day and tented with Moses, Conductor, and others near Lost Mountain Shelter.

Just as I got in my tent and zipped up inside my sleeping bag, the sky opened up and a massive thunderstorm hit. Although lightning and falling trees can harm a hiker inside his tent, I always considered my tent a safe refuge. Once inside, I enjoyed the sound of rain pounding against my tent and the occasional lightning flashes. Even in the worst of storms, I was able to sleep like a puppy.

Day 48 – Lost Mountain Shelter to Thomas Knob Shelter
12.3 miles, 497.1 cumulative miles

Despite rain throughout the morning, I was motivated because today I would reach the highest point in Virginia, Mount Rogers, and the scenic, wild pony-filled Grayson Highlands. Near the summit of Whitetop Mountain, Moses caught up with me and we took a snack break on two large rocks next to a bush (that wasn't burning).

While talking about a mission trip he had scheduled for later in the year, we saw two deer approach, wiggle their white tails, spot us, and freeze.

After staring at us for a few moments, they wandered off. "That's not something you see every day," I commented. "Another of God's gifts," Moses replied.

After descending the mountain, Moses, Olive Oil and I took a long break at the VA 600 parking lot. I spread out my wet rain fly and ground cloth so they could dry in the sun, and laid in the thick grass checking my beard and armpits for ticks.

Late that afternoon, I stopped at Thomas Knob Shelter, well within the southern boundary of wild pony country. While I'm not much of a horse guy (that's Janet's domain), for some reason I was pretty excited to see and interact with some midget wild ponies. Unfortunately, my first interaction was anything but positive. As I traveled for water at a spring 50 yards behind the shelter, I approached a momma pony just standing there two yards off the path.

Her baby pony lay motionless at her feet with flies buzzing around. We believe it died in the heavy thunderstorm the prior evening. A hiker returning from the spring told me the mom had been standing over her little foal for three hours. She would occasionally nudge it, trying to wake it up. It was so sad to watch. I wondered how long she would stay there before realizing all hope was gone. Whether it be humans or ponies, there is something very special about the love and care a mother shows to her offspring.

When I went to hang my food bag near the shelter at dusk, two wild ponies emerged from the woods and walked up to me. The scene was strange, exciting, and magical. I started channeling my inner Dr. Doolittle, and struck up a conversation with the ponies. I asked them why I should hang my food bag, when surely a bear would choose a fresh wild pony over packaged Beef Stroganoff. Clearly offended, they remained silent. With *unbridled* enthusiasm, I asked if they were from *Filly* and whether they were *Spurs* fans. They remained quiet, but I could tell they thought I was a *stud*, maybe even the shelter *mare*. I told them I had Ramen noodle-induced *trots*, was not *stable*, and couldn't talk *furlong*. They shook their heads and walked away.

A short while later, just before sunset, I explored an area north of the shelter and came across a campsite with more wild ponies. All I could think of was that every parent who has a kid who loves horses needs to camp here and give them the experience of a lifetime.

Still channeling my inner Dr. Doolittle, I fulfilled another AT bucket list item by interviewing a wild, talking pony. I chose one based on her pleasant disposition, wide girth, and ability to speak English. While videoing, I *harnessed* my courage and asked if she had ever seen a long-distance hiker better looking than me (answer: neigh); whether it bothered her being a midget horse and having people call her names like "Colt Shorty-Five" (answer: neigh); and whether she would like to go to *"mane"* with me (answer: neigh). Off camera, she told me, "I *canter* do this interview anymore," and then left the area with a handsome *mustang*.

I returned to the shelter, ate some cheese with *thorough bread*, and took a position next to Conductor in the shelter's *hind quarters*. All *horsing* aside, I needed a good night's sleep in order to get out of the *gait* early and get a *leg up* on the other hikers. For those of you who object to these horse puns, quit being *neigh*-sayers.

Day 49 – Thomas Knob Shelter to Dickey Gap
21.1 miles, 518.2 cumulative miles

Despite my daily routine of mountain Kegel exercises, my bladder alarm sounded at 6:00 a.m., informing me it was time to visit the woods. As I exited the shelter full of sleeping hikers with regular-sized prostates, I heard a sound by the picnic table. I looked and there was a wild pony grazing only 10 yards from the shelter. Her presence was an early indication that this was going to be a magnificent day two on the magical wild pony mystery tour.

I gathered my belongings and headed AT north towards Grayson Highlands State Park. After transiting the park, I crowned a new trail champion. Yes, in my humble opinion, the five-mile section from the Mount Rogers side trail (mile 497) to the northern end of Grayson Highlands State Park (mile 502.4) was the overall best section of trail to date.

What makes it so special? Start with wonderful vistas in every direction. Throw in varied terrain, including rock climbs, rolling balds, majestic forests, and even a Fat Man's Squeeze. Finally, top it off with dozens of midget wild ponies roaming freely. This place was truly magical. It was a section you might create if you were designing a perfect AT section on a computer. I stopped a few times to visit the ponies and promised myself I would return someday with my wife and grandchildren.

Near the end of this incredible section, I crossed the 500-mile mark on my AT journey. Like so many hikers who had gone before me, I paused for a moment, took a picture, and joined The Proclaimers in singing, "I would walk 500 miles, and I would walk 500 more." Then I added, "And then I'd walk 500 miles, and then I'd walk 689.1 more." If I planned to hike that far, I might as well proclaim as much.

Shortly after reaching this milestone, I came across trail maintainers from Konnarock, the Appalachian Trail Conservancy's flagship crew program. The crew, volunteers of different ages and backgrounds, worked on the AT from Rockfish Gap, near Waynesboro, Virginia, to the Trail's southern terminus at Springer Mountain. I stopped for a few moments to thank them for their service and discuss their plans for the week. I appreciate people who volunteer to cut fallen trees, move rocks, shovel dirt, and do whatever else is necessary to give hikers a much better path to traverse.

As I approached The Scales livestock corral, a longhorn bull stood directly on the trail, just staring at me. What little I know about farming and cattle I learned earlier this year from Sam, the 81-year-old father of Jaye Trovillion, a family friend. During a visit to Florida, Sam offered me a tour of his 160-acre ranch. We got in his pickup and he drove all over the ranch, explaining the layout, facilities, farming equipment, and cattle operations in general.

As a person who has spent my life in mostly suburban settings, I was taking it all in. He had me open a gate and we drove onto a sprawling pasture and through a herd of cows. They seemed to recognize him and his truck and were unfazed.

Sam and I came to a stop in the middle of his ranch and he put the truck in neutral. That's when, after nearly 50 years of living and fathering two children, I finally got "the talk." Yes, THE talk...the one that would have been nice to hear when I was 13 or at least before my wedding night. This was not how I imagined it happening...in the middle of a pasture, with an 81-year-old man I had just met, parked in a pickup truck surrounded by cows. The talk went like this...

Sam: "This farm is all about breeding. Are you familiar with that?"

Fob (*hesitates*): "Breeding? No, not really. Well...yes and no. I've done some...myself. But not with cows."

Sam: "I should hope not."

{*a few seconds of awkward silence*}

Sam: "See the big one over there? That's the bull."

Fob: "So he's in charge?"

Sam: "You could say that. He services all the rest of them."

Fob: "The rest are the women?"

Sam: "We call them heifers...or cows when they get older. We've got 55 of them split into two pastures, each with a bull."

Fob: "So that one bull services all 25 heifers?"

Sam: "That's his job...to eat and to service heifers."

Fob: "He's like a fat Charlie Sheen."

Sam: "I suppose."

Fob: "That's a lot of heifers for one bull. When does he service them?"

Sam (*looks me in the eye, and his voice starts to sound like the guy in the Dos Equis commercials*): "When they are ready... they'll let him know."

Fob: "Like with a wink and a nod?"

Sam (*laughs and shakes his head*): "Not exactly. When the heifers go into heat, they emit an odor."

Fob: "Like the odor when you drive by a Five Guys? I love that smell."

Sam: "Not exactly. In addition to the odor, when the heifers are ready, they will start to mount each other."

Fob (*breaks eye contact and looks out the window*): "Uh, well, we should probably be getting back now. I bet lunch is ready."

As Sam put the truck in gear, I took a final picture of the Bull (who I secretly named "Charlie"), and we drove back across the pasture. It had been a wonderful ranch tour and a strange bonding moment. I had finally received "The Talk." The veil had been removed from my eyes. I was now much wiser about the "ways of love" on a farm. My world would never be the same.

While staring down this longhorn bull on the AT, I wondered what Sam would tell me to do. I assumed those horns could be used to defend against a coyote, scratch oneself, or gore a long-distance hiker. I gave him some space and apologized for all the beef I had eaten, and will continue to eat, in my lifetime. He eventually moved a few feet off the trail and I quickly hiked by without incident.

Later that afternoon, I was happy to see Cambria and a few other hikers who had stopped along the trail to eat supper. Cambria, you may recall, was the young lady who was not only born in the same state as me, but at the same hospital. However, since I am roughly 30 years older than her, I suspect our mothers used different fobstetricians.

After an incredible, 21.1-mile, wild pony-filled day, my longest mileage day to date, I stealth camped by a stream with Conductor, Tumbleweed, and Princess Grit. I learned Princess Grit is a section hiker from Nashville, Tennessee, who models at Nissan car shows around the country. She was named Princess because she looks like one, and added Grit because she always feels gritty after a few days of hiking. I waited for her to ask if I, too, was a model, but the question never came.

Day 50 – Dickey Gap to Glade Mountain
19.4 miles, 537.6 cumulative miles

"The first thing you have to know is yourself. A man who knows himself can step outside himself and watch his own reactions like an observer."
- Adam Smith

The big goal today was to make it to Partnership Shelter and order a pizza. It's one of the few trail shelters where hikers can call and have a pizza delivered. The shelter also has a shower, another rarity. I arrived just before 3:00 p.m. and went in on a large pizza and family-sized cheese bread with Reading Man, who reads a lot. We devoured our meal at the shelter picnic table and shared some with Dirty Deed, Buckles, Princess Grit, Olive Oil, and others.

Around 4:30 p.m., I checked the forecast and saw that rain was expected to begin in three hours and last for three days. Given the crowded shelter and likelihood of at least one loud snorer who would need to be shanked in the temple with a spork, I decided to hike on.

As I climbed Glade Mountain, I could feel the storm approaching. I accelerated to a flat spot at the summit. At mile 537.6, after a 19.4-mile day, I pitched my tent, hung my food bag, and crawled into my tent just as rain started to fall. I called Bobby, a friend of mine from Florida who is currently battling cancer. While my goal was to offer him encouragement, he ended up encouraging me, which will come as no surprise to his friends.

I estimate the closest human being north of me that night was 1.5 miles away at the next shelter, and more than five miles away to the south. My mountaintop isolation raises a question I was frequently asked by friends and family: "Does it bother you to hike alone or sometimes camp alone atop mountains and other remote places?"

I will answer in a way only my youngest, Myers-Briggs-loving son, Kyle, aka Trail Pooper, could appreciate. Isabel Briggs Myers and her mother, Katharine Briggs, developed a personality inventory to make C. G. Jung's theory of psychological types understandable and useful in people's lives. (I used to teach AP Psychology so bear with me as I put on my geek hat.)

By answering a series of questions, one can find to which of 16 personality types one belongs. Kyle and I are ENTJs—Extraverted, iNtuitive, Thinking, and Judging—which explains why we are so much alike. ENTJs are nicknamed "The Commander" or "The Executive," which can be a good and bad thing on the trail...

The Good...
- Driven, determined...loves a big challenge (explains my #4 reason for hiking the AT).
- Confident...given enough time and resources, believes any goal can be achieved, sometimes through sheer willpower.
- Extremely rational. Helps with AT decision-making related to logistics, mileage, etc. For big decisions, Kyle and I nerdily write pros and cons on a sheet of paper to help analyze major decisions. If I am feeling especially nerdy, I'll put said pros and cons into an Excel spreadsheet. What gets me into the Nerd Hall of Fame (and sucks the joy out of life) is when I weigh each factor by importance, multiply, and then sum the columns in order to mathematically compute the right, rational, best choice. I still make plenty of bad decisions, but rarely because I haven't analyzed the pros and cons involved.

- The Extroverted (E) nature, which I am just barely (52 percent to 48 percent), makes me comfortable and able to draw energy from groups (at shelters, campfires, etc.). I enjoy good conversation and being around people.
- The 48 percent score for Introverted (I) nature makes me just as comfortable and able to draw energy from being/hiking alone, solo camping atop a mountain, reading by a quiet lake, etc. My best thinking and writing happens in solitude. Thus, while I missed my wife and family, I was never unhappy as a result of being alone on the trail.
- Thinks strategically, with a long-term focus (summiting Katahdin), while executing each step of my plans with determination and precision (five million steps actually!).
- Strong-willed...unlikely to give up when the going gets tough. Time would tell.
- Inspirational...hopefully I am to some—at least to my two sons. They are my pride and joy and the ones I most want to inspire, encourage, and mentor. If I leave any worthy legacy after I'm dead and gone, it will be those two fellas.

"Strengthen me by sympathizing with my strength, not my weakness."
- Amos Bronson Alcott

The Bad...
- Sometimes ENTJs are not emotionally expressive. I am more likely to rationally analyze with a fellow hiker who is hurting than to give the needed hug and shoulder to cry on. "Of course you're struggling, you have a 12-lb. stove!"
- Impatient with people viewed as inefficient, incompetent, or lazy.
- Can sometimes be condescending, insensitive, and arrogant. I assume this applies to other ENTJs, but not me!
- Too much willpower and confidence can lead to pushing my vision and agenda, and mine alone. As a mostly solo hiker, it was good that I didn't have to regularly confer or negotiate with others on when to start and stop, where to stay, and the myriad other daily decisions that couples and groups hiking together deal with. All decisions were mine alone, whether good or bad.
- Sometimes intolerant. I am more likely to confront (rationally, of course) or walk away from a pot smoker, than to sit breathing it in and "tolerating" it. Because of this personality trait, I struggle at times with the AT golden rule, "Hike Your Own Hike."

Fob Fundamental #21 – Someone who has made a fair and objective assessment of his strengths and weaknesses is well-positioned to leverage those strengths and mitigate those weaknesses.

Among the famous ENTJs in history are Julius Caesar, David Letterman, and Jeb Bush. I can see some of them in Kyle and me. On the other hand, Adolf Hitler was reportedly an ENTJ, the knowledge of which has kept me up many nights.

I encourage everyone to take the Myers-Briggs test and see how well it captures your personality. The self-awareness can help you to leverage personality strengths and be aware of and mitigate potential weaknesses. If you disagree with me, you are clearly irrational and need to reconsider your position. I'll loan you my spreadsheet.

Before dozing off to heavy rain, I received a message from my friend, Darrell Brimberry, with a video clip of Heart performing Zeppelin's "Stairway to Heaven" at the Kennedy Center Honors. I took note of verse three because tomorrow a new day would dawn. I would stand strong. Unless I were to trip and fall...and then the forest would echo with laughter.

Day 51 – Glade Mountain to Atkins
6.2 miles, 543.8 cumulative miles

"Into each life some rain must fall."
- Henry Wadsworth Longfellow

Light rain, especially on a warm, muggy day, is refreshing on the trail. Heavy rain and rain that lasts for several days gets old quickly. Rain makes everything more challenging—the trail becomes muddy or turns into a stream; the hiking pace slows; rocks become slicker; and visibility drops, making the "money views" not so grand.

While the contents of a well-packed and covered backpack can be mostly kept dry, the same cannot be said for the hiker. I typically ended up soaked to the bone in heavy rain. My attempts to cover up with rain gear only left me soaked in sweat instead of rain. Either way I got wet. Wet socks and feet made me more susceptible to blistering, and when the rain was accompanied by cold, I was more susceptible to getting sick.

On the other hand, there are upsides to hiking in the rain. In rainy conditions, water sources are more frequent and reliable. Hikers who together endure lengthy rainy conditions and other difficulties form bonds more quickly. As with other challenges, overcoming extended rain often makes hikers tougher and more resilient. After enduring long periods of

119

rain, I appreciate the eventual sunshine all the more.

Day 51 was a rainy day. My approach was to wear very little—shorts, boots, and sometimes a shirt. As the rain pelted me, I prayed and thought about my family. I focused on positive, happy thoughts and putting one foot in front of the other...the next right thing. I tried to remember the good that comes from rain.

One prayer was answered quickly when I stumbled upon some much-needed trail magic. The historic Lindamood School, part of the Settlers Museum, is a one-room, 1890s schoolhouse. A local Baptist church stocks the school with free food, drinks, and supplies for hikers. It would have been magic enough to simply have a place to get a break from the rain. All the goodies inside were a much-appreciated bonus. Another church group letting their light shine on the AT!

After a short, rainy day, I decided to stop in Atkins and dry out at the Relax Inn. After checking in, my first stop was...you guessed it...the delicious all-you-can-eat buffet at the nearby Barn Restaurant, a hiker favorite. By mid-afternoon, the rain stopped and I was able to lay out my wet tent and boots in the parking lot while I did laundry. Since the laundry room was next to my room, I put all my clothes in the washer and then sprinted to my room wearing just a towel.

As I entered my room, I glanced back and noticed a trellis on the far side of the parking lot that would be a perfect spot to dry my tent. Not seeing anyone around, I grabbed my tent and bolted across the parking lot in just my towel. After hanging it up and beginning the return sprint, I looked over and Princess Grit was entering the far side of the parking lot. She yelled, "Is that you, Fob?" and I yelled back, "Never heard of him!" and ducked into my room. I couldn't be certain, but assumed she was on her way over to suggest I consider a modeling career.

That night, Buddah Jim, Princess Grit, several other hikers and I ate at a Mexican restaurant attached to, quite appropriately, a gas station. Buddah Jim told me about his work at a psychiatric hospital. Based on his description of the patients, I believe most aspiring thru-hikers would feel right at home there.

Day 52 – Atkins to Lick Creek
18.4 miles, 562.2 cumulative miles

Before leaving the motel, I grabbed a couple of items from the hiker box, including a package of beef jerky. A few miles after crossing the I-81 underpass out of Atkins, I reached mile 547.275—the exact one quarter mark on the Appalachian Trail!

Later, atop Brushy Mountain, I started getting hungry and remembered the beef jerky I had picked up from the motel's hiker box. Jerky sounded good so I reached into the package, pulled out two pieces, and stuffed them into my mouth. Instantly, I knew something was wrong. They tasted like wet cardboard that had been sautéed in bacon grease. I gagged for a moment and then swallowed them simply for the calories.

Thinking maybe I had just gotten a bad piece, I shoved two more pieces into my mouth and got the same nasty result. A little while later, I commented on the disappointing beef jerky to a fellow hiker. He looked at the package and said, "Dude, you're eating dog treats!" I couldn't believe it! There was no mention of dogs or pictures of dogs on the package. There were some Spanish phrases on the package, but nothing about *perros* (dogs).

Later, I complained to Conductor about the misleading labeling…

Fob: "If a company sells dog treats, the package should clearly indicate that's what it is."

Conductor: "Who makes them?"

Fob: "Gravy Train."

Conductor: "Fob, Gravy Train is a well-known dog food company."

Fob: "Never heard of them."

Conductor: "Most folks have. They're a big-time company. So, the package really doesn't need a warning saying, 'These are dog treats. Not to be consumed by hikers.'"

Fob: "Well, having stuffed four pieces of bacon-flavored cardboard in my mouth, I would say that a warning is exactly what the package needs."

Conductor: "That bad, huh?"

Fob: "I don't even think my dog, Mandy, would eat them."

Atop Lynn Camp Mountain, I checked the forecast and saw heavy rain was due to hit in about 30 minutes. I descended the mountain in full beast mode and arrived at a pretty campsite on the edge of Lick Creek. I had just enough time to pitch my tent, heat some instant potatoes to accompany my Mike and Ike's candy, and hang my food bag.

With the sun setting and a light rain beginning to fall, I caught my second AT fish using a piece of Slim Jim. I would have used beef jerky for bait, but a wise man once told me that Gravy Train is really just for dogs.

Day 53 – Lick Creek to VA 623
11.6 miles, 573.8 cumulative miles

"When your values are clear to you, making decisions becomes easier."
- Roy E. Disney

Shortly after beginning the long ascent up Chestnut Knob, the rain began. Once again, my strategy was to wear as little as possible. This may sound strange, but I rarely wore my rain jacket in the rain. With enough rain, I was inevitably going to get wet and the added perspiration caused by a rain jacket only made me wetter. I preferred to have just my quick-drying synthetic tee shirt get wet, and keep my rain jacket dry and available for duty around camp at night.

When I reached Chestnut Knob Shelter, a fully enclosed concrete shelter, heavy rain began to pour. I quickly stepped in and ended up staying three hours with Hopscotch, a southbound section hiker. He was on his way to Damascus for Trail Days, and we shared notes on the trail ahead. He is a military Intelligence Analyst and Cryptologist, so we exchanged a few war stories. Since my Top Secret clearance (and need to know) had long expired, he was not able to tell me any of the really interesting stuff and spoke only in generalities.

The rain subsided and I headed back out across a long, rocky ridge along Garden Mountain. The rocks took a toll on my feet and legs, with the feet alternating between pain and numbness. After a long, rain-filled day, I headed 25 yards downhill from the ridge to stealth camp. Shortly after hunkering down in my tent, the rain started to fall again.

Unable to sleep, I conducted a rational examination (complete with pros and cons) of key issues that hikers debate. I've mentioned the overused AT expression that hikers should, "Hike Your Own Hike." The phrase means hikers "own" their AT hike and get to decide for themselves the right way to hike the trail. Hikers shouldn't criticize others who hold different views. Still, there was plenty of friendly banter between hikers as we discussed our respective positions on a host of issues.

Here, then, are my personal opinions on some of these issues. This is how I was "hiking my own hike." I didn't judge or criticize others for holding different views—at least not to their face.

1. Should one hike the 8.8-mile Approach Trail from Amicalola Falls State Park to Springer Mountain in Georgia?

The case for hiking it:

- It's incredibly scenic, with diverse forest and terrain, mountaintop views, and a waterfall.
- It doesn't require backtracking southbound before starting the northbound AT hike.
- Some hikers consider hiking the Approach Trail part of AT tradition.
- For those without access to a vehicle, it's the only way to get to Springer Mountain from Amicalola Falls State Park.

The case against hiking it:

- Quite simply, the Approach Trail is not part of the designated 2,189.1-mile AT. The goal is to thru-hike the AT, not trails that feed the AT.

- It's a very difficult, strenuous way to begin the hike, which makes a raw hiker more susceptible to injury.
- For those with family and friends wanting to join them for the first mile of the AT, it's easier to meet at the Springer Mountain parking lot and take the much shorter hike to the southern terminus together.

Verdict: I opted not to hike the Approach Trail, primarily for family reasons and because it's not part of the AT.

2. Is it acceptable to take blue-blazed shortcuts in order to dodge a difficult section or hike through a prettier section? Similarly, is it acceptable to "aqua blaze"—canoe parallel to the trail?
The case for it:

- Less experienced, less able, or older hikers may want to skip an especially dangerous section in order to avoid injury, which might end their hike altogether.
- No need to worry about hiking exactly 2,189.1 miles. If one can travel the same number of miles, or close to it, and see a prettier section, one should feel free to do so.
- Canoeing is fun, provides a refreshing break to one's legs and feet, and the canoer is still traveling near the AT.

The case against it:

- A successful thru-hike occurs when one hikes all 2,189.1 miles.
- One is *hiking* the AT—not canoeing, kayaking, horseback riding, or snowmobiling it. The goal is to be a thru-hiker, not a thru-traveler.

Verdict: As an AT purist, I would have forever regretted taking any shortcuts that lessened the AT mileage by even a foot. In fact, I always exited a shelter on the same path I came in on so as to not miss a single white blaze or inch of trail. To me, hiking it all meant: hiking...it all.

3. Is it best for an aspiring thru-hiker to travel northbound (NOBO), southbound (SOBO), or do a flip-flop (typically, Harpers Ferry to Maine, and then Harpers Ferry to Georgia)?
The case for traveling SOBO:

- More aloneness and solitude, if that's desirable. In particular, one can avoid the early (March-April) crowds of NOBO hikers.
- Fewer crowds, especially at shelters, decreases the likelihood of catching a disease, such as norovirus.
- A great option for college students and others who can't begin their hike until summer.
- Enjoy the Fall colors in Virginia.

- Avoid the October 15th deadline to finish the hike faced by NOBO hikers. Baxter State Park, where Mt. Katahdin resides, closes on this date.

The case for doing a flip-flop:

- More aloneness and solitude, if that's desirable. In particular, one can avoid the early (March-April) crowds of NOBO hikers.
- A great option for college students and others who can't begin their hike until late spring.
- Provides for the longest window of mild weather.
- Begin the hike on some of the AT's easiest, flattest terrain.
- Avoid the October 15th deadline to finish the hike faced by NOBO hikers.

The case for traveling NOBO:

- Save Katahdin, arguably the AT's toughest climb, for last, when one is in optimal shape.
- End the journey with your hands in the air at the summit of Katahdin, the AT's most iconic mountain.
- Take advantage of the early crowds by interacting and building friendships with other hikers.

Verdict: I chose a NOBO hike primarily because I wanted to be standing at Katahdin's summit, with my hands in the air, at the END of my journey. That is the iconic photo—the one I saw posted on photo boards at hostels, restaurants, and elsewhere. I enjoyed interacting with the numerous other NOBOs early in my journey. While that led to the occasional crowded shelter or campsite early on, the herd quickly thinned and there were plenty of opportunities for solitude and stealth camping away from shelters. Finally, I wanted to avoid climbing Katahdin and facing Maine's 100-Mile Wilderness at the beginning of my hike, as an inexperienced, overweight rookie.

4. Is it okay to "slack pack," which means hikers have someone else—a friend, family member, or hostel owner—carry (drive) their backpacks for them for a day or more so they can hike unencumbered and achieve bigger and easier mileage days?

The case for slack packing:

- Achieve higher mileage days, which helps one to finish the trail sooner.
- Enjoy easier hikes, especially on strenuous sections of trail.
- More opportunities to spend comfortable nights at a hostel or the home of whoever transported you.
- The *person* is the thru-hiker…not the backpack.

The case against slack packing:

- Part of the AT's appeal is the high level of difficulty, and a big part of that is carrying a loaded backpack.
- Slack packers typically have to rush to achieve the big miles and rendezvous with their backpack. The AT should not be rushed.
- Slack packers have no flexibility to stop early for the day in really bad weather or as the result of an injury or sickness. They have to get to the pickup point by the agreed upon time.
- There is usually a fee for the shuttle service, and possibly also for a second night at the hostel if you hike back to it. Thus, slack packing the trail is more expensive, although that's somewhat offset if you finish the trail sooner.
- By rushing, slack packers risk missing, or not fully enjoying, the sights, sounds, and experiences along the way.

Verdict: I never slack packed. I felt carrying my pack was my job—not someone else's. I wouldn't go whitewater rafting and have someone else paddle for me. I wanted to rise to the occasion and overcome the high level of difficulty of hiking the AT, not lower the level of difficulty for an easier experience. If I wanted an easier experience, I would have chosen an easier trail, or just gone bowling.

Furthermore, rushing was the last thing I wanted to do. My goal was to slowly savor the trail, rather than achieve big, easy miles. Case in point: one female slack packer zoomed by me to reach her 30-mile day, with thunderstorms in the forecast. I asked her what her intentions were regarding McAfee Knob, arguably the second most famous landmark on the trail. Out of breath, she said, "I don't have time to stop there. Gotta hit my pickup point. Will have to return some day to get a pic and enjoy." Then she sped off. Seriously? I'm not suggesting all slack packers missed all the cool sights. I am suggesting a hiker is more likely to miss cool things when he is rushing.

Along those same lines, I came across this note in an AT shelter log by a fellow hiker named Arrow: "How many of us gazed off Black Rock, splashed in the waters of a 200' falls, relaxed in the sun on Apple Orchard Mountain, and scrambled over the massive boulders of the Devils Marble Yard? Since when did big mileage become so important that we are willing to skip wonderful side adventures? Since when did we begin to focus so much on a number that we miss the things that make the AT so beautiful and exciting? Many of us came here to escape the busy, over-productive, hurry-hurry civilization, but perhaps we have brought it along with us?" She nailed it!

Most importantly, for me, was that my mom's ashes were in a pouch inside my backpack. She would remain there—and it would remain with me. My backpack was an extension of me on many levels, and I wasn't going to delegate its transport to someone else.

Those are my personal views on what it meant for me to hike my own hike. Each hiker resolves these issues in a way that works for them and doesn't violate their conscience. At the end of the hike (however defined), we each need to be able to look in the mirror and feel good about the journey. That same principle applies to how you live your life, and how you'll feel about your life as you reflect on it towards the end of life's journey.

Fob Fundamental #22 – Live your life in such a way that one day, at the end of your life, you'll be able to look back and be proud of the way you lived.

Days 54 & 55 – VA 623 to Bland
16.1 & 0 miles, 589.9 cumulative miles

I rolled over on my air mattress, checked my body crevices for ticks, threw down a pop tart, and departed. It didn't take long for light rain to begin, and it continued for most of the day. Mentally, I played a little game and told myself that every drop of rain that hit me today was going to make me stronger and more determined. That may sound silly, but it beat letting multiple days of rain wear me down mentally and physically.

I played whatever mental games I had to in order to stay motivated and moving. Several hikers had already quit the trail because several weeks of rain had taken a toll and they were no longer having fun. I reminded myself of the commitment I had made to finish the trail, regardless of how fun or hard it was on any given day. The pain and inconvenience of the rain was not greater than my desire to finish.

By mid-afternoon, the rain let up, and I passed a series of poster board signs on trees announcing "Trail Magic ahead!" Signs are not necessary to attract hikers, but they do build anticipation. After all the rain, the magic couldn't have come at a better time. As I approached the tent and chairs, I could tell this was going to be something special. The trail angels had a generator running to charge hikers' electronics. Anyone who goes to that level of trouble to meet hikers' needs is about to deliver some real magic—and they did!

The trail angels were DeAnn and Dave Werner, from Pennsylvania, along with DeAnn's sister, Deb, and her husband, Vince. Dave informed me that their daughter's fiancé, trail name J-Bird, thru-hiked the AT in 2010 and had a wonderful experience. He appreciated all the trail magic and wanted to return to the AT in 2011 and serve as a trail angel himself. Unfortunately, and sadly, he was diagnosed with colon cancer, died in 2012, and never got the chance to be a trail angel. In his honor, DeAnn and Dave have been returning to the trail as trail angels every first week of May since he died, giving the magic to hikers that J-Bird himself had so badly wanted to give.

Their trail magic was magnificent. There was a ton of food, including scrumptious meatball sandwiches, hot dogs, fruit, vegetables, desserts, and drinks. They offered a mini hiker store, with everything from batteries to wet wipes to hygiene supplies—yet it was all free.

To top it all off, cards and pens were available so we could write messages to our loved ones. They took care of the postage and mailing. Thanks to them, I was able to send a Mother's Day card to Janet. I thanked them from the bottom of my heart. They had truly honored J-Bird's memory. Deann gave me their cell phone number and told me to call when I got to Pennsylvania. They wanted to treat me to lunch. What awesome people!

I left with not only a re-charged phone, but a full belly and an overall better outlook. That's what trail magic can do for a tired hiker who has been busting his butt up and down mountains in the rain for several days.

I hiked on and eventually rolled into Bland, Virginia. I hitched a ride with Bubba to the Big Walker Motel. I was initially reluctant to stay at a town called Bland, but after looking at the map, I realized it was a better option than Boring, Iowa or Mediocre, Minnesota.

Bubba was quite a character for a Bland guy. As a man who makes a living shuttling hikers, he has seen his share of interesting things. Two of his stories are noteworthy:

- Bubba once shuttled two female German hikers who rode in the back of his pickup truck with their gear. He noticed a car swerving behind him and looked back to discover the girls had removed their wet tops to let them air out. (In this context, I was not entirely sure what his term "them" referred to.) He told the "ladies" that public highway nudity was not allowed in this country, with the possible exception of Mississippi. As hikers hailing from Boobvaria, they were surprised to hear this. I told Bubba it was a good thing he handled the situation; otherwise, the town risked being renamed *NotSo Bland*.

- Bubba also gave a ride to, and later received a thank you card from, a hiker with the trail name Bismarck. Bubba found out later that Bismarck had been hiking the AT for six years to avoid being arrested for embezzling $8.7 million from Pepsi, his employer. The law eventually caught up with Bismarck at Trail Days in Damascus. He ended up in prison, and authorities recovered less than $1 million of the money. There are rumors Bismarck stashed the remainder at various spots on the AT. I made a mental note to begin looking for the money beneath shelters, behind trees, and under rocks.

Once in my room at the Big Walker Motel, I looked at the forecast. It was supposed to be cold and rainy the following day. Thus, I decided to take a zero day. That night, I ordered spaghetti and meatballs, a salad, and a large, family-sized order of cinnamon rolls, and had them delivered to my room. After eating a few thousand calories of food, I took a hot bath and shower, and then hand-washed my clothes in the tub. I went to bed that night thankful for the trail magic I had received, and grateful to be clean, out of the rain, and full of pasta and cinnamon rolls.

Not wanting to do anything too exciting in a town called Bland, I spent most of Day 55 resting in my motel room, eating more cinnamon rolls, watching TV, and blogging. I ventured out for a couple of hours to re-supply at the Dollar Store, have dinner at a gas station Dairy Queen, and pick up a foot-long Spicy Italian sub for the next day's hike. I called Janet in order to hear her sweet voice and get caught up on family events. She told me she loved me, was glad that I was surviving, and was proud of what I was doing. Hearing that was more filling than the 18 cinnamon rolls I'd eaten in the past 24 hours.

Days 56 & 57 – Bland to Woods Road
16.1 and 17.1 miles, 623.1 cumulative miles

"So, if you think you are standing firm, be careful that you don't fall!"
- 1 Corinthians 10:12

After chowing down the last two cinnamon rolls, I left the motel and took a shuttle to the trailhead. The hike today was unusually flat, with overcast skies. I was beginning to wonder if the sun ever shined in Virginia. Just before passing Jenny Knob Shelter, I reached the 600-mile milestone and celebrated with a Pay-Day candy bar.

As the skies darkened, I checked the forecast and saw yet another thunderstorm was headed my way. After an uneventful 16.1-mile day, I stopped near Woods Road and quickly set up camp. As the rain started to fall, I took care of some business while hugging a tree at the recently named 20-Cinnamon-Roll Gap.

Day 57 was the first of two consecutive rough days. Some days are like that. When I hit a wall, physically and/or emotionally, I just had to grind it out and keep my head up. Today I would hit a wall.

A couple of miles into the morning hike, I took a side trail .3 miles west to investigate the beautiful Dismal Falls. The scenic waterfall and surrounding campsites were the best water-based places to camp on the AT thus far. I had the place to myself. I set my pack and trekking poles down, ate a snack, took pictures, and decided to explore the surroundings. Specifically, I wanted to walk along the edge of the water and look for fish.

That's when it happened. As I nonchalantly walked around some large, wet, flat rocks, not really paying attention, my feet slipped out from under me and I went airborne, landing flat on my back! Actually, my back, butt, and right elbow all hit at the same time, with my elbow bearing the brunt of the fall. I was in immense pain and felt embarrassed.

Before getting back on my feet, I paused briefly to consider how it was possible for someone to be alone and feel embarrassed. I also found it interesting that after hiking 610 miles in all kinds of weather and terrain, my first AT fall occurred on a side trail with my backpack off. I was thankful I hadn't cracked my skull, otherwise you might be reading my fobituary rather than my book.

I gathered myself, assessed the damage (a severely bruised right elbow, muddy shorts, and dislocated ego), and then continued northward. I walked alongside various streams and crossed bridges throughout the rainy day. In the afternoon, my feet began to pulsate with pain. They became especially sensitive to stepping on sharp rocks, which happened hundreds of times throughout the day. On top of that, the elbow pain from my fall worsened and I wasn't able to push off on my right trekking pole during climbs. It felt like someone had popped me in the elbow with a hammer. As a hiker who relies heavily on forearms and trekking poles for power and balance during climbs, this was a problem.

In addition to the physical pain that afternoon, I was depressed to be missing the graduation ceremony for my son, Kyle, and future daughter-in-law, Laci. Yes, Kyle had overcome the trail pooping incident and was about to graduate from college. Realistically, hiking the trail meant I had to choose between attending their graduation today or their wedding the following weekend. The wedding prevailed.

Although Kyle and Laci understood and supported my decision, I felt terrible. They had both had remarkable college experiences and the whole family was there to celebrate except me. It's one of those sacrifices I had to make to hike the AT, and emotionally it crushed me. Exhausted, bummed, and with intense foot and elbow pain, I had simply had enough. I stopped in my tracks and decided to set up camp on that spot.

Day 57 had been a tough 17.1-mile day, both emotionally and physically. As I sat there alone cooking Chili Mac, watching my elbow swell, and feeling sorry for myself, Conductor and Whistler (aka Mowgli) passed by and asked how I was doing. I answered, "Fine, thanks."

I lied.

Day 58 – Woods Road to Pearisburg
11.1 miles, 634.2 cumulative miles

"My life before the trail was often a bit white-washed, as if someone had trimmed the peaks and valleys from each day. The trail has brought a vivid color back to each day, both in good and bad ways. The reality is that you can't have the highs without the lows out here."
- Slice, 2016 thru-hiker

I'm a side sleeper and that made for a restless night. Every time I rolled onto my right elbow, the pain woke me. As I crawled from my tent to retrieve my food bag, excruciating pain shot through my feet. This was the sorest they had ever been. I hobbled to a nearby tree, retrieved my food bag, and walked gingerly back to the tent. I sat there for a few minutes rubbing my foot with one hand, and eating a pop tart with the other.

A quick glance at my phone reminded me today was Mother's Day, the first since my dear mother passed away from cancer. Emotion overwhelmed me. I'm not much of a crier—ENTJs tend to not be all that emotionally expressive. But with a mouth full of pop tart, I laid back on my air mattress and had my first good, long AT cry. I thought about my mom, how much I missed my wife, and what a jerk I was for missing my son's graduation.

To make matters worse, I was alone in the middle of the Virginia wilderness, nursing an injured elbow, and dealing with foot pain that made it difficult to take a single step. Of my 58 days on the AT, I had reached rock bottom.

Writing has always been therapeutic for me. It allows me to unscramble and process my thoughts and emotions. Prayer has a similar effect. God knows my heart and struggles and gives me whatever I need to get through the day. After drying my eyes, popping a few Advil, and pouring my heart out to God, I wrote this poem for my mom.

The Voice from My Pack

Woke up this morning, felt the weight of my heart,
Didn't feel like hiking, didn't even wanna start.
It's been just nine months, but the pain feels so real,
Some wounds do persist; some hearts never heal.

A pouch with her ashes, a voice from my pack...
"Keep hiking son, I'll forever have your back."

My dear mother loved me, and my sisters too,
Hearts as big as hers, there are so few.
But no phone calls today, nor sweet cards to sign,
No flowers to send, to this precious mother of mine.

A pouch with her ashes, a voice from my pack...
"Keep hiking son, I'll forever have your back."

I don't call the shots, didn't hang the stars and moon,
But from my vantage point, God took Mom too soon.
Guess he needed an angel, and she fit the bill,
He'll put her to work, but I miss her still.

A pouch with her ashes, a voice from my pack...
"Keep hiking son, I'll forever have your back."

So, I'm hiking the AT, hike most every day,
Told Mom I would do it, she told me she'd pray.
I know Mom's in heaven, but today I shed tears,
We just have her ashes, and memories to hold dear.

A pouch with her ashes, a voice from my pack...
"Keep hiking son, I'll forever have your back."

Got out of my tent, and laced up my boots,
What's in store today, Mom? Probably more rocks and roots.
One step at a time, in the snow and the rain,
With mom in my backpack, we'll make it to Maine.

A pouch with her ashes, a voice from my pack...
"Keep hiking son, I'll forever have your back."

At Katahdin's summit, I'll see Mom's smiling face,
I'll kneel to the ground, where her ashes I'll place.
Our journey will have ended, as mother and son,
But she'll remain in my heart, I'll still miss her a ton.

A pouch with her ashes, a voice from my pack...
"Keep hiking son, I'll forever have your back."

I thank God for her life, and all she means to me,
Our moms are so special; I think you'll agree.
If your mom is still living, I so envy you,
Tell her you love her; cards alone just won't do.

To the pouch with her ashes, to the voice from my pack...
"I'll keep hiking, mom, and never look back."

Taking a moment to count my blessings pulled me from my funk. God has been incredibly good to me my entire life and I wouldn't trade lives with anyone. Still, just like the AT's terrain, life has its peaks and valleys and I was in a temporary valley.

I thought about people and families I know courageously dealing with cancer and brain injuries and other things far worse than the sadness and foot pain I was experiencing. I realized I needed a break from the trail and, fortunately, a break was coming! All I needed to do was hobble 11.1 miles into Pearisburg. So, that's what I did.

Conductor caught up with me and we hiked together for the last few miles. He is one of my favorite hikers and I'm glad our paths crossed several times. We both are retired military and love the AT, so there was plenty to talk about. As a guy who thru-hiked the AT a decade earlier, he had tremendous credibility in answering trail questions.

When asked, Conductor humbly offered advice, so he didn't come across as a know-it-all. Today's lesson was on poison ivy, and he dispensed advice on how to spot, avoid, and treat it. The lesson came with relevant pictures of the nasty vine from his smart phone.

Next, Conductor taught me how to identify and appreciate the many Junco birds that nest near the trail. We discussed why so many of these little sparrow-like birds build nests so close to the trail. As hikers approach, Juncos flutter away from their nests, chirping and flapping their wings. One theory is they nest near the trail because that's an area where their natural predators avoid. Then, as hikers approach, they protect their nests by creating noisy diversions away from the nest. I don't know whether that theory is true, but it made me pay closer attention to Juncos from that moment on.

After hiking into Pearisburg, checking into the motel, and showering (separately), Conductor and I headed across the street for some great Mexican food and more conversation. He really lifted my spirits, as did the motel manager who offered to do my laundry for free.

That evening, after a hot bath, my feet were feeling better. I decided to walk to the other side of town to attend worship services. I arrived a few minutes before 6:00 p.m., the publicized start time. No one was there. I called the number for the contact person to get more information but there was no answer. Disappointed, I walked back across town to the motel, stopping at Pizza Hut along the way for pizza and salad.

My original plan was to take a zero day in Pearisburg and then rent a car the following day to travel to Alabama for the wedding festivities. While sitting at the Pizza Hut, I decided to accelerate that by a day because I missed my wife and family.

I decided to keep my early arrival a secret from Janet, and just told our friends, the Diamonds (with whom she was staying) about the plan. In just a matter of hours, I had gone from the valley of pain, exhaustion, and sadness to the mountaintop of anticipation in seeing my wife, other family, and friends. I needed rest, a break from hiking, and some normalcy. Most of all, I needed my family. I needed to be with them and be a part of the wedding festivities. I needed some extended time on the mountaintop. And God was about to pour out all those blessings on me big time.

Fob Fundamental #23 – When you find yourself in troubled times, traveling the inevitable valley, there's nothing quite like a loving family and close friends to help you weather the storm and get you back to the mountaintop.

Days 59 to 66 – Pearisburg to Birmingham and back eight 0 days, 634.2 cumulative miles

"When you realize you want to spend the rest of your life with somebody, you want the rest of your life to start as soon as possible."
- Harry from *When Harry Met Sally*

If I couldn't get excited about today, there was no hope for me. In fact, I was downright giddy. I left the motel and walked a mile downhill to the rental car place. They put me in a brand-new car and I headed west toward Alabama and wedding week. I felt weird driving again, as did the other drivers in whose lanes I kept weaving.

I cranked up the radio and sang my heart out for the next 7+ hours. One song, for King and Country's "The Proof of Your Love," hit home. It speaks of the importance of love, and that without love, it doesn't matter what you believe, say, or do. I added this song to my morning AT playlist. My hope was that by listening to it every morning for the next several months, its message about unconditional love would be driven deep inside my brain.

The closer I got to Birmingham, the more excited I became about seeing and surprising Janet. Ten minutes out, I picked up Starbucks coffee for her, my friend Brad, and myself. Just before entering the Diamond's driveway, I texted Janet to tell her I missed her and looked forward to seeing her tomorrow. Right after she responded, I came walking through the basement door where she, Brad, and Jenny were working on wedding signs. I asked, "Did someone order coffee?" Janet looked up in shock and came running over to hug me.

Surprising Janet with something that makes her happy is one of the greatest joys in my life. All the better when that something is me! I was thrilled to see her and the Diamond family, who kept my early arrival a

133

surprise. The only downside was she wasn't wearing the yellow, springy, reunion dress, but she still looked amazing!

The entire week could not have been more perfect. We had a great, informal pasta dinner with the wedding party at the home of our friends. It was refreshing, and a bit odd, to sit among people who were clean, smelled good, and peed indoors. I had to concentrate on eating slowly, using utensils, and not doing anything socially unacceptable.

On the health, hygiene and appearance front, Janet and I discussed grooming in general and my beard in particular...

Janet: "So what's the plan for your beard? Are you shaving it off?"

Fob: "No, honey. It'll be fine. Everyone will be focused on the bride and groom."

Janet: "You can't go like that. You'll be in wedding photos. It looks...scraggly. Kind of mossy."

Fob: "No one cares about the groom's dad. Much less the groom's dad's facial hair. But if it will make you feel better, I'll put my hand over my chin during photos...like I'm deep in thought."

Janet: "You should at least clean up your beard."

Fob: "Deal."

Clean up. The two magical words I was looking for! I knew that if I could get her to agree to just a "clean up," I could later define that phrase to a barber. My skillful negotiating skills had saved my beard! This was a win.

Another win was getting the 50-minute, deep tissue massage from a local spa. The masseuse focused on my feet, legs, and shoulders. I enjoyed being pampered and having her comment on my "rock-hard calf muscles." She never mentioned my beard.

At the rehearsal dinner, I was pumped to see my extended family and friends. They peppered me with all sorts of questions about my hike. The amazing Diamond family singers sang the song I wrote, "My Favorite Trail Things," along with a song of blessing for the bride and groom. The evening was full of bubbling over love between two families, friends, and the wedding party. We were truly being blessed by the merging of these two families. I thoroughly enjoyed this extended time on the "mountaintop" and feeling normal again!

The wedding was wonderful on many levels. The only one missing was Mom, who would have enjoyed the family being together, seeing the wedding cakes, seeing Laci's dress, and the love evident between the bride and groom. As Kyle watched my dad walk down the aisle unaccompanied, he was the first of several to tear up over the missing family matriarch. Moments later, Kyle's face lit up as his bride turned the corner and walked down the aisle with her dad.

The wedding reception was a blast! There was food, dancing, celebration, and conversation. Several guests asked me questions about the trail, my blog, and a possible future book. People I had just met encouraged me to continue hiking and writing. I guess I never realized that something I wrote, using a phone and my right thumb, while alone on a mountaintop or down in a valley, could impact someone hundreds of miles away. These comments gave me the shot in the arm I needed to continue putting my thoughts out there for everyone to read.

Sadly, the time came to say farewell to my family, kiss my wife, and drive back to Virginia and the AT. Saying goodbye was difficult. I had to remind myself of my commitment to finish, along with my other ten reasons for hiking the trail. Knowing Janet and I had another rendezvous in a month, I knew I could do it. Fortunately, I was returning to the trail rested, restored, and rejuvenated.

As previously planned, I left behind my Oboz Sawtooth hiking boots and switched to Salomon XA Pro 3D trail running shoes. The Salomons were lighter, quicker drying, and more agile, while giving up some stability in return. I was anxious to try them in AT conditions.

After the 7-hour return trip to Virginia, I returned the car and walked back to the motel. I laid out my clothes and tent and sprayed them with Permethrin, an insecticide that not only repels but kills ticks, mosquitos, chiggers, and other insects. After spraying them inside my motel room, I noticed the instructions said to "spray outdoors." So, I went to bed that night with a Permethrin buzz, assured that any bugs in my ears, nose, and mouth had been decimated. I was in a good place mentally and physically, and it was time to get back on the trail and continue my journey to Katahdin.

CHAPTER 11

MIDDLE VIRGINIA –
COME RAIN OR…MORE RAIN

May 17 – 29, 2016

"Everywhere is walking distance if you have the time."
- Stephen Wright

Day 67 – Pearisburg to Dickenson Gap
15.9 miles, 650.1 cumulative miles

With more rain in the forecast, I started the day wearing my new Salomon trail shoes without any socks. They worked like a champ right out of the gate, easily handling the climbs, mud puddles, and rocks. As I climbed the first hill out of Pearisburg, I passed a hiker who asked about the origin of my trail name. I told him the story of Sir Fob W. Pot. I then asked him about his trail name, Stan. He said his parents gave him that name when he was born and it stuck. I wasn't sure if that was a joke or not, so I half-laughed to cover my bases.

As I approached the Rice Field Shelter at noon, the Virginia skies opened up and rain began to fall. I ducked into the shelter along with Cambria, Two Soles, Blade, a German Shepherd dog, and several others. Two Soles earned his name because, like me, he had foot troubles and the foot guy at the Damascus outfitter suggested he try a new pair of insoles. He agreed, but after hiking in them the next day, his feet hurt even worse. His hiking companion examined the situation and discovered that rather than replace his old insoles, he kept them in his boots and just put the new pair on top. The two pairs of insoles used simultaneously not only painfully crushed his feet but earned him a trail name.

Sitting at the edge of the shelter with rain falling just inches in front of me, I peeled the wrapper on a Slim Jim, which is not made by Gravy Train. The German Shepherd which had been dozing in the middle of the shelter suddenly jumped to her feet and ran to me, drooling. I gave her half my Slim Jim, overly generous by hiker standards, and she licked me on the mouth. This wasn't nearly as satisfying as my last kiss with my wife, but seemed like a fair exchange. Our interaction made me miss my own dog, Mandy, who I decided not to bring with me on my AT hike. It was an easy decision, really, because you see…Mandy is dead.

Given the number of times I have reflected on Mandy's passing, including this reflective moment under the shelter, let me share the account of her final day. The year was 2011, and I was at school for teacher orientation. Kyle, the Trail Pooper, was at home alone relishing his last few days of sleeping late before his high school senior year began.

Kyle called me at work and said, "Dad, I think Mandy's dead." This came as no surprise given her age and recent lethargy, but I pressed him on the issue. "Why do you think that, son?" "Well, Dad," he replied, "She's not breathing; her eyes are closed; her tongue is sticking out; and there's fluid coming out of her butt." After mulling over these symptoms for a moment, I said, "That's not good. Not good at all. I'll be there in 10 minutes."

I returned home, took our sweet canine's pulse, and with my hand on Kyle's shoulder, made the official pronouncement, "Mandy's dead." It was a sad moment for Kyle and me, as Mandy had been an integral part of our family for more than a dozen years.

"What do we do now?" Kyle asked. "I guess we need to bury her," I replied. "I've never buried a dog before, but it can't be that difficult." Those words would come back to haunt me. I realized this was an important moment between father and son, an opportunity for bonding and mentoring. I wanted to honor Mandy's life and appear competent to my teenage son.

I went to the garage and retrieved a large black garbage bag, a pair of work gloves, and a shovel. "You're putting her in that?" Kyle asked. "Yes, these are 2-ply strength and can hold up to 30 gallons of leaves…or a beagle," I confidently answered. He looked skeptical but continued watching my every move. When done well, mentoring is beautiful.

I gently picked Mandy up, placed her in the bag, and we solemnly carried her to the backyard. I sat the Mandy-filled bag down by Kyle's feet and began digging a hole at the edge of the backyard of our Lithia, Florida home. After I finished the hole and wiped my brow, Kyle asked, "Is that hole gonna be deep enough, Dad?" "It should be fine, son," I said. "If I go any deeper I might hit a gas line or sink hole."

We each said a couple of thoughtful words about dear Mandy and the joy she had brought our family. After saying a final goodbye, I carefully placed Mandy in the hole, which was just wide enough for her body to fit into. I looked down and noticed something wasn't right. "Dad, her head is sticking out a couple of inches!" Kyle declared. "The hole's not deep enough!"

Up to this point, I had tried to be sensitive and careful during this trying time. What happened next remains, to this day, perhaps the most shameful, inappropriate thing I've ever done. With my impressionable son looking on, I lifted my right leg and, with full force, brought the heel of my right foot crushing down on top of the garbage bag. As Kyle stood there shocked and horrified, I realized that if Mandy wasn't dead before, she was certainly dead now.

With one stomp of my shoe, I transformed a sweet father and son bonding time into a canine horror scene on par with *Cujo*. In apparent denial about what I had just done, I asserted, "That should do it," and shoveled dirt into the hole, just barely concealing Mandy's corpse and the Hefty body bag which covered it. After placing a small stick cross by Mandy's shallow grave, I put my arm around my shaken son and guided him back inside to contemplate all that had happened.

While mowing grass the following afternoon, I passed by our makeshift grave and discovered Mandy had been dug up and all that remained was the hole. To this day, we don't know what became of her corpse, or what had caused me to handle the situation the way I did. All I know is that whenever the topic of Mandy comes up, my friends and family avoid talk of the botched burial, and simply remind me that "Mandy's dead."

Fob Fundamental #24 – Competency lies at the heart of effective mentoring. That is to say, dig a deep enough hole.

My thoughts turned back to the task before me, hiking the AT. Once the rain lightened up, I headed out and continued along fairly level terrain. While climbing Dickinson Gap, I spoke briefly with Princess Grit. She asked me to tell the story of my trail name to her hiking companion. I obliged, but decided afterward that the story was becoming repetitive and needed enhancements to keep it fresh. I considered having the Trail Pooper defile numerous famous trails around the country and perhaps even an amusement park or two. These embellishments wouldn't be any more shameful than what I had done to the deceased family pet.

A short time later, I stopped for the night and stealth camped among some tall, barren trees. My new trail shoes had passed their first test, even without socks. Still, I planned to wear socks on most days as that made the shoes more comfortable. Despite mud splashes from my ankles to my knees, it had been a good, mostly rainy first day back on the AT. I was alive and well, which, sadly, is more than I can say for my sweet dog, Mandy.

Day 68 – Dickenson Gap to War Spur Shelter
16.7 miles, 666.8 cumulative miles

Today was dark and cloudy the first half of the day. I spoke briefly with Sasquatch, a south bounder, at Stony Creek Valley. I always thought he would be taller, hairier, scarier, and have bigger feet. Instead, he was very friendly, spoke English, and was able to convey information about the upcoming terrain and water sources.

In the early afternoon, the rain started falling again, and would continue off and on the rest of the day. A mile after Bailey Gap Shelter, I hit a several mile-long section of rocky terrain. I had to concentrate on each step to keep from rolling an ankle. The rocks and mud slowed my pace considerably, but I trudged on.

I eventually camped with Two Soles, Princess Grit, and others near War Spur Shelter. The talk around camp centered on the tremendous amount of rain we had experienced in Virginia. Someone said they talked to an elderly local man who said it was the rainiest month of May he could remember in the past 80 years.

I was once again asked about my trail name and told a story about the time Kyle, a third grader at the time, pooped himself on the Runaway Mine Train at Six Flags over Georgia. Security was called and he was taken away in handcuffs. I felt mild regret later over this blatant fabrication, but that should subside with each false re-telling of the story.

Day 69 – War Spur Shelter to Niday Shelter
18.2 miles, 685 cumulative miles

The ascent to Kelly Knob was brutal. I gained nearly 2,000 feet in altitude in a little over two miles. It wasn't presently raining, but the terrain was muddy from all the previous rain, and the vegetation I frequently brushed up against was wet. All that, plus the high humidity and my profuse sweating, led to one soaked, muddy hiker by 9:00 a.m. As I guzzled a full liter of water and caught my breath at the summit, two deer darted by, a small reward for a tough start to the day.

Later, I passed Keffer Oak, a 300-year-old oak tree with an 18-foot circumference. It's the largest oak tree on the AT in the South, with Dover Oak along the AT in New York being slightly larger. I stopped to consider the long line of hikers who had passed by this tree throughout the decades and how many had posed for pictures with it or camped at its base. I thought to myself, if that 300-year-old tree could talk—well, that would be messed up.

A little while later, on a rock scramble near Sarver Hollow Shelter, I met a hiker named Crisco. Before starting the AT, most hikers are aware that it is not possible to replenish the 5,000-6,000 calories burned on a typical hiking day. Food is heavy and it's not realistic to carry enough grub to offset the calories burned.

Crisco took that as a personal challenge. He began the trail carrying and consuming pure Crisco vegetable shortening, which provides 110 calories of pure fat per tablespoon eaten. Thus, the trail name. So, if he carried and consumed three cups of Crisco daily, over the course of five months, he was getting...well, I really don't want to do the math.

At the north end of the ridgeline on Sinking Creek Mountain, I arrived at a sign marking the Eastern Continental Divide. Curious, I conducted an experiment in which I relieved myself on a large boulder near the sign. Sure enough, the flow went evenly in each direction down the sides of the boulder. I made a mental note of this experiment and plan to contact a scientific journal in order to publish my findings.

I finished my hiking day at Niday Shelter, along with several hikers, including Tennessee Troy, Little Bear, Patrice, Crisco, Sprinkle Toes, ETA, Future Dad, and White Owl. We covered a lot of ground in the camp conversation that evening. Little Bear informed me that Lindsay, who, along with Patrice, was filming a documentary about women thru-hikers, had to get off the trail to have surgery. I was sad to hear this but happy to know the filming would continue and Lindsay would continue with film editing and such after her recovery.

As for Sprinkle Toes, she earned that name during a cold, very windy afternoon in the Smokies. As she relieved herself behind a tree, she didn't realize the wind was blowing her pee all over her left shoe and sock. She ended up with a pee-soaked sock and a trail name. I was glad I was not the only hiker to be named after a bodily function.

Last but not least, we have the fascinating, 70-year-old White Owl from Maine. We immediately hit it off and began trading stories. He has a great sense of humor and, with his tall, lean body and white beard, could easily be my Uncle Phil's twin brother. He showed me a picture of a nature scene he had recently encountered—two crawdads trying to eat a fish that was being digested by a snake. Now that was awesome!

White Owl and I also traded vasectomy and colonoscopy stories, much to the delight of the younger hikers who were just a few years removed from puberty. I don't remember all the details from his colonoscopy story (perhaps a good thing), but his last sentence was, "And then, after raising my bare butt in the air, the nurse looked at me and said, 'That's where I remember you from!'"

Day 70 – Niday Shelter to Newport Road
16.8 miles, 701.8 cumulative miles

"Fairy tales are more than true: not because they tell us that dragons exist,
but because they tell us dragons can be beaten."
- Neil Gaiman, *Coraline*, paraphrasing G. K. Chesterton

I hit the trail, crossed several footbridges, and began the climb up Brush Mountain. At the summit was a wooden bench, uncommon and highly appreciated on the AT. Along the Brush Mountain ridge line, at mile 690.1, I took a short side trail to the Audie Murphy monument. Murphy is the most decorated American soldier of World War II. After the war, he acted in movies for over 20 years and eventually got a star on the Hollywood Walk of Fame. On May 28, 1971, the 45-year-old Murphy died when the private plane he was in crashed on Brush Monument, not far from the monument that now bears his name. I stopped to pay my respects to this hero, a great soldier from what has been called the greatest generation.

As morning turned to afternoon, I set my sights on the famous Dragon's Tooth. Like Albert Mountain, Jacob's Ladder, and other notable trail challenges, Dragon's Tooth has a reputation for being a very tough climb with rewarding views. The ascent was long and rocky, but not too steep. Upon arriving, I was impressed with the giant boulders and the views they afforded.

I also thought Dragon's Tooth was a bit over-rated in terms of level of difficulty. The climb was tough, but not super tough. I took that as a good sign that maybe I was toughening up. Then came the descent, and I realized where Dragon's Tooth's reputation came from. It was very tricky, especially as light rain began to fall. I scrambled down and around rocks using both hands, at one point passing the 700-mile mark on my journey. In a few spots, I slid down rocks on my rear. In other places, metal rungs were inserted in rocks to provide a foothold. After considerable effort, I finally made it to the bottom of the mountain. I had beaten the dragon.

I hiked .3 miles east along Newport Road to reach Four Pines Hostel. The hostel consists of a 3-bay garage with a shower (no towels), along with a separate barn that contained additional sleeping platforms. There is no fee but the owners accept donations.

The place was packed when I arrived, with hikers sprawled out on cots, couches, and the floor. They were playing cards, drinking beer, eating, sharing stories, napping, picking at their feet, and airing out tents and clothes. One couple, obviously committed to Lyme Disease prevention, was off in the corner checking themselves for ticks in a highly sensual and seductive manner. I stared at them, but only for three minutes.

The entire scene reminded me of a place where Charles Manson would have recruited followers. I managed to find a recliner that wasn't taken, next to a couch occupied by a sweet lady hiker in her mid-60s. Her name, Gamel, is a combination of "Georgia (GA) to Maine (ME)" and her nickname, Mel, which is short for Melanie. Being from East Tennessee, she filled me in on the towns and things to do there, as it is a region where Janet and I have discussed putting down roots someday.

I also met the owners, Joe Mitchell and his wife, who walked around checking on hikers. His wife offered me a delicious brownie. The Mitchells are friendly people who love and serve hikers and don't appear to have any previous affiliation with Charles Manson.

The highlight of the evening was set in motion moments later when the shuttle driver asked if anyone wanted to go to the all-you-can-eat, family style Homeplace Restaurant. His question prompted the same response as if someone had yelled "Rabbit!" in a room full of hound dogs. Most of us either stood up, raised a hand, or grunted, indicating a desire to get in on the action. One exception: the couple in the corner, who were unfazed and continued checking themselves for ticks.

Certain words and phrases, like *all-you-can-eat*, excite hikers, and even cause frenzies when we are in groups. Other popular phrases include:
- trail magic
- REI sale
- hot shower
- reliable spring/water source
- free Wi-Fi
- free {insert any word}
- easy hitch (to town)
- flat terrain
- milkshake
- Ramen Bomb
- summit
- campfire
- hot tub or bath
- trail legs
- outfitter
- buffet
- zero day
- Katahdin

My personal list also includes...
- Janet
- yellow, springy dress
- Outback

- Mountain Dew
- Darn Good Chili
- Gold Bond

"We never repent of having eaten too little."
- Thomas Jefferson, 1825

The gaggle of hungry hikers piled into a large van and truck and headed to the Homeplace restaurant. One hiker was on the floorboard and two were in the trunk. The arrangement resembled a prison work crew, only smellier. Upon arrival, 11 of us were seated at one table, including three other Air Force veterans (sponsored by a program called Warrior Expeditions) and four Marines. It was the most heavily defended restaurant table in Catawba that evening. We were a scraggly, hairy bunch, and most of us had not showered or eaten.

What happened next will go down as one of the most prolific displays of eating in American history. The sweet country waitress delivered the initial round of roast beef, chicken, ham, mac 'n cheese, pinto beans, green beans, mashed potatoes, biscuits, and coleslaw. She told us to let her know when we wanted seconds on anything. I pulled her aside and said, "Ma'am, we are long distance hikers and we haven't eaten in nearly three hours. You may want to go ahead and get started on seconds and thirds now."

We were like vultures devouring fresh highway roadkill. With elbows extended, we aggressively postured to get our share of the feast. The large bowl of pinto beans began a table rotation, and was empty by the third person. As the ranking military guy at the table, I didn't pass the mac 'n cheese at all. Instead, I selfishly made the family-style bowl my personal bowl. Selfish? Perhaps so. But what good is it to make rank if you can't leverage it for a private bowl of mac 'n cheese on the AT?

The Marines were sucking on chicken bones and piling them in a mass grave at the center of the table, as grease ran down their chins and hands. Farmer, a former Air Force TACP (Tactical Air Control Party specialist, a special operations guy), sat next to me, helping himself to nine servings of roast beef, six pieces of chicken, and four large pieces of ham. I started to ask him if he had a tapeworm but thought better of it. I looked under the table by his feet to see if anything was coming out the other end.

Each time the waitress came by, we were out of something and ready for more. Each time, I would point to Farmer and tell her, "And he'll need some more roast beef." He would grunt and nod his head, too busy eating to speak. Given his epic trail beard and mammoth appetite, I felt a personal responsibility to keep him from running out of roast beef.

There was little table conversation that evening as we were too busy stuffing our faces and asking for more, as if our very survival depended on it. The whole spectacle was fun to watch and quite embarrassing. Later, the waitress, with perhaps the most unnecessary question ever, asked if we would like peach cobbler with ice cream. On behalf of the group, I said, "We would, please, with coffee, and my friend here, Farmer, would like his cobbler with just a couple more slices of roast beef." He looked up, nodding approvingly. During this brief reprieve from hiking, all was right in our hiker universe.

Day 71 – Newport Road to Tinker Cliffs
14.9 miles, 716.7 cumulative miles

I was one of the first hikers out of the gate, but five or six slack packers passed me during the first two hours of the day. Without backpacks, they were rushing to hike 27 miles to Troutville where the shuttle driver would pick them up, return them to the hostel, and then return them to Troutville the following morning. As previously discussed, I didn't slack pack because, in my opinion, the AT is meant to be enjoyed, not rushed. That was especially true on this section of trail.

Around noon I stopped at Catawba Mountain Shelter to get water. An hour later, I was standing on McAfee Knob, the most famous ledge on the AT. It is second only to Katahdin's summit as the most photographed spot on the trail. I have read about this ledge and looked at hiker photos of it for nearly two decades. Now I was standing on it!

McAfee Knob is where Robert Redford and Nick Nolte are standing in the movie poster for *A Walk in the Woods*. I read this was a photo-shopped picture as neither actor has been to the famous ledge. If true, they missed something special. Standing on McAfee Knob felt surreal, even though the cloudy day limited my view.

Terrence, a young day hiker, agreed to take several pictures of me on the ledge, the last of which had me sitting down dangling my feet. While I was carefully making my way to the edge, I recalled the promise I had made to my mother-in-law about not taking unnecessary risks. Maybe when she saw this picture, I could tell her it was photo-shopped. Sitting on the ledge with the drop off below was another small step in overcoming my fear of heights. Posing for this photo was my second scariest AT moment to date, just behind the climb up Shuckstack fire tower in the Smokies.

Towards the end of the day, as storms once again threatened, I stopped to say hello to ETA and Training Wheels, who had already set up camp for the night. Training Wheels earned her name by falling down several times during the first two weeks of her hike, including once just casually walking by the campfire. ETA was based on the hiker's initials, E.T., and the fact he hailed from Alaska.

I made a final climb to Tinker Cliffs and the stunningly beautiful views they offered. Revolutionary War deserters supposedly hid out on these cliffs, repairing pots and pans for money. They came to be known as "tinkers" and the area as Tinker Cliffs. The trail followed along the edge with drops of up to 150 feet. It was a perfect spot for tenting with a view, so I called it a day.

I cooked Ramen Bomb on a large, flat rock on the edge of the cliffs. As I dozed off to sleep that night, I wondered what it must have been like to live there as a war deserter, repairing pots and pans, while others were down below fighting for independence and the creation of a new nation.

Day 72 – Tinker Cliffs to Roanoke
10.8 miles, 727.5 cumulative miles

I began the day on another outstanding section of trail. In fact, the hike from yesterday's McAfee Knob to today's Hay Rock placed in my top five favorite sections of the AT so far. Five scenic overlooks, with views stretching for miles, were God's special gifts to AT hikers today.

Having exhausted my water supply on the cliffs, I stopped at the creek by Lamberts Meadow Shelter to refill my bottle. This was another shelter that had been closed indefinitely due to bear activity. While filtering water faster than normal, my head swiveled in anticipation of a bear charging and going all *Revenant* on me.

The final few miles into Daleville/Roanoke were scenic and relatively flat. I looked forward to arriving because Debbie Freeman, a longtime family friend, was picking me up and treating me to some southern hospitality. Long ago, my family got to know the Smyth family (Debbie's maiden name) through the school friendship between Debbie and my oldest sister, Ellen. My mom and Debbie's mom also became close friends and kept in contact for over 40 years.

My first memory of the Smyth family was as an 8-year-old, in 1974, when my family returned from our military assignment in Germany. Before moving into our home in Dover, Delaware, we stayed with their family in a big home outside of town. My main memories are of a house full of cute girls of various ages, a bumper pool table that I was allowed to play on, and a rope swing in the backyard. What more could an 8-year-old boy want from his homeland?

Their dad, Joe Smyth, is a long-time newspaper man and, at the time, served as Editor of the Delaware State News. I remember him sitting in his big chair with a pen and newspaper and marking it up. The Smyth family was very kind to us. It was no surprise that 42 years later, Debbie and her husband, Bill, would once again show hospitality to a tired long distance hiker.

The first treat was observing Debbie's latest hobby, beekeeping. I learned the ins and outs of starting and maintaining a hive and the role of each type of bee. The magnificence of their design, unique roles, and coordinated effort to survive once again pointed to a Grand Designer. Surely, God made them. It was all new and fascinating. I considered surprising Janet with a beehive starter kit for her birthday. If I were to ask for her permission, I bet she'd say, "No, honey."

After starting my laundry, I headed straight for a shower and bath. Debbie provided me muscle-soothing Epsom salt and lavender essential bath oil. I had never bathed with oil before, essential or otherwise, and it was luxurious! I laid back, breathed deeply, and closed my eyes. Once again, all was right in the universe. I imagined snapping my fingers and having two beautiful, toga-clad women enter. One held a platter with grapes and cheeses and the other a cold Mountain Dew. I had been away from my wife too long.

I snapped back to reality, put on Bill's bathrobe, and headed down to supper. I smelled like a bouquet of flowers and my muscles were relaxed. Debbie prepared a scrumptious meal featuring chicken, asparagus, bread, and more. We enjoyed catching up on what our respective families had been up to the past several years.

Day 73 – Roanoke to Wilson Creek Shelter
11.2 miles, 738.7 cumulative miles

Debbie filled my tank again with a wonderful breakfast, took me to Wal-Mart to resupply, and returned me to the trailhead at Daleville. She and Bill were excellent hosts and I truly appreciate their kindness. After eating pasta and salad at Pizza Hut, I got back on the trail at 2:15 p.m.

Journeying northward, I reflected on how good God has been to me. I have been through some tough times, for sure, but God has sustained me. I am thankful He placed wonderful people in my path to encourage me, most recently the Freeman family.

As I hiked, I reflected on Psalm 23. I considered how David, a young shepherd, saw the Lord as his shepherd. Just as David protected, provided for, and cared for his sheep, God did the same for him.

I then wondered—because on the AT there was plenty of time for wondering—how Psalm 23 might have been worded if David had been a long-distance hiker, rather than a shepherd. This resulted in a revised Psalm 23 of sorts—a poem that went like this...

The LORD is My Sherpa

The LORD is my Sherpa, my Leader, my Model, my Defender and my Protector.
He hikes in front of me, showing me the path to follow
to reach the finish line and the crown that awaits.
He hikes behind me, nudging and encouraging me to stay focused
and to take it one step at a time.
He walks beside me, as a friend, and we talk things out, like good friends do.
He surrounds me with Trail Angels, both seen and unseen.
I don't want Him on my team; rather, I am on His team...
a team that has already defeated Satan and this fallen world.

Please refer to Appendix C to read the entire poem.

I arrived at Wilson Creek Shelter and tented nearby with several hikers. I enjoyed chatting with Gamel again, and also meeting Tree from Indiana. Fellow hikers named him that because, around a campfire one night, he knew and shared too much detailed information about AT trees. As I dozed off to sleep, I caught a final faint whiff of lavender and then it was gone.

**Fob Fundamental #25 – To gain fresh, new
insights from a well-known passage of Scripture, try
re-writing it from your own perspective, based on
your current struggles, challenges, and blessings.**

Day 74 – Wilson Creek Shelter to Bryant Ridge Shelter
20.8 miles, 759.5 cumulative miles

Just a few miles into my morning hike, I saw the first of many views and crossings of the Blue Ridge Parkway. Given its beauty and popularity, I was surprised not to hear or see any traffic. I learned later they occasionally shut down sections to trim branches and do maintenance. As I relieved myself behind a tree just off the trail, I was suddenly overcome by the smell of toxic, radioactive nuclear waste. Initially alarmed, I then remembered I had eaten asparagus with the Freemans two days earlier.

The Virginia rains I had become accustomed to had been replaced by high humidity and oppressive heat. Sweat poured off me. I decided to take off my shirt, which didn't cool me, but provided a scary sight for SOBO hikers. The hotter it got, the more motivated I became to reach today's big goal, Jennings Creek. Two words in my AT guidebook drew me like a magnet to the creek—swimming hole!

I crossed the VA 614 bridge and arrived at Jennings Creek at 4:15 p.m. As two male hikers eating lunch on a boulder watched in amusement, I stripped down to my quick drying, synthetic underwear and waded into the frigid waters. Once I got over the initial shock and caught my breath, it was a wonderfully refreshing moment. I swam out to the whirlpool and fobbed up and down like a manatee playing in a tidal pool. I then waded over to a large boulder and stretched across it to dry out and nap.

Later, as I waded back to shore, I caught a large crawfish, named him Cajun, and looked for another in order to have a crawfish duel. I couldn't find another, so Cajun remained the Jennings Creek champ, uncontested and undefeated. As you might suspect, the next item on the agenda was fishing. Unfortunately, I was shut out, moving my record versus AT fish to 2-1. I think the fish might have been spooked by my earlier frolicking in my underwear.

Feeling refreshed, I continued hiking. Five minutes into my ascent of Fork Mountain, I saw a six-foot-long black snake. Knowing they can bite but are non-venomous, I reached out and grabbed his tail and he spun around. I chose to show him mercy and not turn him into a belt.

After a 20.8-mile day, I stopped at a deep, wooded ravine and stayed in the large, 20-person Bryant Ridge Shelter, along with Tree, Big Stick, and several others. The shelter was built in 1992 as a memorial to Nelson Garnett, an architecture student from Catholic University, who died in 1991. His fellow architecture students did a magnificent job designing the shelter, which was built with funds provided by the Bryant family. One of the nicer AT shelters, it features two levels, a skylight, covered picnic table, and wrap-around seating.

One hiker about my age, while going down steps to the creek, lost his balance and wiped out. All the other hikers, myself included, started laughing at his misfortune. Then we went to the bushes to check on him and confirm that he wasn't dead. In retrospect, we should have checked on him before laughing.

Day 75 – Bryant Ridge Shelter to Marble Spring Campsite
17.1 miles, 776.6 cumulative miles

Today was brutal. First of all, it was once again unbelievably hot and humid, and there were no swimming holes to provide relief. Second, the morning featured a 3,000-foot climb and the afternoon a 2,000-foot descent. There was very little flat terrain to catch a breather. Third, I awoke with a small outbreak of poison ivy on my right forearm, which served me right for laughing at the hiker who fell yesterday. I am very susceptible to getting poison ivy, so I was surprised that my first bout on the trail didn't happen before my 75th day.

Despite these tough conditions, I had my trail legs and water sources were plentiful. I made it through the day by drinking lots of water, powering through the ascents and descents, and ignoring the poison ivy. Today's top man-made sight was a large, impressive Federal Aviation Administration tower at the summit of Apple Orchard Mountain. I remembered from my earlier visit to another FAA facility not to trespass or tamper with it in any way because people could die. So, I hiked on, wondering what would really happen if someone trespassed.

Less than half a mile later, I hiked under The Guillotine, a large boulder suspended directly above the trail, held in place by two even larger boulders. Maybe this was where they cut off the heads of people who trespass at the FAA facility?

After a hot, exhausting, 17.1-mile day, I tented at Marble Spring Campsite, along with Big Stick, Smiley, and David and Sarah from Washington, D.C. I also met Tree Beard, whose long beard was in a ponytail, and his hiking partner, Waterfall, who once fell while trying to position himself higher on a waterfall.

The discussion around the evening campfire concerned an aggressive bear that had been harassing hikers at the Thunder Hill Shelter, leading to its closure. The bear knew how to knock food bags down and one evening helped himself to several bags of hiker food. The bear allegedly stalked a group of hikers from the shelter down to the Harrison Ground Spring camping area. Once authorities were alerted, the bear had to be put down near Petites Gap.

There was no way to know whether all the details from that story were true, but it made for interesting talk around the campfire. There was also a rumor that a male model was posing in his underwear for a *GQ* photo shoot at Jennings Creek. I don't know where all these crazy rumors come from.

Day 76 – Marble Spring Campsite to Punchbowl Shelter
18.2 miles, 794.8 cumulative miles

"We don't even know how strong we are until we are forced to bring that hidden strength forward. In times of tragedy, of war, of necessity, people do amazing things. The human capacity for survival and renewal is awesome."
- Isabel Allende

For four-year-old Ottie Cline Powell, November 9, 1891, began as a typical day. The fifth of Edwin and Emma Belle Powell's eight children, little Ottie awoke, got dressed, and went with his siblings to the one-room schoolhouse near his family's farm. It was a chilly, overcast day in Amherst County, Virginia. A few inches of snow had blanketed the ground.

Upon his arrival at the Tower Hill schoolhouse, his teacher, Miss Nancy Gilbert, welcomed little Ottie, an intelligent young man with blue eyes and a fair complexion. She noticed the wood pile had been exhausted during the recent snow. During recess, she instructed her students to return with sticks to fuel the school's wood-burning stove.

Little Ottie, barefoot at the time, went looking for wood, wandered off, and never returned. Miss Gilbert frantically searched for him and became increasingly concerned. She sent her students home with instructions to tell their parents that little Ottie was missing. More than 1,500 locals and several dogs searched for him, in the rain and then ice, in ever-widening circles. "Ottie! Ottie Powell! Where are you? Come here, Ottie!" There was no sign of him. The entire community was baffled by his disappearance and his parents were heartbroken.

On April 5, 1892, nearly five months later, a hunting dog picked up a scent and led a hunter to an old hunting and Indian trail at the top of Bluff Mountain. It was there, seven miles from the schoolhouse, at 3,372 feet, that little Ottie's remains were found. Experts believe he got lost, panicked, and started to run. After climbing the mountain, he collapsed and succumbed to the freezing temperatures. An autopsy showed he had undigested chestnuts from school in his stomach, an indication that, thankfully, he didn't suffer long.[10]

On Day 76, I made the long descent from Highcock Knob and crossed James River footbridge, the longest foot-use only bridge on the AT. I then began the exhausting 2,700-foot climb up Bluff Mountain. This ascent was the toughest climb in Virginia for me due to the humidity and lack of water sources. I carried a woefully inadequate two liters of water. Completely drained and soaked to the bone with sweat, I eventually summited.

At the summit, I spotted the memorial to Ottie Cline Powell, placed at the location where his body was found over 124 years ago. Emotions ran through my mind. More than anything, I felt sad for little Ottie, and imagined the despair and panic he likely felt as he ran and ran and couldn't find his schoolhouse. I wished there wasn't a 124-year gap between our Bluff Mountain summits, so that I could have rescued that little boy.

I was amazed that such a young boy, one-month shy of his 5th birthday, in his bare feet, in those conditions, could have traveled seven miles, much of it uphill in rugged wilderness. Simply remarkable. I'm thankful he likely didn't suffer for long on that mountain. I'm also thankful he's in heaven now. Perhaps someday I will meet little Ottie and give him a fist pump, a standard greeting between long-distance hikers.

---

[10] Youngblood, Beth. "The Sad Disappearance of Ottie Cline Powell." http://bethyoungblood.com/2016/01/11/the-sad-disappearance-of-ottie-cline-powell. Accessed 15 January 2017.

I descended Bluff Mountain and arrived at Punchbowl Shelter after a physically grueling 18.2-mile day. Clearly dehydrated, my first priority was to filter and consume nearly two liters of water. My second priority was to retrieve my fishing gear and try to catch a fish at the nearby mountain pond. I got some nibbles but ultimately struck out, bringing my record versus AT fish to 2-2.

I ate dinner at the shelter picnic table, along with Training Wheels, Shoe Leather, Big Stick, and Uno. One of them, reading from the shelter journal, informed us that the shelter is reportedly haunted by the ghost of Ottie Cline Powell. I doubted that, but kept my 1-inch Swiss Army knife close by just in case.

Since a light rain started to fall at the end of supper, and I hadn't set up my tent, I decided to sleep in the shelter. I was joined there by Shoe Leather (a south bounder) and Uno. Seeking refuge in the shelter would turn out to be an awful decision. As I settled into my sleeping bag, the bugs descended on Punchbowl Shelter.

First came the mosquitos. I could hear them loudly buzzing my ears. Each time they came close, I slapped myself in an attempt to kill them. I probably slapped myself upside the head 25 times between 9:00 and 9:30. I didn't kill any mosquitos but gave myself a slight concussion.

Next came the black flies. I hate black flies with a passion. They feasted on my exposed skin, already in bad shape from the poison ivy. I was miserable and fighting a losing battle. My only option was to pull my sleeping bag liner over my head. This technique kept the bugs at bay, but also meant sleeping in a 100-degree, sweat-filled cocoon.

Between the bugs and heat, this was my worst night on the AT so far. I might have slept an hour. If I could live that night over, I would have summoned the ghost of Ottie Cline Powell to have him club me over the head with a piece of firewood, ending my misery.

Rest well, sweet Ottie.

Day 77 – Punchbowl Shelter to Buena Vista
11.3 miles, 806.1 cumulative miles

After a night of relentless bug attacks, sweltering humidity, and getting only an hour of sleep, I was thrilled to say goodbye to Punchbowl Shelter and any ghosts that reside there. I was glad today would be a short day, just 11.3 miles, as I was heading to Buena Vista to shower, do laundry, and resupply.

After crossing Pedlar River Bridge, I passed the AT 800-mile marker, spelled out in sticks. While on the surface insignificant in the context of a 2,189.1-mile journey, I had come to appreciate these milestone markers. They provided opportunities to pray, eat a candy bar, reflect on the progress made, and consider the physical and mental work remaining.

Whether one's goal is to write a book, lose weight, raise a child, or hike a trail, I suggest breaking the goal into a series of smaller, more manageable pieces and celebrating the accomplishment of each one of them. I wasn't sure I could hike 2,200 miles, but I thought I might be able to hike 100 miles 22 times.

Fob Fundamental #26 – You can conquer mountain-sized, seemingly impossible to achieve goals by breaking them into smaller, more manageable pieces. Celebrate each milestone, and use it as fuel to conquer the next.

Shortly after crossing the 800-mile marker, I approached a historical sign next to a bench. The sign informed hikers that the next 1.4-mile section of trail featured the remnants of the Brown Mountain Creek community.

In the early 1900s, freed slaves built and lived in this community. They worked hard, lived in small homes, and ate simple but nourishing food. Living as sharecroppers, they raised tobacco, corn, wheat, and oats. It was a simple life and, most importantly, they were free. The community disbanded when they sold their land to the National Forest Service in the early 1920s. I didn't see any remnants of their community as I passed through, but I'm sure this forest area has stories to tell. I highly regard people who are willing to work hard in tough conditions to make their lives better.

I emerged from the woods at a parking lot on US 60, 9.3 miles east of Buena Vista. I tried hitchhiking for 15 minutes, but many vehicles just passed by. It wasn't a great first impression of the town, but I was a smelly, sweaty male hiker so I understood the reluctance.

Forty-five minutes and $15 later, a shuttle delivered me to the Budget Inn. I was so hungry that I opted for Burger King over a shower, which didn't happen often. I managed to spend $16 at Burger King, eating a sampling of food from each section of the menu. After eating, I stepped outside, belched loudly, and smelled myself. I was unquestionably the foulest, most disgusting living thing in Virginia that afternoon.

After showering and doing laundry, which once again involved a sprint across the hotel parking lot wearing nothing but a towel, I walked to town to re-supply. I found what I needed at Family Dollar and Amish Cupboard, which has a variety of canned and dried foods, jerky, and other snacks. Traveling on, I stopped at Don Tequilas for excellent Mexican food. After dropping my stuff off at the hotel, I walked next door and finished the day with a cherry-flavored shaved ice.

Day 78 – Buena Vista to Hog Camp Gap
6.3 miles, 812.4 cumulative miles

The first thing on my agenda today was to walk downtown to be the first customer when the barber shop opened. Madam Barber was friendly and quite interested in my hike. I told her to shave my head but not touch the beard, because it only grows one centimeter per year. She laughed and gave me a good, close haircut.

She told me about the town, its economic struggles, and history of flooding. After the haircut, I ate a foot-long sub and then walked to the town intersection to give hitchhiking another try. This time it only took two minutes! Kara, a very kind lady in a convertible, pulled in and offered me a ride to the trailhead, restoring my faith in humanity.

Given my late start, I hiked only 6.3 miles, but half of that was up a fairly steep mountain to Bald Knob, which isn't bald. I tented at Hog Camp Gap, a sprawling grassy meadow, along with Gamel, Jelly and his dog (Peanut Butter), Verge and Legs (really cool sisters), Pantry and his dog, and several others. Pantry earned his trail name by having unquestionably the largest food bag on the AT, with a wide assortment of food, herbs, and spices. My dog, Mandy, was not there, and that's all I want to say about that.

Twenty-five yards from us was an impressive encampment of Boy Scout Troop 27 from Newport News. Just prior to sunset, Scoutmaster Tommy, their leader, walked over and said, "Hey guys, we have plenty of leftover spaghetti and bread if you guys are interested." We looked at each other, grinned from ear to ear, thanked him, and quickly made our way to the Troop 27 encampment. We were like pigs running toward a trough at feeding time. It was Hog Camp Gap, after all, and if aspiring thru-hikers are anything, we are ravenous hogs.

Day 79 – Hog Camp Gap to The Priest Shelter
14.3 miles, 826.7 cumulative miles

"Whoever conceals their sins does not prosper,
but the one who confesses and renounces them finds mercy."
- Proverbs 28:13

With the taste of leftover Boy Scout spaghetti still lingering in my mouth, I headed north toward Maine. At mile 818.2, I crossed the north fork of the Piney River, an area one hiker accurately described as a Yoda marsh due to its swampy, bog-like, moss-covered appearance. Described, he did.

Initially surprised by the large number of day hikers on the trail, I remembered it was Memorial Day weekend. I spoke with several of these clean, smiling people with Fannie packs and answered a few questions about my hike. Passing most of these day hikers on the climbs boosted my ego which had taken an earlier hit when I was passed by a woman and her wiener dog. Along with several other hikers, I stopped and scrambled up the scenic, frequently visited Sky Rock.

By mid-afternoon, rain started to fall. Rather than take on Virginia's steepest descent in the rain, I ended my day at The Priest Shelter atop Priest Mountain. I was joined at the shelter by an assortment of hikers, including Hawaii, Clancy and his dog (Findley), Spaghetti Legs, Gamel, and Pantry.

The Priest is one of the more famous shelters along the AT because of the tradition for hikers to write confessions to "The Priest" in the shelter log book. As the rain fell, I blew up my air mattress in the shelter, exited my wet clothes, and began nibbling on and sharing the dried, salted green peas from the Amish Cupboard in Buena Vista. I spent the next hour reading confessions from the log and writing several of my own. Other hikers confessed to...

- Not digging cat holes (to bury human waste) six inches deep
- Getting another hiker's Nalgene "pee bottle" from a hiker box and using it as a drinking bottle for a month. (One could only hope that the hiker who placed their pee bottle in the hiker box also confessed.)
- Not liking certain other hikers—even hiding in the woods to avoid them
- Not believing in God
- Not having showered or brushed their teeth in several weeks

I added my own dozen confessions, including...

- Attempting to smell southbound women hikers as they pass by, just in case they're wearing perfume
- Fishing without a license in various states along the AT
- Cheating on an 8th grade music test at Caesar Rodney Junior High School. One of the questions involved a series of musical notes written on the chalkboard. We had to figure out the song. While the teacher stepped out of the room for a second, a fellow student hummed the tune which gave me the answer. That has bothered me since 1978. I let it go at The Priest Shelter.

**Fob Fundamental #27 – Regularly confessing
your sins to God opens channels
for His amazing grace to flow.**

Later that evening, I chatted with Hawaii, a mid-20s guy from...well, you can figure it out. We began torturing ourselves by naming the food we most craved. His number one craving was duck, a food introduced to him by his Chinese girlfriend. I went with Outback's Victoria's Filet Mignon with horseradish crust...with a blooming onion, bread and butter, a loaded baked potato, and salad. I count that as one item—deal with it.

We also discussed why, according to Hawaii, older people tend to complete the AT at a higher success rate than the younger, fitter crowd. His answer, based on his experience hiking with many in their 20s, consisted of three main reasons:

1. Younger hikers tend to let their egos go wild and make unwise decisions about mileage, causing injury. They hike for too many miles, too soon, and their bodies don't play along. Older, wiser hikers generally have aged, less fit bodies to work with, and yet they understand how to get more out of their bodies without injury.

2. Younger hikers tend to run out of money, often the result of spending vast sums on beer in trail towns.

3. Many younger hikers begin the trail not having experienced as many hardships in life. They may not have experienced the kind of physical and emotional challenges (e.g., serving in combat, dealing with loss or loneliness, etc.) that tend to harden and toughen those who have.

While I agreed with Hawaii's perspective, there were exceptions. I met millennials on the trail who were as tough as nails from day one, having survived domestic violence, horrific war wounds to the face, and other hardships much more daunting than anything I have endured.

As I laid there in the shelter with rain falling outside, I thought of a few more confessions I should have made. I relieved myself too close to Ottie Cline Powell's memorial, and for that I am truly sorry. I also might have shouted an inappropriate word when I landed on my back and elbow at Dismal Falls.

There's more. Earlier in life, while Janet was shopping, I may have put thick winter gloves and coats on my young sons and had them box each other in our basement. When Jason knocked his somewhat chunky brother down, Kyle lay on his back like a helpless, overturned turtle. Rather than help him up, I may have laughed. And then there was the most unfortunate burial of Mandy. I let it all go. Deep, cleansing breath.

Before dozing off to sleep, I gagged and coughed up a dried, salted Amish green pea onto Hawaii's air mattress. I must confess to reaching over, picking it up, putting it back in my mouth, chewing it some more, and then re-swallowing. I am not proud of what I did. When it comes to confessions, we rarely are.

CHAPTER 12

NORTHERN VIRGINIA TO WEST VIRGINIA –
THE HEADQUARTERS MARCH

May 30 – June 12, 2016

"Accept the pain, cherish the joys, resolve the regrets; then can come the best of benedictions—'If I had my life to live over, I'd do it all the same.'"
- Joan McIntosh

Day 80 – The Priest Shelter to a Stream
17.3 miles, 844 cumulative miles

"I discovered that if one looks a little closer at this beautiful world, there are always red ants underneath."
- David Lynch

I began the day with the steepest descent in Virginia, a 3,100-foot, rock-infested plunge over three miles. At the base, I crossed the Tye River suspension bridge and then reversed the process, climbing 3,000 feet over six miles. Whoever said the AT in Virginia is flat has never hiked the AT in Virginia.

Halfway up the mountain, I caught Gamel. We stopped for a spell at Harpers Creek Shelter. Gamel lost her husband to cancer not long ago. She was honoring him by hiking the AT, rather than sitting at home mourning. As we finished off the last of the dried, salted Amish green peas, I told her I was sorry for her loss, and that I was proud of her for being here doing what she's doing.

Her face lit up and she said, "Thanks, Fob, you are the first person to tell me that!" Her comment reminded me it only takes a few seconds to recognize someone and give them a boost. I had been on the receiving end of such kindness from family, friends, and readers of my blog. I needed to make a greater effort to be a giver of such kindness. I needed to take the previously stated Fob Fundamental #13 to heart.

Our long climb to the top of the mountain was rewarded with a spectacular view from Hanging Rock Overlook. Later, Gamel and several other hikers decided to exit the trail at Reeds Gap and go to a nearby brewery for dinner and to camp. I pressed on and ended the 17.3-mile day camping alone.

After a tortilla with hard salami and sharp cheddar cheese supper, I felt a pain and sharp rumbling in my stomach. I blamed the Amish and their dried peas. Nature was calling and I was the only hiker around to answer. I rarely did my business in the woods these days, as I could usually wait to get to a privy, hostel, or trail town. There would be no waiting tonight.

I grabbed my toilet paper and quickly traveled around some bushes and found a nice, secluded tree 20 yards off the trail. I dropped my shorts and underwear around my ankles and assumed the 90-degree position with my back against the tree. With my recent weight loss, and trail legs firmly under me, I could stay in that position for as long as I needed to—even overnight.

About mid-movement, I happened to glance down and, to my horror, noticed that my left foot was firmly planted in a nest of fire ants! They had built their mound under the leaves I was standing on, and had every intention of defending it. Faced with a contingency I had never considered or prepared for, I did what any other hiker would do—I panicked!

My first instinct was to hop directly toward their position, so I did. Then, as the lead ants established a perimeter on my underwear, another platoon began scaling my left hiking sock toward my bare shin. I took a deep breath and dropped a bomb on their home base, striking the edge of their nest. The impact knocked several off their feet, and completely ruined the day of several others.

As the first ants summited my left sock, I raised that foot and started shaking it, then swung my left hand down to swat them. I hopped again, positioning myself directly over enemy lines, as hundreds of ants emerged from the nest. Just as the first ant stuck his mandibles into my left shin, I carpet bombed them, complete with sound effects. This was Day 3 at Gettysburg, and they were General Pickett. Their scouts were firmly entrenched all over my underwear and shorts now, but the villagers were in a full sprint to avoid the heavy bombardment. Once again, I raised and shook my left foot, and swung my hand down to swat at their "antfantry" maneuvering through my thick leg hair.

My counter-offensive continued for a solid minute—hop, drop, shake, and swat. Collectively, this technique is called *Doing the Fob*. Put it to music, and you have a dance that could be every bit as popular as *The Stanky Leg*. Sometime when you're alone, or with that special someone, give it a try— hop (with half turn), drop (simulate by bending knees and wiggling rump), raise and shake a foot, and then swat your ankle or knee. I found that it worked best while listening to "You Dropped a Bomb on Me" by The Gap Band, or the American Idol classic, "Pants on the Ground."

Out of ordnance, I hopped away from the carnage, swat killed the remaining ants from my drawers, and then cleaned up. Although they inflicted a dozen bites on my left leg, I rendered their entire community uninhabitable. I suspect the survivors will move to Reeds Gap and start over.

Days 81 & 82 – A Stream to Waynesboro
17.3 & 0 miles, 861.3 cumulative miles

Wayne's-boro! Wayne's-boro! Party on, Garth! Excellent! Yes, I was motivated today because my destination was Waynesboro, a popular trail town. Near Humpback Mountain I passed a mother and daughter who were looking for and photographing butterflies. They were having the best time together and it made me miss my family. Jason and Kyle used to love going into the woods with me to photograph butterflies. Not true. Going in the woods—yes. Photographing butterflies—never.

After a 17.3-mile day, I emerged from the woods at Rockfish Gap. Waynesboro, to its residents' credit, has a sign posted where hikers exit the woods and enter civilization. It contains the names and phone numbers of locals who identify themselves as trail angels and are willing to give hikers free shuttle rides to town. I greatly appreciated the handy list and wished all trail towns would follow suit.

The highway ramp ended at a gourmet popcorn vendor's stand. Hungry, sweaty, and tired, I opted for a standard issue hot dog instead of the signature gourmet popcorn. After reviewing the list of trail angels, I called Tom "Southerner" Brown, who said he'd be there in 10 minutes to shuttle me to town.

Southerner welcomed me to Waynesboro and gave me a quick driving tour of the town, pointing out restaurants, the grocery store, laundromat, and other points of interest. He has been giving rides to hikers for more than a decade and is very personable and helpful. Southerner previously served in the Army Reserve, the IRS Criminal Division, and some other security related positions I'm not at liberty to share.

Fresh off my soul-cleansing time at The Priest Shelter, I started to confess to Southerner that on my 2013 federal tax return, I may have overvalued a Goodwill charitable donation. Specifically, the bag of old clothes I donated probably wasn't worth the $30 I claimed. I decided to keep that to myself, so that Southerner wouldn't feel any pressure to make a phone call to his old IRS office on my behalf.

I planned to spend two nights in Waynesboro so I could take a full zero day. I opted to take advantage of a hostel run in the basement of Grace Lutheran. Good call! They opened their doors at 5:00 p.m., took our picture, and told us to set up a cot in their air-conditioned Fellowship Hall. I took full advantage of the showers (best so far on the AT), Wi-Fi, breakfast, and hiker lounge. All this was free, although donations were graciously accepted.

After showering away trail dust, I walked across town to do laundry, re-supply, and eat a terrific Western omelet dinner at Weasie's Kitchen. I looked around for George Jefferson at the restaurant, but he was nowhere to be found!

Other hikers taking advantage of the hostel that night included Gamel, Legs, Verge, Hawaii, and Arrow. While sitting in the hiker lounge thinking the evening couldn't get much better, a fellow hiker popped in a VHS of *The Shawshank Redemption*—one of my Top 5 all-time favorite movies. I sat on the couch with Legs and Verge, two funny and adorable sisters, and a few others, happy to be off the trail for a while and enjoying a great movie with my fellow hikers.

I started my zero day with a wonderful bagel and Oreo cookie breakfast, courtesy of Grace Lutheran. Knowing it's fun to stay there, I headed to the YMCA, hoping for a hot tub. There was no hot tub, but they did provide scales, and I came in at 199.5 pounds—down a whopping 35.1 pounds since starting my journey. I hadn't been under 200 pounds since college in the late 1980s and the new me felt great.

That sub-200 weight wouldn't last for long as I was heading to Ming Garden's all-you-can-eat Chinese buffet. A Chinese gentleman, possibly Ming himself, stood in the corner and watched me down four full plates of food and two desserts. With each return trip to re-load, he eyeballed me, like a spectator at a ping pong tournament. He was losing money on Sir Fob!

After 75 minutes of non-stop eating, I was full to the point of wishing those fire ants would return and mount a final, fatal attack to put me out of my misery. I spent the rest of the afternoon at the Waynesboro public library, digesting, resting, and blogging. I did some research and tracked down John and Linda, a sweet older couple willing to give me a ride to Wednesday evening Bible Study at the Waynesboro Church of Christ.

The congregants were another friendly bunch and I enjoyed my time with them. I knew I would be better off returning to the trail having been fed spiritually, physically, and emotionally. John and Linda not only drove me to the hostel, but stopped at the Cook Out restaurant on the way so I could get a burger and shake to go.

That night, hikers were spread out on cots across the Fellowship Hall in the church basement, chatting, organizing food, and treating battered feet. One young lady shared with me that she was hiking the trail, in part, to get away from an abusive situation at home. She wasn't sure if, or when, she would return home, or how long she would be on the trail. I felt bad for her and tried to offer encouragement.

Our conversation reminded me of a quote, attributed to various men, which reads, "Be kind, for everyone you meet is fighting a hard battle." Aspiring AT thru-hikers were, by virtue of this pursuit, fighting a hard battle. Still, I was reminded that some among us faced battles deeper and harder to win than others.

I called Southerner and he graciously agreed to pick me up in the morning and return me to the trailhead. I went to sleep that night thankful to have stopped in Waynesboro, a trail town that lived up to its lofty reputation. I was also excited to take on the next leg of my journey—the magnificent Shenandoah National Park!

Day 83 – Waynesboro to Turk Mountain Trail
11.2 miles, 872.5 cumulative miles

"Pain is temporary. Quitting lasts forever."
- Lance Armstrong

After eating my second and final breakfast at the hostel, I headed to the Waynesboro library. I was able to FaceTime with Mr. Reeve's and Mrs. Wilkinson's classes at Foundation Christian Academy. I always look forward to talking to these kids. They're so full of energy and questions.

One of the students asked if I had been scared of anything on the trail. So far, I hadn't been scared of any people, wildlife, or the trail itself. I had been frightened climbing the Shuckstack fire tower and dangling my feet over the edge at McAfee Knob. I also had experienced distress trying to find flat spots to tent when big thunderstorms with lightning flashes were bearing down on me.

I hoped that I would be able to return to the school someday and talk to these amazing young people about my successful thru-hike. I also hoped my journey would inspire them to dream big dreams and push the boundaries of their comfort zones. Perhaps someday one of them would grow up and decide to hike the AT.

At 11:00 a.m., Southerner picked me up and returned me to the trailhead. As I was getting out of his truck, he said, "Fob, I've been giving rides to hikers for more than a decade. You've hiked over 860 miles. People who make it this far rarely quit. A family emergency or injury could take you out. But listen—just don't quit." I appreciated his pep talk and thanked him again for the two rides during my time in Waynesboro.

Just don't quit. Just—don't—quit. There was a lot of power and potential in those three simple words. On the trail, there was always a voice in my head giving me a good reason to quit. Whether the voice was a shout, a whisper, or just a buried thought, it reminded me that I was tired, in pain, and homesick, with the prospect for more rocks, biting insects, bitter cold, searing heat, high humidity, and the like.

Fortunately, there was another voice in my head reminding me of the 10 reasons I was on this hike, and each was compelling. Part of my strategy, which had worked so far, was to have the reasons for staying counteract and overwhelm any reasons for quitting. The "stay" voices had to drown out the "quit" voices. So, barring an injury or family emergency, I re-committed to staying. Southerner told me not to quit and I wouldn't. Ever. As a result of re-stating that pledge, the "stay" voices in my head got a little louder.

One mile into today's hike, I filled out a registration form and entered the 103.2-mile long Shenandoah National Park (SNP). If you ever want to get an idea what hiking the AT is like, don't base it on hiking the SNP. Hiking the AT in SNP is more like spending a week at Disney World. For starters, the terrain is fairly easy, with only a few moderate hills. At times, it felt more like walking through an airport on a moving walkway.

On top of that, there are several eateries throughout the park, but they're not cheap. I entered the park with only three days' worth of food and would eventually exit six days later with one day's worth remaining. The park is also full of bears, deer, tourists, and other wildlife. After 862.3 challenging, sometimes grueling, miles on the AT, I was ready for a week of pampering—or so I thought.

Given my late departure from Waynesboro, I managed to hike only 11.2 miles. I passed a couple of SOBOs getting water, along with a day-hiking couple from the Netherlands, who told me a storm was approaching. Moments later, I heard the first rumblings of a massive thunderstorm headed my way. I had about 30 minutes before the storm and sunset would arrive, so I picked up my pace and began looking for a flat spot on which to camp.

With 15 minutes to go until the yellow/red band (severe thunderstorm) on my weather app hit the blue dot (me), I climbed toward Turk Gap as fast as I possibly could. At mile 872.5, the wind picked up, lightning struck nearby, and I felt the first drop of rain strike the middle of my forehead. I was tense, out of breath, and in an increasingly dangerous situation. Heavy rain can make for a miserable day, but one bolt of lightning can kill a hiker.

Unsure of what to do, I stopped in my tracks. I took a deep breath, said a quick prayer, gathered myself, and quickly reviewed my options. It seemed the best option was to immediately get off the trail, go into the woods, and quickly carve out a place to camp. I walked through thick brush and around trees to a borderline acceptable spot, cleared some space big enough for my tent, and set up camp in record time.

Realizing that surviving a thunderstorm does one no good if one is eaten by a bear, I grabbed a few granola bars from my food bag and hung the bag in a nearby tree. As the leading edge of the thunderstorm hit and the heavy rain began to fall, I jumped in my tent and zipped up. A minute later, lighting struck nearby. I can't say how close it was, but there was a deafening flash-bang that rocked my world.

While I was still in danger from a lightning strike or tree falling on me, I felt safe and secure inside my tent. I stripped off all my clothes, blew up my air mattress, and stretched across it. As the heavy rain, thunder, and lightning continued, I laid there in the buff, sweating and eating three granola bars. I thanked God for, once again, providing relative safety, warmth, and comfort inside my tent.

I thought about my first 10 miles in Shenandoah National Park, the supposed Disney World of AT hiking. Should I have vacationed on a cruise ship instead? If lightning strikes my food bag, will my pop tarts be warm in the morning. If I'm struck dead by lightning, will the person who finds me cover my nakedness before dialing 911? I thought about a lot of things that night, but not about quitting. Why? Well, as my friend Southerner might say, you "Just don't quit."

Day 84 – Turk Mountain Trail to Ivy Creek Overlook
20.5 miles, 893 cumulative miles

I awoke bleary-eyed, after a stormy, restless night. While stopping for water near Blackrock Hut, I met a hiker and his injured dog. The dog's paws were torn up from the trail and the hiker was cutting back on miles to give the dog time to heal.

Although I understand a hiker's need for companionship, I am not an advocate of hikers bringing dogs on the AT. Logistically, dogs make everything more difficult—carrying provisions, negotiating rock scrambles, shopping at stores, and staying at hotels. Some sections of the trail, like Great Smoky Mountains National Park and Baxter State Park, don't allow pets. The journey extracts a major toll on the dog physically, as evidenced by this dog's bloody paws. The same is true for hikers, but the dog doesn't get a vote.

Of course, under the principle of "hike your own hike," each hiker chooses whether or not to bring a dog. Moreover, as a hiker who botched the burial of his dear, sweet family pet, I was not in a position to judge others on cruelty to animals.

A half-mile later, I climbed Blackrock, a massive pile of boulders and perhaps the most interesting geological feature in Shenandoah National Park. I was told boulders are there, rather than trees, because the rocks are still shifting positions. Later that day, I took a .5-mile side trail to my first park eatery, the Loft Mountain Wayside. I downed a cheeseburger, fries, and milkshake in under five minutes, got water, and charged my phone.

Partially full and completely happy, I hiked on and crossed Ivy Creek. I entered an area that had been burned by the April forest fire. The fire, second largest in the park's 80-year history, burned 10,326 acres, caused the evacuation of hikers, and temporarily closed Skyline Drive. I stealth camped in this area, finishing a 20.5-mile day. After crawling into my tent, I had a good milkshake belch, breathed in the light smell of burnt forest, and dozed off to sleep.

Day 85 – Turk Mountain Trail to Lewis Mountain Campground
22 miles, 915 cumulative miles

Choosing the most difficult section of the AT in Shenandoah National Park is like choosing the ugliest Dallas Cowboys cheerleader. If pressed, I would go with the section between miles 892.1 and 911.9, which contained enough challenges to put me into a full sweat. I saw a few deer and hikers going in each direction. By then, most hikers had reported seeing at least one bear in the park. So far, I'd only seen large mounds of bear poop.

As I hit the 19-mile mark on the day, I was tired and more rain was approaching. I looked at my guide and saw that the Lewis Mountain Campground and Cabins, featuring a camp store with laundry and showers, were only three miles away. Decision time. Option 1 – immediately stop and camp, stay dry, and rest my tired feet and body. Option 2 – press on, risk getting wet, further tire my body, but reach the campground. My feet voted for Option 1, but they were overruled by the rest of my body. I pressed on and hiked to the campground, just as rain started to fall. This would turn out to be one of two 22-mile days for me, my longest on the AT.

At the Lewis Mountain Campground store, I met the manager, Randy, who has been working there more than 30 years. He is a friendly, outgoing person who loves telling stories and jokes. My first priority was to take my first-ever coin-operated hot shower. Fortunately, I was able to lather and rinse my body and purge the bugs from my beard before my supply of quarters ran out.

As the rain continued to fall, I put in a load of laundry and purchased a Stromboli and a container of chocolate ice cream. As I sat on the porch eating, Tree Beard approached and said, "Hey, Fob, a bunch of us went in on the hiker cabin if you want to join us. It's rustic, and all the bunks are taken, but you're welcome to sleep on the floor or on the covered porch under the picnic table. It would save you from having to tent in the rain." I replied, "Yes! Absolutely! Thank you so much! I'll be over in 10 minutes."

The AT changes perspectives. In the real world, it was so easy to complain if a hotel room temperature was too cool or warm or a church pew was uncomfortable. Here I was, on the AT, absolutely thrilled to be offered a 6-foot by 3-foot section of dirty floor in a small, rustic cabin with five other tired, smelly hikers. The AT changed my perspective and made me appreciate what I had, rather than complain about what I was missing. Incidentally, mission trips to third-world countries have a similar effect, and don't require six months of hiking.

**Fob Fundamental #28 – Ironically, a person
who frequently complains about his life
might actually have too good of a life.
For an attitude and perspective adjustment,
spend time serving the less fortunate…
or living in the woods.**

Several of us sat around the small cabin porch that night telling stories and enjoying each other's company. I met Happy, an older military veteran doing a section hike. We were joined by Arrow, Tree Beard, Waterfall, Pantry, Too Tall, and Tree. Arrow, a short, friendly hiker in her early 20s, is considering a military career, and asked my advice on the differences between the military services, types of jobs within the military, and the pros and cons of military life.

Having grown up as a military brat and then having served a 23-year Air Force career myself, I have some opinions on these subjects. Among other things, I told her the most successful people I knew in the military had two things in common:

1. People skills—the ability to understand, relate to, and get along with people. No one likes to work for or with a self-centered jerk. On the contrary, people who respect you and enjoy working with/for you are generally going to be highly motivated, which makes it easier to accomplish the mission.

2. Communication skills—the ability to sell your ideas through speaking, writing, or giving a presentation. If you have good ideas on how to fix things—how to "work your boss's problems," and you can effectively pitch your solutions, you will stand out from the crowd.

As an Air Force personnel officer, I had given career and other forms of counseling to literally thousands of Airmen and their families through the years. I enjoyed wearing that hat again and trying to help a young lady in the midst of planning her life. I told her to finish her thru-hike, because that feat would look good on a résumé when applying for many different types of jobs and would give her a great sense of accomplishment.

I checked the forecast and saw it was supposed to rain most of the following day. Tree Beard, who was quickly becoming one of my favorite hikers, said, "You know, we could take a zero tomorrow and avoid the rain. One of the nicer, regular cabins is available. If we split the cost, it'd be cheap. Randy, the manager, told me he'd loan me his truck to go into town for some grub and re-supply."

He had me at "zero and avoid the rain." By hiking in the rain almost every day during the month of May, we knew we could do it again. But if we were truly trying to enjoy the journey and not rush, why not call an audible and spend the day hanging with friends, resting the body, and staying dry? Everyone wholeheartedly agreed with Tree Beard's proposal.

Day 86 – Lewis Mountain Campground
0 miles, 915 cumulative miles

"The only normal people are the ones you don't know very well."
- Alfred Adler

I slept well on the floor wedged between Tree and an old wood-burning stove. Tree Beard began the morning on the porch, plotting a strategy. I had already been amazed with the boldness with which hikers ask for things. I knew of a hiker who saw an older woman working on some landscaping and other yard work on the main drag in Hot Springs. He approached her and offered to do any yard work she needed done in exchange for a bed or couch to sleep on. She counter-offered that in exchange for his work, she would pay the $20 fee for his hostel stay that night. Deal! That is how one does the AT on a budget.

I don't know what he said or how he did it, but somehow Tree Beard convinced Randy to loan us his truck not once, but twice! I appreciated Tree Beard's initiative to ask and Randy's kindness to loan us his vehicle. Perhaps after 30 years of running this campground, he had a good sense of who he could trust.

We all piled in the truck and headed to Big Meadows Wayside for a delicious hiker's breakfast. At the gift shop, I got several park postcards for my family. Tree Beard dropped $40 on a red bear onesie with a trap door opening in the back. It reminded me of something Jason, my eldest, would have worn to play intramural softball at Harding University.

We returned to the campground and checked into our new, upgraded cabin. This one had two bedrooms with queen beds and a shared bathroom in the middle. Although it was designed for four people, our plan was to double that number, plus a dog, by bringing in two cots and using the remaining floor space. Tree Beard offered the 8th and final spot to Fire Starter, a rare 30-something hiker. We spent the afternoon resting, reading, napping, blogging, calling family, and snacking.

That evening, we once again piled into Randy's truck as rain started to fall. Tree, bless his heart, volunteered to sit in the bed of the truck and endure the rain for our 20-minute drive to Elkton. I was scrunched in the backseat with two other hikers, including Fire Starter. With our knees jammed next to each other's, Fire Starter told me she was from the Nashville area and graduated from Harding University. Imagine that—the same school from which both of my sons graduated! Meeting her in that setting reminded me that we live in a small world. Here at Shenandoah National Park, you could almost say it's a small world after all.

After a delicious meal at Ciro's Italian restaurant in Elkton, we stopped at a grocery store and then returned to the cabin. Since I slept on the floor the previous night, I qualified for a highly coveted spot on the queen bed. Tree Beard earned the other spot by virtue of having suggested the zero day and for acquiring the use of the truck. Pantry, his dog, and his massive food bag were on the floor. Arrow took a spot on the cot, and the four other hikers were in the adjoining room discussing politics and religion.

As I laid on the bed, Tree Beard emerged from the bathroom wearing only his red bear onesie with a trap door.

Fob: "You're wearing that to bed?"

Tree Beard: "I am. That's what it's designed for."

Fob: "So there's over 4,000 people who will attempt an AT thru-hike this year, and I somehow managed to end up in bed with a guy named Tree Beard wearing a red onesie."

Tree Beard: "You drew the lucky number."

Fob: "Well, I just want to say thank you for getting this cabin for us and convincing Randy to let us use his truck."

Tree Beard: "No problem. It was a good zero day."

{Tree Beard crawled into bed next to me and turned off the light.}

Fob: "Oh, and one other thing."

Tree Beard: "What's that?"

Fob: "Just want to remind you, I'm happily married and you need to keep your trap door shut!"

Tree Beard: "No worries."

Day 87 – Lewis Mountain Campground to Skyland Lodge
16.7 miles, 931.7 cumulative miles

After enjoying a final cup of coffee at the Lewis Mountain Campground store, I headed north on the trail. While approaching the Big Meadows area, I saw a deer laying in the grass off to the right. I stopped for a snack and sat by a tree 15 yards from her. She looked at me but didn't move. I chugged water and retrieved a Clif energy bar. As I did so, the deer stood and stared at me. She had that "Fob, I want a bite of your Clif energy bar" look in her sultry eyes.

She cautiously took a step toward me. With my heart racing, I grabbed my phone and started recording. Next, I violated the principle of "keeping wildlife wild" by extending my Clif bar. Intrigued, she took another step toward me and then another. At this point I should have just left. After all, she should eat only natural food. She should fear humans. She could get spooked and injure me or maybe give me a disease. My head told me this wasn't a good idea. My heart told me it was a once in a lifetime opportunity and I should go for it.

My heart won. I wiggled the Clif bar and she moved closer and closer. Just a foot from me, she stuck her neck out and licked the bar. I wet myself. I didn't have a good grip on the bar and it fell, causing her to jump back a step. Continuing to film, I picked it up and held it out again. She approached and gave it a few more licks. She was so close I could smell her breath. I guess she preferred a different brand, because she backed away. Clif bars are nutritious and delicious, but they require a lot of chewing to get down. Or perhaps she found my breath offensive.

She slowly walked away. It was a really cool wilderness moment that I will never forget. It wasn't the right or textbook thing to do, but it was certainly fun, cool, and memorable. I won't do it again because I've done it once. But would I do it again a first time? Absolutely! These moments don't come along often.

Fresh off this wildlife encounter, I took a short side trail to the Big Meadows Lodge where I had a Caesar salad and seven glasses of pink lemonade. Why? Because I could. This was Shenandoah National Park, the second happiest place on earth—just behind Disney World. I hiked on, passing more deer and snakes, and arrived at the Skyland Resort and Restaurant around 4:30 p.m.

Skyland is an upscale place so I assumed a room would be out of my price range. But since I was close, it was worth a shot. The normal price was well out of my unemployed, RV-living, AT-hiking, fixed income, gypsy price range. The "thru-hiker rate" was substantially less, but still more than I wanted to pay. Then I thought to ask if they had a military rate. Bam! Bada-Bing! It was even less than the hiker rate and within my fair and reasonable range. So, I got a 1-room cabin and took a nice hot shower.

I donned my less funky set of clothes and headed to the Skyland Restaurant for the fried chicken basket (1,807 calories, according to the menu) which included half a fried chicken, garlic mashed potatoes, cranberry relish, and steamed cauliflower. The waitress brought the dessert menu and I selected three large scoops of ice cream--vanilla bean, chocolate, and signature blackberry—which combined for 1,026 calories. I suppose most restaurant patrons use menu calorie counts to manage or limit their food consumption. I, on the other hand, used them to identify the most caloric bang for my buck.

As I swallowed the last bite of ice cream, a guitarist took the stage, sang, and played his guitar for the next couple of hours. He asked the audience where we were from. I didn't answer because I didn't know. It's complicated. My mailing address, voter and car registrations, rental house, and wife were all in four different states…and I was in a fifth! I'm just an American who lives, serves, and hikes in all sorts of places. He then asked the 30 audience members—day hikers, vacationers, and me—who had seen a bear this week. Every single hand went up but mine. That hardly seemed fair.

As I laid in my soft cabin bed that night, I reflected on my near perfect day. Where in the world do you have a close encounter with a deer, a Caesar salad with lemonade, a fried chicken dinner, three scoops of ice cream, live music, a hot shower, and a soft pillow and bed on which to sleep? At Shenandoah National Park, I say, the second happiest place on earth.

Day 88 – Skyland Lodge to Rattlesnake Point Overlook
19.2 miles, 950.9 cumulative miles

"Since it is so likely that [children] will meet cruel enemies, let them at least have heard of brave knights and heroic courage.
Otherwise you are making their destiny not brighter but darker."
- C. S. Lewis

Before getting out of bed, I re-read the letters that had been written by Mrs. Wilkinson's 5th grade class at Foundation Christian Academy. Their assignment was to write a story about Fob on the AT. Allow me to share some excerpts from the creative minds of these young people:

"One day Fob was doing the AT. He heard something in the bush, so he went out to check it out. It was a bear!! The bear swallowed him whole. He stayed in there for five days. The bear threw him up. Fob came out and said, 'It was a good thing I had pepper.' And then he hiked the rest of the AT.

And he lived a happy life til he got eaten by a bear again."
- Jessie, 5th Grader, FCA

"Fob was walking through a soup trail. He was trying to get through the soup but a deer was eating the soup and licked his face. It was made of chocolate. The deer ate Fob's face off and skipped away."
- Karisa, 5th Grader, FCA

Inspired once again by these students, I left my comfortable cabin to face the heat, humidity, and face-eating deer Karisa had just warned me about. Before leaving the Skyland Lodge area, I recalled the 1996 murders of two female hikers, just one-half mile from the lodge. While one is safer on the AT than in a city or on a highway, bad stuff happens from time to time. So, I began with a little prayer asking for my safety today and always.

Near the Pass Mountain Hut, I stopped to get water and use the privy. A fellow hiker standing by the hut looked at me and said, "Hey, you're Fob! Do you know Larry Alexander?" I answered, "Maybe. What did he do?" (Caution should be used when associating oneself with Larry in case any crime has been committed.) The hiker replied, "We have something in common. Larry gave both of us our trail names. I'm called Little Brother now but on the PCT (Pacific Crest Trail) I hiked with Larry for a while and he named me Young Gun. I know through your blog post on Larry's Facebook page that he named you Fob W. Pot." I said, "Wow! It is a small world (after all). Larry is a great dude. His two AT books inspired me to be here. It's great to meet you, Little Brother."

Speaking of inspiration:

"Once upon a time, Fob was in the woods on the AT. He woke up and a bear got his bag! He got up and ran but the bear got away! He was lost with no tent and no food but there was a creek full of clean water. He saw his yellow tent but it was about 7 miles away. He got to his tent but it suddenly burned. I don't know why or even how. He found his food and picked it up and it burned. 'Wow, I can't even make a fire but I burn everything I touch,' he said. He prayed and prayed then God sent angels down. They picked him up and brought him to heaven. He was happy in heaven and he spent his time there worshipping God."
- Brock, 5th Grader, FCA

At mile 943.9, as I descended Pass Mountain, I looked up and saw... (*dramatic pause*) ... (*play Kentucky Derby bugle call*) ... (*all rise as judge enters courtroom*) ... (*drum roll*) ... a BEAR! A real-life Shenandoah National Park black bear! Yes! Finally, I had joined the club of aspiring thru-hikers and every visitor at the Skyland restaurant who'd seen a bear in the wild! No longer would I be made fun of at shelters, campsites and lodge restaurants.

Instinctively, I crouched to one knee and, for just the second time on my journey, raised both trekking poles in the air in the single troop phalanx formation. I bowed my head and whispered, "Spartan, prepare for glory." I had seen *The Revenant* movie and now I was Hugh Glass, about to be charged and mauled by a bear in the wild.

The bear, still 25 yards away, continued to calmly forage for berries and grubs along the trail. She (or maybe he, I didn't check) completely ignored me. Like the attitude of girls at the middle school dances of my youth—I didn't exist. There was not even a warning growl or threatening glance. I eventually stood up, exhaled, and returned my trekking poles to a non-defensive position.

This was not my day to die and for that I was grateful. But a problem remained. The bear was directly in my path, right on the trail, and was taking her sweet time foraging and enjoying the day. I got a little closer for the obligatory photo and video, and then sat on a rock to wait her out. I ate a granola bar, drank water, wiped sweat from my arms and face, and waited. And waited. I started to throw a warning rock or yell, "Excuse me, Winnie the Pooh, hate to bother you...but I'm hiking the AT...trying to survive out here in the wild by living off the land...and I need to get to the next park eatery for a blackberry milkshake before they close. Any chance you could move it along and forage elsewhere?" Of course, only an idiot would have a conversation with a bear.

Eventually, on her own schedule, without regard to my feelings or agenda, she moved her black hairy behind along. I continued northward, but I was a different Fob now, a battle-hardened Fob who had survived a close encounter with a distant, non-threatening, berry-eating wild bear.

"So one day Fob wanted to hike the Aplachin Trail so he did but when he got there he felt a tickle in his backpack so he turned around and saw a bear taking a samwhich so he chased him for awhile and gave up so he saw a deer and tried to get a selfie but the deer hid in the pond and Fob was not happy but he went to get his phone and it fell in and he said why did i do this."
- Aidan L, 5th Grader

Delayed by my near bear attack, I shifted into high gear to reach Elkwallow Wayside before closing. I arrived just in time and ordered a pretzel, grilled cheese, and blackberry milkshake. Why? Because I could. I was in Shenandoah National Park, the second happiest place on Earth. And this is how we roll here—no apologies.

I was joined at the Wayside picnic table by a trio of aspiring thru-hikers: Happy Feet, Pharmacist, and an Idahoan. I enjoyed talking to them. They told me they were hiking *on* Skyline Drive some of the time because it was "more scenic" than the actual AT. They were right, but as a white blaze loving purist, this was like hearing someone's nails scraped across a chalkboard. But, hey, they get to hike their own hike.

As the sky darkened, I ended my day stealth camping near Rattlesnake Point Overlook. After surviving my near wrestling match with a giant black bear, surely I could survive tenting where rattlesnakes come to view the valley below. Before dozing off to sleep, I contemplated and was encouraged by one final statement written by Eian, another Foundation Christian Academy 5th grader: *"Sir Fob will make the hike because God made that his journey."*

Day 89 – Rattlesnake Point Overlook to Front Royal
18.2 miles, 969.1 cumulative miles

About mid-morning I stopped at Gravel Springs Hut to get water and use the privy. Just after exiting the privy, I heard a loud cracking sound and spun around just in time to see a large tree branch fall on the privy! Had the branch fallen three minutes earlier, I would have been trapped inside. Within seconds, my skin would have started to peel. Within minutes, the putrid privy smell would have caused asphyxia-induced hypoxia. Authorities eventually would have found me in a fetal position, moldering away at the bottom of the tank.

I removed the branch and hiked on. Near Little Hogback Mountain and South Marshall Mountain, respectively, I saw my second and third bears. I was a little more confident following yesterday's encounter, so I attempted to pose for a selfie with the second bear. (Do not try this yourself.) However, by the time I got my phone positioned and the angle just right, the bear had scampered off. Thus, I ended up taking the worst bear selfie in history, as there was no bear in the photo! At mile 965.5, I said farewell to Shenandoah National Park. It had lived up to its lofty reputation and my memories of the friendly deer, ferocious bears, and delicious blackberry milkshakes will remain with me forever.

Not quite ready to give up my week of comfortable backpacking, I spent the night at Mountain Home Cabbin (yes, with two b's) near Front Royal. The owners, Scott and Lisa, are extremely helpful and friendly hosts. After Scott thru-hiked the AT, they bought the abandoned, dilapidated historic property and are renovating and restoring various structures.

The property was once owned by Samuel Gardner, a magistrate and horse and cattle farmer. He owned over 3,000 acres and used the hostel where I stayed, which dates to 1847, as slave quarters and later as the tri-county courthouse. Scott and Lisa are still renovating the main house which will one day become an upscale bed and breakfast. Scott shuttled me to town to grab a bite and resupply, and Lisa gave me a great tour of the property and historic buildings.

171

We had a mixture of folks staying at the hostel that night. Four of us were upstairs, including another hiker with a leg injury who would seek treatment in Front Royal. Next to him (in nearby beds) were Matt and Sarah, who were finishing a 3-week long archaeological dig at the nearby Belle Grove Plantation. They were trying to locate the plantation's slave quarters in support of Matt's doctoral work at Syracuse University.

Scott and Lisa were downstairs, since their living quarters in the main house were still being renovated. They were joined by a Fulbright scholar on her way to a conference in Washington D.C. Her future plans are to teach English in Indonesia. Each of these hostel guests were on missions and had compelling stories. Getting to know them certainly enriched my own AT story. I suspect the slaves who once slept in these same quarters also had compelling stories worth knowing.

Day 90 – Front Royal to a Stream
22 miles, 991.1 cumulative miles

"Excellence in any pursuit is the late, ripe fruit of toil."
- W. M. L. Jay

I left the hostel and headed north. There was a massive fenced-in area nearby, which I learned is the Smithsonian Conservation Biological Institute. The 3,200-acre campus houses a variety of endangered species, including the cloud leopard, mane wolf, American bison, and cheetah. As a conservative Christian, I should have been on that side of the fence. Prior to its use for conservation, the area was used to train war horses during World War I.

My priority today was to coordinate a time and place to meet my friends, Darrell and Alicia Brimberry. My wife and I became friends and attended church services with the Brimberrys during my military assignment at the Pentagon. We share a love of the outdoors, and they are planning to thru-hike the AT in 2018 after he retires from the Army.

Their plan was to set up a trail magic station and then Darrell would hike with me for a couple of days. Alicia would then pick us up in Harpers Ferry and take us to their home on Bolling Air Force Base in Washington, D.C. for some rest, recuperation and resupply. Needless to say, I was really excited.

Plan A had them setting up at Manassas Gap, but the timing worked better to shift that northward. I suggested Plan B which involved them setting up at Ashby Gap, mile 989.1. It made sense as the map showed a road crossing the AT. My job was to hike at least as far as Dicks Dome Shelter, so I would be within five miles of their position the following morning. Here, then, are how the best laid plans can unravel.

When I arrived at Dicks Dome Shelter, I called an audible. Rather than face a mile ascent and five-mile hike in the morning, I decided to hike an extra mile. This would shorten my journey the following day and my AT guide showed a spring a mile ahead on Signal Knob. Being nearly out of water, finding some was paramount. So, I climbed the mile to Signal Knob only to discover the spring was completely dry. Not good. Not good at all. Given my increasingly desperate need for water, I had to continue hiking.

A mile later I entered Sky Meadows State Park. It is a beautiful park, but unfortunately camping is not allowed in the park along the AT. There are also no water sources in the park along the AT. Thirsty, tired, waterless, and with no place to camp, I hiked on. A few miles later, I arrived at Ashby Gap, our Plan B meeting point.

The good news—there was a little creek running beside the highway so I was able to get some much-needed water. The bad news—this was a terrible spot for the Brimberrys to do trail magic. It is among the most dangerous, divided highway road crossings on the AT. So, with the sun starting to set, I called Darrell and told him we needed a Plan C, but my priority at the moment was to find a place to set up my tent before it got dark.

Exhausted, I continued northward and eventually found an ideal spot by a stream at mile 991.1, just as it was getting dark. After settling in, I called Darrell. He proposed a new trail magic and rendezvous point at Snickers Gap, about 12 miles north. I agreed, mainly because I heard him say "Snickers." After my difficult, 21.7-mile day, I just wanted to go to sleep— so I did.

My takeaways from the above narrative:

1) It is not easy to coordinate a time and place to meet someone on the AT because there are so many variables. I'm glad the Brimberrys were patient and flexible.

2) A hiker can't always rely on water being available where the AT Guide indicates, unless it is a major source like a river. Thus, I learned to have a backup plan, preferably one that didn't require hiking at night or in bad weather.

3) The butterfly effect is alive and well on the AT. One seemingly small decision, to hike just one more mile, can have a much larger ripple effect, like having to actually hike seven more miles (a bad effect) and discovering the planned rendezvous point needed to be changed (a good effect).

Along those same lines, I considered how my life might have been different had I made different decisions which flipped different levers. According to Romans 8:28, "...*in all things God works for the good of those who love him, who have been called according to his purpose.*" This verse reminds me that if I love God and try my best to live faithfully, he will ultimately bring good outcomes in my life. This is true regardless of the lever flipped, be it the choice of career, college, or mate. I would continue to make bad choices on the AT, and those choices would often have bad consequences. Still, I slept, and continue to sleep, easy at night knowing God is in control and my future with Him is secure.

Day 91 – A Stream to Blackburn AT Center
19.5 miles, 1,010.6 cumulative miles

After getting water near Rod Hollow Shelter, I strapped on my seatbelt and began the famous AT Roller Coaster, a 13.5-mile stretch of non-stop ups and downs. Over dozens of steep, rocky hills, this section has a total elevation gain of more than 5,000 feet. It is Virginia's parting shot to hikers before they cross into West Virginia.

More than halfway up and down the Roller Coaster, I came across a sign marking the 1,000-mile point for NOBO hikers. I had to stop for a moment and let that sink in. I had just hiked 1,000 miles! I took a picture, of course, and said a prayer of thanksgiving. I didn't ask God for anything. I just thanked Him for bringing me this far on the journey without serious injury or incident.

I posted the photo on my Facebook page, and received a comment from Rex Dutton, our former preacher from Florida, which I found quite profound. Rex wrote:

> *"Congratulations! These adventures are going to make an awesome book one day soon. God will work through this journey of yours to do many great things! I have so enjoyed your posts! And for the rest of us who will never accomplish anything so significant, and may feel useless from time to time, I could not help but think about that tree behind you bearing that sign... It has never been anywhere, and yet, there it stands and it still serves an important purpose."*

By "anything so significant," I think Rex was referring to noteworthy, out of the ordinary *physical* feats. I reminded him that preaching over 40 years, as he has done, is an amazing, world-changing accomplishment that far exceeds hiking a trail—even a really long one. I appreciated his final point about the tree holding the sign. No glory. No fanfare. It wasn't the biggest, oldest or prettiest tree on the AT or even that mountain. But it had a purpose—a job to do—and it did that well. By doing its job, it allowed the sign, and the thousands of hikers who would pose in front of it, to get the glory.

I suspect some of those who followed my journey, and perhaps some readers of this book, have felt useless or unappreciated at times. Maybe your life seems boring or insignificant. You may think, "All I do is *(fill in the blank*)." Maybe it has been a while since your boss, customers, parents, children, or spouse have thanked you for who you are and what you do.

Let me remind you, your life has significance because God made you in His image! Your life has significance because Christ made the ultimate sacrifice, giving His own life, to make your salvation possible. God has a plan and a purpose for each of us. According to Ecclesiastes 9:10, "*Whatever your hand finds to do, do it with all your might...*" Whether you are a plumber or teacher, a janitor or doctor, a tree or a sign, be a good one. Do it well. Whether you aspire to hike the AT or just get through the day, know that what you do matters and makes a difference. You are a hero to someone, so keep on keeping on.

Fob Fundamental #29 – Whatever role God has called you to in life, however important or unimportant it may seem, do it well. You are a hero to someone.

By mid-afternoon, I arrived at Snickers Gap. I crossed the road and made my way over to the Brimberry's trail magic station. Alicia ran up and hugged me, which meant she would need to throw her outfit away. I was beyond funky from my AT Roller Coaster ride. The two of them had been there for a few hours, providing drinks, fruit, cookies and other goodies to hikers. A crowd of hikers was partaking of the goodies when I arrived. Alicia had prepared a private cooler of drinks and snacks just for me which made me feel special.

After resting, eating, drinking, and visiting, we said farewell to Alicia, and Darrell and I headed northward. For the first time in my journey, I was hiking with a long-time friend. He was eager and fresh, mostly because he had missed 12 miles of the Roller Coaster that morning. I enjoyed hiking with him and getting caught up on his children, career, and future plans. Not surprisingly, he had several AT-related questions as he continues to prepare for their 2018 thru-hike. At mile 1,005.7, we stopped for a photo at the sign telling us we were crossing into West Virginia, my 5th state on the AT!

After a 19.5-mile day for me, we stopped for the night at Blackburn AT Center. It wasn't a challenging first night on the trail for Darrell, as we were offered big bowls of soup by the caretaker and slept on the Center's large screened-in porch. It had been an interesting couple of days, featuring a 1,000-mile marker, trail magic stop, roller coaster, border crossing, and multiple changes of plans. Ultimately, God worked everything out, as I knew He would. I was especially thankful He saw fit to provide me a good friend to hike with, if only for a couple of days.

Day 92 – Blackburn AT Center to Bolling Air Force Base, Washington, D.C.
12.5 miles, 1,023.1 cumulative miles

"Hey, Fob, the coffee's ready when you are," Darrell whispered just inches from my face.

I slowly opened my blurry eyes and tried to focus them. Darrell's eyes seemed disproportionately large for his face and his voice was disproportionately eager for someone over the age of seven. Before responding, I looked at my watch. It was 4:37 a.m. That's early—even for AT hikers. Really early. It was so early that it was almost yesterday. There are clearly differences between an active duty Army colonel on his first morning on the AT and a retired Air Force colonel on his 92nd AT morning.

I didn't know whether to thank Darrell for alerting me about the coffee, or stab him in the temples with my carbide-tipped trekking poles. Not wanting to squash his enthusiasm for the AT, void the warranty on my poles, or hurt my good friend, I half-heartedly thanked him for waking me in order to enjoy fresh coffee. I was sure it would taste good after I slept four more hours.

Shortly after 7:00 a.m., Morning Coffee (Darrell's temporary trail name) and I left Blackburn AT Center, along with a hiker named Hammer. Just as we got on the trail, I asked Morning Coffee if he would lead the three of us in prayer and he obliged. (Back in March, just before getting on the AT, I received a call from Darrell and he said a prayer over the phone with me. After 1,000 miles of hiking, it made sense for him to say another one.)

The morning hike was mostly flat, but the heat and humidity were unbearable. I didn't have a lot of energy. This may have been a result of hiking a combined 80 miles, including the Roller Coaster, over the previous four days. Or maybe it was my 4:37 a.m. wake up call. We enjoyed hiking with and talking to Hammer about his past business successes and difficulties, along with politics, religion and other topics.

By mid-afternoon, we crossed into West Virginia again and made our way toward Harpers Ferry. It had only been a 12.5-mile day, but I was exhausted, completely soaked, and the most private crevice in my body was chafing. We stopped for a photo at Jefferson Rock, where Thomas Jefferson once stood with a gorgeous view of the Shenandoah River just prior to its confluence with the Potomac River. We then headed down the hill into downtown Harpers Ferry, where a smiling Alicia awaited us.

Our next stop was the Appalachian Trail Conservancy Headquarters which, unfortunately, was .6-miles uphill. That may not seem far for a long-distance hiker, but I was completely spent and had two miniature loggers in my underwear sawing my butt crack with sandpaper. After trudging along behind Morning Coffee and Alicia for 50 yards, I saw a woman exit a car parked on the side of the road. She said, "Hey, Fob, it's Kailah! Wanna ride?" I started to ask, "Is there room for two miniature loggers?" but thought better of it.

Kailah, in addition to being a sweet trail angel, is the niece of Chuck and Jana Leasure, friends from our Virginia days. I met Kailah years ago at a wedding. She had been keeping up with my AT journey and knew about when I would be arriving to Harpers Ferry. She figured I might want a ride up that hill. She figured right!

Kailah handed me an ice-cold Gatorade (pure magic), a bag of snacks, and some unnecessary but appreciated lunch money. I thanked her from the bottom of my heart and invited her to lunch. Unfortunately, she was on her way to a wedding and had to decline. While exiting her car, she wished me well and told me to finish strong. If I finished at all, it would be because of people like her, the Brimberrys, and others who came along at just the right time to meet a need. Serendipity? No, that's God's providence.

Despite my exhaustion and being drenched in sweat, I excitedly marched into ATC Headquarters with the Brimberrys and the miniature loggers in my underwear. (A point of clarification: Only the loggers were in my underwear.) Although I am more into actual halfway points than psychological ones, it felt special being at Harpers Ferry. I had been at the Headquarters a decade earlier with Janet, and told her I would be back some day as an aspiring thru-hiker. Today was that day. I had my photo taken and signed the hiker book with my information. I was northbound hiker #607. Ninety-two days to Harpers Ferry wasn't bad for a 50-year-old who had taken two weeks off for a wedding and a spousal rendezvous.

The Brimberrys and I invited Hammer and another hiker named Pocahontas to have dinner with us at a nearby Italian restaurant. Upon arrival, I headed to the restroom to rinse the loggers and sandpaper from my nether regions and to apply a copious amount of Gold Bond. It stung in a good way, like watching your final child graduate and leave the nest. I changed into a clean set of Morning Coffee's clothes that Alicia was thoughtful enough to bring me.

We headed to the Brimberry's lovely home on Bolling Air Force Base where the magic continued. I took a hot shower and then a cold one and then a hot bath. It was not just any hot bath, but a bubble bath, featuring bath bubbles from *Frozen*, the movie. I laid back and closed my eyes, feeling extremely blessed to be in that place at that moment. After dozing for a few minutes, I opened my eyes and *Frozen's* Elsa was staring at me from the bubble container at the other end of the tub. Like Morning Coffee recently, her eyes seemed disproportionately large for the rest of her head. I didn't appreciate her bug eyes staring at my fobness, so I leaned up and turned the bottle around. Little *Frozen* creep.

After my long, hot bubble bath, I stepped on the scales and weighed 192.5 pounds. I had lost 44 pounds and was now at my college weight. I knew Janet would tell me to eat more, and she did. The gorging began moments later as I feasted on a magnificent steak dinner, courtesy of Team Brimberry! Janet's instructions to Alicia involved feeding me almost non-stop for the next 32 hours. Thus, I would leave the Brimberry's home having gained six pounds.

As I laid in a soft, comfortable bed that night, I read the Father's Day cards from my family. It was a great ending to an enjoyable day with two very special people.

Day 93 – Bolling Air Force Base, Washington, D.C.
0 miles, 1,023.1 cumulative miles

Day 93 was a special zero day because I would be worshipping at the Manassas Church of Christ where Janet and I were members from 2004-2008. I was excited to see many familiar faces and reconnect with brothers and sisters in Christ. After services, I went to lunch with the Brimberrys, Leasures, and Paul and Trish Johnson. I enjoyed being with long-time friends and eat a filling pasta meal. I also appreciated the two bags of home-made cookies that Jana Leasure gave me.

That evening we returned to Bolling Air Force Base for my final night of pampering. I got my laundry together and made a few gear and clothing adjustments. Since I hadn't used my stove in a couple of weeks, I left it behind. While I enjoyed cooking at night when it was cold, I didn't feel as motivated to cook in hot, humid weather. Unlike many hikers, I was perfectly content to go weeks eating only tortillas with salami and cheese, or tortillas with peanut butter and honey or coconut oil. No stove meant a quicker dinner and not having to clean up afterwards. Also, not carrying a stove and fuel would save weight and space in my backpack. I also left behind my gloves, thick socks, and puffy winter jacket, which would eventually be sent to me with the stove when it started to get cold again.

Alicia and Morning Coffee had a final surprise up their sleeves. They set up a vibrating, heated, bubbly foot bath in the living room, which made me consider quitting the trail and moving in with them. As I sat relaxing and soaking, I downed two large bowls of Corn Pops. I read a Facebook message from Larry Alexander, congratulating me on making it halfway and offering advice for the second half of my journey.

Just before going to bed, Morning Coffee gave me some great news. We could sleep in and didn't need to leave until 8:00 in the morning! He seemed less eager than before, and his eyes were in proportion to the rest of his head. I might start calling him Darrell again.

178

To Be Continued in...

Sir Fob W. Pot's Journey to Katahdin, Volume II

Thank you for joining me on the first-half of my incredible, life-changing journey to Katahdin. I encourage you to take a break, get a bite to eat, and rest up. You'll need your energy as you lace up your hiking boots and join me again for the remainder of my journey in Volume II. For wildlife lovers, you'll experience riveting encounters with mice, bears, and moose. For people lovers, you'll meet a whole new cast of interesting characters, and learn the fate of some familiar ones. For AT lovers, get ready to take on Pennsylvania's foot-crushing rocks, New Hampshire's formidable White Mountains, and Maine's remote 100-Mile Wilderness. Fob's goal: Katahdin. Fob's pathway: the Appalachian Trail. Are you ready for your next adventure?

For more information on the release of Volume II, and to see photos from my journey, check out my Facebook author's page at: https://www.facebook.com/authorstevejohnson/

Appendix

Appendix A – Gear List

The Big Three

Big Agnes Fly Creek UL2, with footprint – 34.4 ounces; ultra-light, 3-season, freestanding, double wall tent. Technically a 2-person tent, but better suited for a large solo hiker + gear.

    Pros: Ultra-light, quick set up, kept me dry.

    Cons: Small vestibule, which allowed some rain in when entering or exiting tent in the rain. Floor seepage on a few occasions in heavy rain when the ground/platform underneath didn't drain well.

ULA Circuit Backpack with pack cover – 41 ounces; 4,200 cubic inches (68 liters) in total volume.

    Pros: Lightweight, durable, very comfortable, large hip and belt pockets.

    Cons: None, unless one plans to carry heavier loads.

Western Mountaineering Alpinlite – 33 ounces; 20-degree, 850-fill down sleeping bag.

    Pros: Warm, roomy, breathable, comfortable, compressible.

    Cons: Very expensive, but worth every penny.

Other Gear & Stuff

Sea to Summit Reactor Thermolite Mummy Bag Liner – polyester, insulated sleeping bag liner which added up to 15 degrees of warmth to my sleeping bag and helped keep it clean. I also used it alone as a warm weather sleeping bag.

Therma-a-Rest NeoAir XTherm Sleeping Pad – inflatable, soft, warm, and comfortable. Only complaint: it was quite noisy whenever I moved/rolled over on it.

Leki Corklight Trekking Poles – adjustable, sturdy; anti-shock system; comfortable cork handles. Could be used to spear trout.

Duct Tape – Tim DeBoef, a friend of mine, once told me that success in life is mostly a result of "duct tape and prayer." I believe him. I kept strips of tape around each trekking pole and used them on several occasions.

Black Diamond Spot Headlamp - lightweight, very bright, dimmable, multiple modes.

Sawyer Squeeze Water Filter – light, compact, easy to use.

Platypus Water Bladder (2 Liter), x2, a primary and backup. I typically used half of a Gatorade bottle to scoop water from the water source, then poured into this bladder, and then filtered the dirty water into my water bottles using the Sawyer Squeeze.

Potable Aqua Chlorine Dioxide Water Purification Tablets – Plan B in case water filtered failed. Never used.

MSR Pocket Rocket with MSR IsoPro fuel – simple, compact, and lightweight canister stove. Boiled a liter of water in less than four minutes.

Only cooked during my first two months and final month on the trail.

Fire Starters – Bic lighter x2, 24 matches in waterproof case, and a UST Mini-Flint Sparker. I only used the Bic lighter.

Snowpeak Trek 900 Titanium Cookset - set includes a 30-fl. oz. titanium pot, a small titanium fry pan and a nylon mesh storage sack; fry pan doubles as a pot lid. Stored fuel insight pot. Used fry pan lid to cover pot during cooking, but not for frying. Only complaint is that the fry pan/pot lid did not fit securely on the pot.

Snowpeak Titanium Cup – Used this light, but expensive item a few times early in my hike to heat instant coffee. Sent home at Harpers Ferry.

Snowpeak Titanium Spork – for eating; could also be used as a shank to kill wolverines or loud snorers. The 6.5-inch length was acceptable, but I wish I had gone with a longer one to more easily reach food at the bottom of freeze-dried food pouches.

Classic SD Swiss Army Knife – I resisted the urge to buy a big, cool, unnecessary hunting knife. This small, 7-function, lightweight knife had all I needed. I primarily used it to cut and shape moleskin and slice salami.

Glasses and sunglasses (both prescription), contact lenses with solution – Regular glasses with transition lenses were sufficient. Sent sunglasses home at Harpers Ferry. Kept contact lenses as emergency backup, but never used them.

Triple-A Batteries – extra for headlamp and flashlight.

Shammy – multi-use towel—cleaned pots, wiped off tent, dried tears, etc.

AWOL's Guide to the AT, **by David Miller** – full of useful information on shelters, elevations, towns, water sources, etc. I used this guide every evening to take notes on the day's events and plan for the following day. I had this in hard copy and another guide downloaded on my phone as a backup.

Guthook's Hiking Guide – While I used *AWOL's Guide* primarily in the evening, I used the Guthook iPhone app throughout the day to gain situational awareness on my location, elevation, next water source or shelter, and myriad other information. Do not hike the AT without this app on your smart phone.

Pen with small light – used for note-taking at night, writing in shelter journals, and writing sentimental, heartfelt letters to my wife.

50' Utility Cord + Small Stuffsack + Carabiner – used together, with a rock, to hang food bag (**OPSAK Barrier Bag** inside **Sea to Summit Ultra-Sil 20L Drysack**), on a high enough tree branch so bears wouldn't get it.

Trash Compactor Bag – lined the backpack, providing an extra layer of water protection for clothes bag and sleeping bag. One bag lasted the entire journey.

Fishing Gear – one spool of fishing line, two bobbers, five hooks, and five lead weights.

Gold Bond Extra Strength Medicated Body Lotion – used regularly and copiously to combat chafing, which I feared more than bears. This was a result of psychological trauma from literally chafing my nipples off during the 2007 Marine Corps Marathon. At the finish line, a young Marine handed me a medal and two Band-Aids. Fortunately, they regenerated like salamander legs. By that, I mean both processes involve regeneration—not that salamander legs grew where my nipples once were. I digress.

Toiletries

Small toothbrush and toothpaste, wet wipes, small hand sanitizer, earplugs, toenail clippers, and Chap Stick w/ SPF protection. In lieu of toilet paper, I began the hike using only sage leaves and pinecones, a technique recommended by my trail mentor, Larry Alexander. He suggested I learn this technique on my own, preferably in a quiet, wooded area far from camp, while listening to Pink Floyd's *The Dark Side of the Moon*. By the third week, I switched to more conventional toilet paper, and carried one-third to one-half of a roll with me the rest of the way.

First-Aid & Medicine

Items taken and used at least once: Band-Aids, moleskin, blister pads, athletic tape, Neosporin, DEET Insect Repellent, razor blade, needle (to pop blisters), tweezers (for tic removal), Vitamin I (Ibuprofen), and Tums. Items taken but never used: Gauze pads, sterile bandages, Imodium, antihistamine, sting and bite pad, acetaminophen, Nexium.

Clothing & Shoes (worn or placed inside REI 15L Drysack)

Columbia Zero Rules Short Sleeve Shirt – super-cooling tech tee, polyester wicking fabric, UPF 30 sun protection, antimicrobial treatment.
American Backcountry Short Sleeve Shirt – polyester, moisture wicking, manufactured by Vapor Apparel. Although this blue shirt with a white AT blaze on the front was an impulse buy at the Amicalola Falls Visitors Center, I ended up wearing it almost every day. I also had "Fob" ironed on it.
ExOfficio Triflex Hybrid Long Sleeve Shirt – durable, comfortable, quick drying.
Patagonia Capilene 2 Lightweight Crew Top & Capilene 2 Lightweight Bottoms – quick drying, highly breathable, moisture-wicking polyester; synthetic base layer top & bottom; 20-UPF sun protection. Used these as pajamas and as an added layer of insulation in extremely cold weather.
Patagonia G1 III Zip Off Pants – tough, lightweight, nylon-taslan pants with zip-off legs; durable water repellent finish and 50+ UPF sun protection.

Northface Paramount II Cargo Shorts – abrasion-resistant midweight nylon; large cargo pockets with secure Velcro closures.

Marmot Essence Rain Jacket – waterproof, breathable; attached hood, integrated cooling vents; chest pocket. Worked well in wind and rain. Used alone or in combination with any of the above shirts, depending on conditions.

Northface Venture Full-Zip Rain Pants – waterproof, breathable, full-zip pants. Worked well in wind and rain. Used alone or in combination with any of the above pants/shorts, depending on conditions.

Mountain Hardwear Hooded Ghost Whisperer – ultralight (2.1 ounces) nylon insulating jacket; wind and water-resistant. Wore it mostly around camp in cold weather.

Darn Tough Vermont Men's Merino Wool Socks (2 pairs) – Comfortable, well cushioned, moisture wicking.

REI Smartwool Merino Wool Sock Liners (2 pairs) – soft, silky merino wool blended with stretch nylon for durability and a good fit; helped minimize blistering.

Smartwool Hunting Heavy Crew Socks (1 pair) – Warm, comfortable, cushioned. Mainly used around camp, especially in cold weather.

ExOfficio Underwear (2 pairs) – soft, durable, breathable, moisture wicking; 1 for hiking; 1 for camp.

REI Smartwool Balaclava – soft, snuggly, pure merino wool. Kept the head/face warm while hiking or at camp.

REI Buff – helped keep sweat off face and prevent sunburn.

Outdoor Research Versaliner Gloves – Breathable, 100-weight fleece insulating liner and removable waterproof ripstop fabric shell. Kept my hands warm enough on all but about the three coldest days on the trail.

Oboz Sawtooth Mid Hiking Boots – lightweight, waterproof, comfortable out of the box. Wore these for the first 634 miles on the AT, where they provided extra ankle protection in the early GA/NC Mountains. Despite some early blisters and foot pain issues, these boots served me well.

Salomon XA Pro 3D Trail-Running Shoes – Synthetic mesh uppers/lining, EVA midsole, rubber outsole. Comfortable, durable, quick drying. These things are beasts and, according to a hiker survey, were the most popular footwear on the AT in 2016. I wore three different pairs, beginning at Pearisburg, Virginia, mile 634.

Spenco PolySorb Walker/Runner Insoles – probably unnecessary, given the quality Sawtooth insoles. Switched to green **Superfeet** insoles in Damascus. Did not wear any additional insoles with my Salomons.

Crocs – lightweight camp shoes. Switched to **Vivo Barefoot Ultras** in Virginia because they are lighter, better looking, and cinch-able. The ability to cinch them would come in handy during river crossings further up north.

Under Armour Fishhook Cap – helped prevent sunburn and keep rain off eyeglasses.

Coghlans Mosquito Head Net – worn over ball cap; it proved to be invaluable in heavy bug traffic areas. Could also be used to strain pasta noodles.

Chums Surfshorts Wallet – lightweight, durable ripstop nylon.

Food and Water

1-Liter Smartwater Bottles x2 – durable, fit nicely in backpack side pockets, easily replaceable. I generally carried two full bottles, although I'd adjust upward or downward depending on the projected distance to and reliability of the next water source.

Food – although a bit more expensive, I re-supplied in the towns along the trail, rather than sending multiple mailings to post offices along the way. I liked not being tied to a post office schedule, e.g., needing to hike 25 miles in the rain to get to the post office before it closed for the weekend. I also liked the flexibility of buying whatever type of food I was hungry for in that town, versus packaged food assembled months earlier. Thus, I paid a bit more for food, but that was offset by not having to pay for multiple mailings.

Loksak Garbage Bag – to pack out garbage.

Electronics

iPhone 6 w/ charger – used as a phone, camera, note taker, e-book reader, weather forecaster, and music player.

Mophie 3X Powerstation – external battery, 2.4 amp, 6,000 mAh; provided three full charges for the iPhone. My iPhone never died.

Yurbuds Ironman Earphones – because not everyone wanted to hear my playlist.

Casio ProTrek Titanium Solar Watch – among other functions, had a compass, altimeter, thermometer, and barometer. As an added bonus, this watch tells the time.

The above checked in at 21 pounds of base weight, and another 7-12 pounds of food and water depending on distance to the next resupply town and water source. This list doesn't constitute the "best gear" or the "right gear" for anyone else. All I can say is it worked for me.

Appendix B – Study Guide

Fob Fundamental #1 – To achieve a challenging goal, the anticipated pleasure associated with achieving it must be greater than the anticipated pain. (Refer to page 10.)

Scripture to Consider: Philippians 3:13-14

Discussion Questions:
1. Why did Fob write down and memorize his 10 main reasons for wanting to hike the AT? Which of those 10 do you think were the most motivational for him? Why?
2. In Philippians 3:13-14, Paul pursues his goal by straining toward what was ahead, and remembering the prize that awaited him. What was that prize? What pain did Paul experience in his life, and how do you think he would balance the pain with his ultimate reward?
3. What are the top few goals you want to achieve in life? For each one, make a list of the pleasure and pain you would anticipate in your pursuit or achievement of the goal.

Fob Fundamental #2 – God can take even the smallest gifts and turn them into something grand and wonderful. (Refer to page 14.)

Scripture to Consider: Mark 12:41-44

Discussion Questions:
1. How might the story have turned out differently if Fob's widow friend had not donated $10 toward the adoption?
2. In Mark 12:41-44, what does it mean that the widow gave "*out of her poverty*"?
3. Describe a time when you have either sacrificially given a gift or been on the receiving end of such a gift. How did it make you feel?

Fob Fundamental #3 – The first step toward a major goal is often the most difficult. Dig deep, take the first step, and your momentum will make subsequent steps a little easier. (Refer to page 22.)

Scripture to Consider: Psalm 37:23-24

Discussion Questions:
1. Why do some consider the first step on the Appalachian Trail the most difficult? What had Fob done prior to the first step to make it

a little easier?

2. In light of Psalm 37:23-24, who orders, or firms up, the steps of a good, faithful man? How should knowing that give one confidence in taking the first, and subsequent, steps toward any goal? For those who fear stumbling, how does this passage provide reassurance?

3. For each of the goals you listed in Fob Fundamental #1, what is the first step you can take to achieve that goal?

Fob Fundamental #4 – Oftentimes the best response to a kind gesture is simply to smile and humbly say thank you. (Refer to page 28.)

Scripture to Consider: Luke 17:11-19

Discussion Questions:
1. Why do you think Fob felt the need to give Sticks $5? What does it mean that by doing so, Fob had turned the magic into a transactional event?

2. In Luke 17, only one of the 10 cleansed lepers returned to thank Jesus and glorify God. According to the text, and your imagination, what other priorities might have interfered with the other nine lepers returning to thank Jesus?

3. When you do a big favor for someone, do you prefer a tangible gift in return or a simple thank you? Do you think one's response to that question changes as he or she gets older?

Fob Fundamental #5 – Take the time to tell your story. You never know how it might lift someone's spirits, change his day, or even his life. (Refer to page 35.)

Scripture to Consider: Luke 8:26-39

Discussion Questions:
1. Why do you think the injured Marine in the story chose to hike the Appalachian Trail? How might his list of reasons have differed from Fob's list?

2. In Luke 8:39, Jesus tells the demon-possessed man he had just healed to, "*Return home and tell how much God has done for you.*" What impact might his testimony have had on his family and those in the city in which he lived? How might the world be changed if Christians simply told their friends and neighbors about the great things God has done for them?

3. Describe a time when hearing someone's story encouraged, motivated, or inspired you?

Fob Fundamental #6 – Pick and choose your cultural battles carefully. Sometimes it's best to remain silent, digest your food, and keep peace at camp. (Refer to page 38.)

Scripture to Consider: 1 Peter 3:15-16

Discussion Questions:
1. In the scene at Deep Gap Knob Shelter, Fob chose to remain quiet, even though he disagreed with some of the political/cultural ideas being shared. What are the pros and cons of remaining silent and of speaking out?
2. According to 1 Peter 3:15-16, how are we to answer those who ask us for the reasons for our hope in Jesus?
3. If you were in Fob's situation, would you have spoken up and given your opinion? What if the conversation and your disagreement had not been over politics, but over religion, sports, or your favorite food?

Fob Fundamental #7 – God is in and over all things for the purpose of our good and to His glory. From an eternal perspective, things will ultimately work out well for those who love and obey Him. As a result, we can rest. (Refer to page 42.)

Scripture to Consider: Romans 8:28

Discussion Questions:
1. Do you believe the good things that happened to Fob were a result of the providential hand of God or simply serendipitous good luck? Why?
2. In Romans 8:28, what does it mean that in all things *"God works for the good of those who love him, who have been called according to His purpose."*? How can a Christian experience great hardship and suffering in this life, and yet ultimately be blessed?
3. Describe a time when something happened to you that you initially thought was good but it turned out to be bad? How about a time when something happened that you initially thought was bad but ultimately turned out for your good? Describe a time when something happened you though was coincidence, but after further reflection, decided it was God's providence.

Fob Fundamental #8 – To get through a tough section of trail, or life, focus on doing the next right thing. Put one foot in front of the other, and remember the pain is temporary and things will eventually get better. (Refer to page 45.)

Scripture to Consider: Hebrews 12:2

Discussion Questions:
1. In the snowstorm and frigid temperatures near Bly Gap, what did Fob think and do to help him endure this hardship?
2. Hebrews 12:2 tells us that Jesus *"endured the cross"* by focusing on the *"joy set before him."* What was the future joy that Jesus was anticipating?
3. Think of a current hardship or difficult situation you're going through. What is the "next right thing" you can do? How might taking a 10 or 20-year perspective change the way you see the challenge? How might God use your situation to ultimately bring about good?

Fob Fundamental #9 – You will eventually see every person you know one final time. Since you don't know when that time will come, leave nothing unsaid and leave no kindness undone. (Refer to page 50.)

Scripture to Consider: Colossians 3:12

Discussion Questions:
1. If you had been on the shuttle, would you have handled Fob's conversation with Baltimore Jack any differently? How would knowing or not knowing about his impending death have influenced your approach?
2. Fob spent a year acquiring specific clothes to wear on the trail. According to Colossians 3:12, with what other things should God's chosen people clothe themselves?
3. Do a mental inventory of your family, friends, co-workers, and others with whom you regularly come in contact. If you knew that you were about to see each of them one final time, what would you tell them? Since it's rare to receive an advanced notice of that nature, what's keeping you from going ahead and sharing those thoughts before it's too late?

Fob Fundamental #10 – If you want to establish credibility and truly have your message hit home, practice what you preach. (Refer to page 51.)

Scripture to Consider: 1 John 3:18

Discussion Questions:
1. In their treatment of Fob, how did John and Linda practice what John was about to teach? Contrast their treatment of Fob, a stranger, with Fob's treatment of Baltimore Jack, also a stranger.
2. According to 1 John 3:18, how are we to love?
3. Describe a time when your parent, teacher, or preacher taught one thing but lived contrary to it. How did their actions undermine their words?

Fob Fundamental #11 – God's gift of His son, Jesus, is like any other gift in that it can be opened, enjoyed, and its blessings reaped...or left unopened. (Refer to page 57.)

Scripture to Consider: Romans 6:23

Discussion Questions:
1. What would it be like to be a traveling missionary on the AT like Fob's friend, Stone? In what sense are all Christians traveling missionaries?
2. According to Romans 6:23, what is the gift of God? What are the benefits for, and burdens on, those who choose to open that gift? What are the consequences of choosing to leave it unopened?
3. Have you ever given a gift that was rejected or not appreciated? How did that make you feel? Do you think God feels the same way whenever someone rejects His most precious gift?

Fob Fundamental #12 – To overcome your greatest fears, focus on being brave for just the most critical 20 seconds. (Refer to page 60.)

Scripture to Consider: Joshua 4:14-17

Discussion Questions:
1. Do you agree with Ralph Waldo Emerson's statement, "Do the thing you fear, and the death of fear is certain."? What are some of the things Fob did to overcome his fear of heights?
2. In Joshua 4, priests carrying the large, heavy, extremely valuable ark of the covenant had to step out into the Jordan River. Given that it was harvest time of year, why would it have been important for them to dig deep and find "20 seconds of courage"?

3. List the top two or three fears that you'd like to overcome. For each one, what would be the most critical 20 seconds in your attempt to overcome it?

Fob Fundamental #13 – Never underestimate the power of your words to motivate, encourage, or inspire someone. If you recognize talent or potential in a person, by all means let them know. (Refer to page 65.)

Scripture to Consider: Deuteronomy 31:7-8

Discussion Questions:
1. Why do you think Booknboot took the time to encourage Fob to write a book? What does that say about her character?
2. In Deuteronomy 31:7-8, Moses, just prior to his death, offers some powerful, encouraging, and motivating words to Joshua, his successor. What was the most important thing Moses said to him? How do you think these words impacted Joshua?
3. What is the most motivating or life-changing thing a person has ever said to you? Who is someone in your circle of influence that you could similarly encourage or inspire?

Fob Fundamental #14 – Nothing binds soldiers, teammates, friends, or hikers more quickly than overcoming adversity together. (Refer to page 66.)

Scripture to Consider: Ruth 1:1-18

Discussion Questions:
1. Why do you think Fob and his traveling companions became friends so quickly in the Smokies? What is it about facing adversity or a common enemy that tends to bring people together?
2. In Ruth 1, what common adversity did Naomi and her two daughters-in-law face? According to verses 16-17, how did the situation affect Ruth's relationship with Naomi?
3. Describe a difficult situation in your life that brought people together. Would those involved have become as close had they not shared a common adversity?

Fob Fundamental #15 – Do as much as you can, as often as you can, to make those around you feel like rock stars. (Refer to page 70.)

Scripture to Consider: 1 Thessalonians 5:11

Discussion Questions:

1. Why do you think Fob and the others received "rock star" treatment at Newfound Gap? Compare and contrast that situation with the one he experienced as a deploying troop at Bangor International Airport.

2. 1 Thessalonians 5:11 commands us to *"encourage one another"* and *"build each other up."* How does encouragement build someone up? How does building someone up encourage them?

3. Describe a time someone made you feel like a rock star. Is there someone in your life you could encourage to the point of making them feel like a rock star?

Fob Fundamental #16 – It's possible to get to know and become friends with someone through many short, casual conversations over the course of several years. To short-circuit that process, have a five-hour uninterrupted conversation with them. (Refer to page 75.)

Scripture to Consider: Acts 20:7-11

Discussion Questions:

1. How was Fob affected by the long conversations he had on the AT? How would making friends quickly be helpful to an AT hiker?

2. In Acts 20:7-11, Paul visited the people of Troas and spoke to them *"until midnight"* and then again *"until daylight."* Why would Paul have invested so much time in talking to these people? Not counting Eutychus, who died, what impact do you think Paul's words had on the people?

3. Have you ever had a really long conversation with someone? If so, did you gain new insights on the person? Were you able to go deeper on certain subjects than you would have in shorter, more casual conversations?

Fob Fundamental #17 – To really understand the joy of giving...while a present is being opened, focus not on the face of the recipient, but on the face of the giver. (Refer to page 80.)

Scripture to Consider: Acts 20:35

Discussion Questions:

1. Why do you think giving his leftover pizza to two hikers brought Fob so much joy? In general, who do you think ends up happier— the hiker who receives trail magic or the trail angel who provides it?

2. Paul quotes Jesus in Acts 20:35 because he wants them to

remember to do what for whom?

3. Do you recall a Christmas where you were more excited about the presents you gave than the ones you received? How does a grateful recipient impact you as a giver?

Fob Fundamental #18 – As Christians, we're called to change the world by being salt and light. We're not called to judge—to bring fire and brimstone, as that is God's domain. (Refer to page 84.)

Scripture to Consider: Matthew 5:13-16

Discussion Questions:
1. Do you agree with Fob's reaction to the drug use and cursing he encountered around the campfire? What were the risks, and potential rewards, of him remaining there? How do you think you would have handled the situation?
2. In Matthew 5 and 7, Christians are called to be salt and light, and not to judge others. However, Hebrews 5:14 tells us to use our spiritual training and instruction to *"distinguish good from evil."* How can a Christian "not judge" but still take a stand and speak out against evil, such as child abuse?
3. Are you more influenced by a person's actions or words? Why do you think that is so?

Fob Fundamental #19 – An experience initially considered difficult, painful, or bad, might ultimately be considered good if it draws one closer to God, develops one's perseverance, or strengthens one's resolve. (Refer to page 102.)

Scripture to Consider: James 1:2-4

Discussion Questions:
1. Do you think Rock Boat had actually forgotten the bad stuff that happened on his thru-hike? Or, was the bad stuff, in the context of his overall hike, eventually considered to be part of the good stuff?
2. In James 1:2-4, why does James tell us to face trials with joy? How does the long-term benefit compare to the temporary pain of the trial?
3. Describe a time that you were drawn closer to God through a trial? Did the experience help you to persevere through subsequent trials?

Fob Fundamental #20 – Appreciate short-term friendships and casual acquaintances, but cherish those friendships that span many miles and decades. (Refer to page 111.)

Scripture to Consider: Proverbs 18:24

Discussion Questions:
1. Why do you think Jeff (Cy Clops) traveled so many miles, on several occasions, to visit Fob? How did their long-term relationship affect their conversation?
2. Proverbs 18:24 warns that unreliable friends can lead one to ruin. What are some ways that can happen?
3. Who are your two or three closest friends? How do you remain close to them? How did they move from being casual friends to close friends?

Fob Fundamental #21 – Someone who has made a fair and objective assessment of his strengths and weaknesses is well-positioned to leverage those strengths and mitigate those weaknesses. (Refer to page 119.)

Scripture to Consider: Romans 12:3-8

Discussion Questions:
1. Which of the ENTJ's traits were most, and least, helpful to Fob on the AT?
2. According to Romans 12:3-8, how should we judge ourselves? What are some of the different functions, or talents, of the members of Christ's body? What is it about a person that makes them better at teaching or encouraging than someone else?
3. Go to myersbriggs.org and follow the instructions to determine your personality type. Did you agree with the findings? What are the strengths and possible downsides to someone with your personality type? Which of the 16 personality types is most helpful to someone trying to thru-hike the AT?

Fob Fundamental #22 – Live your life in such a way that one day, at the end of your life, you'll be able to look back and be proud of the way you lived. (Refer to page 126.)

Scripture to Consider: 2 Timothy 4:6-8

Discussion Questions:

1. Why was it important for Fob and the other hikers to "hike their own hike"? Once Fob defined what a successful thru-hike was to him, how would he have felt about violating those principles? What if he was the only one aware of the violations?

2. In 2 Timothy 4:6-8, Paul, nearing the end of his life, looks back on his life. How does he feel about the way in which he has lived his life? Compare and contrast "keeping the faith" with "hiking your own hike"?

3. Imagine today is your final day on this earth. Think back over your life. What are your proudest moments? What are your biggest regrets? If you had more time, what would you do over the next several days, weeks, or years to turn the regrets into positives?

Fob Fundamental #23 – When you find yourself in troubled times, traveling the inevitable valley, there's nothing quite like a loving family and close friends to help you weather the storm and get you back to the mountaintop. (Refer to page 133.)

Scripture to Consider: Job 4:7-8

Discussion Questions:

1. How did anticipation of seeing his family and friends at the wedding affect Fob's morale? How does the climate and terrain along the AT compare to life's journey?

2. Job was shaken and in a valley, having lost his family, possessions, and good health. Review Job 4:7-8, 8:20, and 22:5-9. How do Job's supposed friends serve as an example of how NOT to help a friend during a time of trouble?

3. Fob sometimes writes and prays to help him work through his emotions. What strategies do you use?

Fob Fundamental #24 – Competency lies at the heart of effective mentoring. That is to say, dig a deep enough hole. (Refer to page 138.)

Scripture to Consider: Philippians 4:9

Discussion Questions:

1. How did Fob's lack of competency and experience in burying a pet undermine his mentoring of Kyle? Do you think his son still learned something from the experience?

2. Unlike Fob, Paul had, in word and deed, set a great example for the church at Phillipi. In Phillipians 4:9, what did Paul tell his

audience to do with what they had seen in him and heard from him?

3. Describe a humorous, shocking, or otherwise memorable moment when your parents demonstrated how to do, or not do, something.

Fob Fundamental #25 – To gain fresh, new insights from a passage of Scripture, try re-writing it from your own perspective, based on your current struggles, challenges, and blessings. (Refer to page 147.)

Scripture to Consider: Psalm 23

Discussion Questions:
1. Fob's re-write of Psalm 23 does not modify, replace, or augment God's inspired word in any way. Rather, he used a technique to relate a well-known passage to his current situation. Given the challenges he was facing, and blessings he had received, how might the penning of this re-write been meaningful to him?
2. Review John 15:5, Psalm 18:2, Revelation 19:7, and Isaiah 64:8. Which of these metaphors for God or Jesus is the most meaningful or relatable for you? Why?
3. Try re-writing Psalm 23 from your own perspective, as a student, parent, employee, etc. Did that exercise provide any fresh insights on the passage?

Fob Fundamental #26 – You can conquer mountain-sized, seemingly impossible to achieve goals by breaking them into smaller, more manageable pieces. Celebrate each milestone, and use it as fuel to conquer the next. (Refer to page 152.)

Scripture to Consider: 1 Samuel 7:12

Discussion Questions:
1. Mathematically, there's no difference between hiking 2,200 miles, and hiking 100 miles 22 times. Yet, to Fob, there was a big difference. How do you explain that?
2. In 1 Samuel 7:12, why does Samuel raise a monument or milestone to God? What does he call it and what does that word mean? Although the defeat of the Philistines was just one battle in a larger war, what affect might the milestone have had on the children of Israel?
3. In Fob Fundamental #1 you listed your top few goals and in Fob

Fundamental #3, you identified the first step in accomplishing each goal. Now, take the process a step further by identify additional milestones on the way to each goal, and brainstorm ways to reward yourself at each progress marker.

Fob Fundamental #27 – Regularly confessing your sins to God opens channels for His amazing grace to flow. (Refer to page 154.)

Scripture to Consider: Psalm 32:1-5

Discussion Questions:
1. Writing down one's errors in The Priest Shelter log is a fun AT tradition. However, actual sin against God is serious business. In Psalm 32:5, who did David confess his sin to and what was the result?
2. According to Psalm 32:3-4, what happened when David kept silent about his sin?
3. In James 5:16, we're commanded to confess our sins to each other. What are some of the benefits of doing that? Do you think that might be easier to do with fellow AT hikers?

Fob Fundamental #28 – Ironically, a person who frequently complains about his life might actually have too good of a life. For an attitude and perspective adjustment, spend time serving the less fortunate...or living in the woods. (Refer to page 164.)

Scripture to Consider: 2 Timothy 3:1-7

Discussion Questions:
1. How did the AT change Fob's perspective on adequate lodging, comfortable temperatures, cleanliness, etc.? Do you think a person used to a comfortable, stress-free lifestyle might have a harder time adjusting to the AT?
2. In 2 Timothy 3:1-7, Paul speaks of troubling times that were coming. Notice how godless people will, among other things, be lovers of money and pleasure, and also ungrateful. Have you known people who seem to have it all and yet constantly complain?
3. Have you ever been on a mission trip to a third-world country or worked amongst the poor in an inner city? If so, did the experience change your perspective? Did you feel more grateful for the blessings you have?

Fob Fundamental #29 – Whatever role God has called you to in life, however important or unimportant it may seem, do it well. You are a hero to someone. (Refer to page 175.)

Scripture to Consider: Colossians 3:23

Discussion Questions:
1. What parallel did Rex draw between the tree that bore the sign and people who may feel useless or unimportant at times? Although AT hikers have undoubtedly taken thousands of pictures at the 1,000-mile marker sign, do you think any of them have paid much attention to the tree that bears the sign?
2. According to Colossians 3:23, how are we to accomplish life's tasks? In accomplishing these tasks, we should work as if who is our boss?
3. Describe a time when you have worked quietly behind the scenes, like the tree, so someone else could get the glory, like the sign. Consider another time when you were out in front, getting the glory. Who were some of the unnoticed people behind the scenes, helping to make your success possible?

Appendix C – *The LORD is My Sherpa*

The LORD is my Sherpa, my Leader, my Model, my Defender and my Protector.
He hikes in front of me, showing me the path to follow to reach the finish line and the
crown that awaits.
He hikes behind me, nudging and encouraging me to stay focused
and to take it one step at a time.
He walks beside me, as a friend, and we talk things out, like good friends do.
He surrounds me with Trail Angels, both seen and unseen.
I don't want Him on my team; rather, I am on His team...
a team that has already defeated Satan and this fallen world.

With Christ as my LORD, I have all I need and many of the things I want.
I trust I'm better off without some of the things I want,
as they might distract me from more godly pursuits.
I need to keep my focus on Him, not the temporary trappings of this world.
Every evening, there is a safe place to lay my head.
I may set up my tent in a green pasture or on a rocky mountaintop.
Or perhaps I'll find myself in a shelter, a hiker hostel, a hotel,
a friend's home, or even the loft of a barn.
I may be alone or surrounded by others. It may be snowy, rainy, or sunny.
Regardless, without fail, every night I am eventually safe, dry, and warm,
and I thank God for that.

God has provided life-giving water.
Sometimes the water is fast moving, a place to get good drinking water.
Sometimes it is a hot shower, a place to wash my tired, dirty body.
Sometimes the waters are calm, a place to fish, soak my feet,
or just sit and reflect on this marvelous world He has created.
I have been thirsty, but never for long.
I have been hungry, but have never run out of food.
God sustains me.

Each morning, I'm renewed and restored.
I feel the prayers of family and friends that have been lifted
for me and my fellow hikers.
I feel a sense of purpose that goes beyond just hiking miles.
He has put me on this earth, and this amazing trail, with a mission in mind.
Perhaps I can help someone to see that this incredible beauty and amazing design
around us is the result not of chance, but the work of an amazing Designer.
Perhaps today I can encourage someone with a kind word or good deed.
Or maybe today I will be the one needing encouragement.
Regardless, God will fill my soul today as only He can.

He leads me on the right, true path, because that path leads to Heaven,
my final summit.
Katahdin is a goal, a dream, and I hope to get there.
But it is an earthly pursuit, with only temporal benefits.
If I fail, so be it...most do. But Heaven! Majestic, glorious Heaven!
May I always strive to follow His Holy Word, the Bible,
as it provides the path, the white blazes if you will,
that lead to a final golden summit and an eternity with Him!
God's Word teaches, comforts, instructs, rebukes, and challenges me.
May I take its messages to heart and encourage those around me to follow it as well.

Even though I hike in dangerous conditions—lighting storms, heavy rain, freezing
temperatures, and searing heat—with bears, snakes, and ticks posing potential trouble,
I'm not afraid of ANY of those things.
God has my back.
He comforts me. He calms me. He protects me.
His Holy Spirit lives and moves and works within me.
He'll bring me home to heaven when He is good and ready
and not one moment sooner.
Even if tragedy were to strike me, do not worry about me, friends.
All is well with me and will remain well with me.
My future is secure.

There are a few enemies, or at least scoffers, here on the trail, who doubt my faith,
reject God's Word, and on occasion put temptations before me.
God is there even then—especially then.
He picks me up and dusts me off and forgives me when I fail.

God provides spray to prevent insect bites, ointment for scratches, sunscreen for
protection, and bandages for blisters.
Like His Word, they must be applied to be effective.
I have all I need, and then some, thanks to God.

As He has watched over me in the past and now on the Appalachian Trail,
my hope and assurance is that He will be with me until the very end.
I have experienced and benefitted from His goodness my whole life.
He has shown mercy to me as a sinner in need of grace.
I am sad Christ so willingly paid my debt, but I am oh so thankful for it.

May I show that appreciation in the way I live my life and treat others,
even here on the trail.
And someday soon, may Christ return and bring me home, along with other
Christians who have staked our hope and future and eternity on Him.

We want nothing more or less than to live forever, together,
in the home Christ has prepared for us.
Come quickly, Lord Jesus!

Appendix D – Glossary

AT – abbreviation for Appalachian Trail. The AT passes through fourteen states and, in 2016, was 2,189.1 miles long. The distance fluctuates from year to year as changes are made to the routing of the trail.

AT section-hiker – someone hiking a section of the AT (e.g., a few miles or a few hundred miles), but not the entire trail.

AT thru-hiker – someone who hikes the entire Appalachian Trail within the span of one calendar year. Others believe a thru-hiker is someone attempting to thru-hike the AT, regardless of how far the hiker gets.

Mount Katahdin – the northern terminus of the Appalachian Trail and the tallest mountain in Maine. For northbound hikers, it is the final summit.

Near-O day – a short day of hiking. Depending on the hiker, this could be any day where the number of miles hiked is below a certain threshold (e.g., less than 10 miles, less than 5 miles, etc.) Near-O days are often taken on the day a hiker arrives or departs a trail town.

Springer Mountain – located in Georgia, it is the southern terminus of the Appalachian Trail. For northbound hikers, it is where the journey begins.

NOBO – northbound or a northbound hiker.

SOBO – southbound or a southbound hiker.

Spork – a utensil which is part spoon, part fork.

Stealth Camping – camping, often undetected, outside of a designated camping area. Can be done legally or illegally in a public or private area.

Trail Angel – a giver of trail magic. A Trail Angel typically loves AT hikers and has an unusually large heart.

Trail magic - any unexpected act of kindness one encounters while hiking the trail.

Zero day – a day off for a hiker. Zero miles are hiked.

ABOUT THE AUTHOR

Retired Air Force Colonel Steve Johnson has traveled the globe. His military career took him to 40 states and 26 countries. Steve has written speeches and Congressional testimony for Air Force general officers, been published in *The Christian Chronicle*, and has a popular travel blog. He has worked with church youth groups for more than two decades and taught at Foundation Christian Academy in Florida. In 2015, Steve and his wife, Janet, sold their home and now travel the country by RV, trying to make a difference in the lives of people they meet along the way. He brought his adventurous passion to the Appalachian Trail.

CPSIA information can be obtained
at www.ICGtesting.com
Printed in the USA
LVOW11s1049191217
560228LV00005B/1541/P

9 780692 838334